TEACHING THINKING ACROSS THE CURRICULUM

Vincent Ryan Ruggiero

State University of New York at Delhi

1817

HARPER & ROW, PUBLISHERS, New York

Cambridge, Philadelphia, San Francisco, Washington,
London, Mexico City, São Paulo, Singapore, Sydney

Sponsoring Editor: Alan McClare
Project Editor: Joan Gregory
Text Design Adaptation: Barbara Bert
Cover Design: Barbara Bert/North 7 Atelier Ltd.
Text Art: Fineline Illustrations, Inc.
Production Manager: Jeanie Berke
Production Assistant: Brenda DeMartini
Compositor: ComCom Division of Haddon Craftsmen, Inc.
Printer and Binder: R. R. Donnelley & Sons Company
Cover Printer: New England Book Components

TEACHING THINKING ACROSS THE CURRICULUM

Library of Congress Cataloging in Publication Data

Ruggiero, Vincent Ryan.
    Teaching thinking across the curriculum/Vincent Ryan Ruggiero.
        p.   cm.
    Bibliography: p.
    ISBN 0–06–045667–1
    1. Critical thinking—Study and teaching.   2. Thought and
thinking—Study and teaching.   3. Interdisciplinary approach in
education.   I. Title.
LB1590.3.R84   1988
370.15'7—dc19   87–18358
                                                     CIP

89 90 9 8 7 6 5 4 3 2

For Krista Lynn Lewis

CONTENTS

PREFACE

In less than a decade thinking instruction has grown from the conviction of a small but dedicated group of scholars and teachers to a national—indeed, *inter*national—educational imperative. The news medias have headlined reports citing students' problem-solving and decision-making deficiencies. Virtually every serious magazine and journal has devoted one or more articles, and sometimes entire issues, to reciting the advantages of possessing skills in solving problems and resolving issues. Many state departments of education have issued directives calling for an emphasis on cognitive skills from kindergarten through high school, and innumerable colleges and universities have instituted required courses in creative and critical thinking.

As welcome as these developments are, they often ignore one vital fact: Few teachers have received formal instruction in thinking themselves, and even fewer have been trained to teach thinking to others. The success of the thinking movement in education will depend, in great measure, on how quickly and how well individuals already in the teaching profession, or soon to enter it, can be prepared to teach thinking skills.

To be meaningful, the preparation of teachers must include much more than a list of commercial materials. It must provide a comprehensive explanation of both theoretical and practical aspects of thinking instruction across the curriculum. Moreover, it must assist teachers in gaining facility in *thinking about thinking* as well as in using the strategies of creative and critical thinking they will be instructing students to use.

This book has been designed to aid in that preparation:

It presents a holistic approach that integrates creative and critical thinking and provides a single heuristic for both problem solving and issue analysis.

It provides comprehensive treatment of teaching objectives and methods.

It identifies the most serious obstacles to students' cognitive development.

It answers the questions teachers most frequently ask about the teaching of thinking.

It details numerous assignments that can be used in a variety of courses across the curriculum.

It demonstrates how instructors can design additional thinking exercises suited to the special requirements of their courses.

It offers guidelines both for assessing student progress in thinking skills and for developing the thinking skills program.

Teaching is likely to be most vital when it reflects the teacher's own genius and not just that of the textbook author. For this reason, the chapters on objectives, methods, and materials have been designed to stimulate the readers' creativity. Readers will find a large assortment of assignments and lessons drawn from various levels of education but *adaptable to virtually all levels.* With a little ingenuity, for example, grade school teachers can adapt a high school or college level assignment for their classes. Even though the specific problem-situation, the wording of the directions, and the level of expectation may be different, the essential assignment can remain the same.

ACKNOWLEDGEMENTS

This book would not have been possible without the contributions of the hundreds of men and women who have enlarged our understanding of thinking and education for thinking. Many of those men and women are cited in the chapter notes or in the bibliographies at the end of this volume.

In addition I wish to give special acknowledgment to Diane Carey of the Los Rios Community College District Office for suggesting the need for this book, and to each of the following individuals, who either shared with me their approaches to teaching thinking, or offered helpful criticism of the early drafts of the manuscript.

James Bell, Howard Community College

Mark E. Blum, University of Louisville

C. Blaine Carpenter, Clayton State College

Lucy Cromwell, Alverno College

Judith S. Engel, Bronx High School of Science

Robert H. Ennis, University of Illinois

Edward Glaser, Los Angeles, California

Jane Halonen, Alverno College

Larry Hannah, California State College, Sacramento

Peter Kneedler, California State Department of Education

Bessie Marquis, California State University, Chico

Tom Mason, College of St. Thomas

Claude Mathis, Northwestern University

Dan P. Miller, Indiana State University

Deborah Morel, Howell Mountain Elementary School

Mary Alice Muellerleile, College of St. Catherine

Ina V. S. Mullis, Educational Testing Service

William Myers, College of St. Catherine

Stephen Norris, Memorial University of Newfoundland

Kathleen O'Brien, Alverno College

Ted Perry, Sacramento County Office of Education

Richard Paul, Sonoma State University

Sam Postlethwait, Purdue University

Kenneth Rich, College of St. Catherine

John Ricketts, DePauw University

George Rochefort, College of St. Catherine

George F. Sefler, Purdue University

Ann Siegrist, Clarke College

Stephen Spangehl, University of Louisville

Robert A. Stager, University of Windsor, Ontario

Richard J. Stiggins, Northwest Regional Educational Laboratory

David J. Stroup, Clemson University

Mary Thompson, College of St. Catherine

Elliot H. Thoreson, University of South Dakota

Ann Trivisonno, Ursuline College

Debbie Walsh, American Federation of Teachers

Richard M. Wolters, Doane College

Mary Diez, Alverno College

Richard Schwab, University of New Hampshire at Durham

Ann Lally, University of Missouri at St. Louis

Terry Thomas, California State University, Sacramento

Ben Cox, University of Illinois at Champaign

Jan Talbot, California State University, Sacramento

Burt Boxerman, University of Missouri at St. Louis

Mike V. Smith, Southeast Missouri State University

Ron Good, Florida State University

Finally, I wish to acknowledge the Exxon Education Foundation and its director, Dr. Richard Johnson, for funding the writing of this book.

Vincent Ryan Ruggiero

chapter 1

QUESTIONS FREQUENTLY ASKED ABOUT THE TEACHING OF THINKING

WHAT MENTAL ACTIVITIES DOES THINKING INCLUDE AND EXCLUDE?

The term *thinking* can be used in a very general way to mean everything that occurs in a person's stream of consciousness. By this definition, everyone would be a thinking person merely by virtue of being alive and awake. The definition of *thinking* used throughout this book is considerably more limited than that. It excludes what John Dewey termed the "uncontrolled coursing of ideas through [one's head]," the "inconsequential trifling with mental pictures, random recollections, pleasant but unfounded hopes, [and] flitting, half-developed impressions."[1] *Thinking,* as we will use the term, embraces only purposeful mental activity over which a person exercises some control.

Our present knowledge of thinking derives from two separate disciplines: philosophy and psychology. (A third discipline, neurosurgery, has made a significant contribution to our understanding of the physiology of thought.) Philosophy's contribution is elder in two senses: its theoretical foundations date back to ancient Greece; and its concern for the practical importance of teaching students

1

how to think can be traced, in modern times, to the late nineteenth century. Even today, the majority of courses devoted specifically to the teaching of thinking are found in philosophy departments, and the authors of most textbooks on thinking are philosophy professors.

The dominance of philosophers in the movement accounts for the fact that teaching thinking has usually meant teaching *critical* thinking: that is, teaching students how to recognize and/or construct sound arguments, applying the principles of formal and informal logic and avoiding fallacies in their reasoning. That analytical, evaluative emphasis is important, but equally important is the dimension of thinking cognitive psychologists have made a special object of study for more than 30 years—the production of ideas, *creative* thinking.

Harvard's David Perkins, researcher and author of *The Mind's Best Work,* has found that though most students are deficient in reasoning skills, they are even more deficient in the ability to *produce* ideas. The latter deficiency, Perkins explains, is evidenced by their inability to generate meaningful scenarios when these are necessary for formulating new premises and evaluating ideas, as well as by their inability to generate counterexamples in the course of argument.[2]

Few thinking situations, whether in decision making, problem solving, or issue analysis, are one-phased. Most involve both the production and the evaluation of ideas. A business entrepreneur, for example, must identify an opportunity for initiative before deciding to pursue it. Similarly, a teacher must generate a solution to the problem of how to present complex material before using that solution; and a professional scholar must conceive of a way to resolve a controversial issue before elaborating and reporting that resolution. True, the production of ideas may in some cases consist of nothing more than remembering what was seen and heard—some business people, teachers, and scholars, after all, never rise above imitation. Yet more than remembering is involved whenever the decision, solution, or resolution is original or ingenious.

The definition of thinking that informs the teaching of thinking, therefore, should reflect the reality of two-phased thought. In other words, it should be a holistic definition. *Thinking, so defined, is any mental activity that helps formulate or solve a problem, make a decision, or fulfill a desire to understand; it is a searching for answers, a reaching for meaning.* One fact about this definition deserves underscoring: whereas it implies that the main mental activity in thinking is conscious, it does not exclude unconscious mental activity, which the evidence suggests can play a significant role in thinking.

IS THE THINKING SKILLS "CRISIS" A MEDIA INVENTION?

The media have not created a problem where there was none; they have merely reported on the studies that have documented the problem. One such study is the National Assessment of Educational Progress, which disclosed that few students are able to offer more than superficial defenses of their views, to elaborate on ideas, or to extend their ideas into a thoughtful discussion. Even more alarming, the study revealed that in all broad areas of learning, the percentage of students achieving higher order thinking skills actually declined during the 1970s.[3]

Moreover, the expressions of concern over the problem, and the recommendations that thinking skills be taught at every level of education have come, not from bureaucrats, but from the most prestigious business, professional, and educational organizations, including the New York State Regents, the National Council of Teachers of English, The Presidential Commission on Excellence in Education, the College Board, the University/Urban Schools National Task Force, the Carnegie Foundation for the Advancement of Teaching, the Exxon Education Foundation (who sponsored the writing of this book), the American Federation of Teachers, the Association of American Colleges, the National Institute of Education, the U.S. Department of Education, the Association of Superintendents and Curriculum Developers, and the National Endowment for the Humanities.

That is an impressive list by any measure. And it suggests clearly that the movement to teach thinking skills is both serious and well-founded. The business community certainly believes it is: the Carnegie Foundation estimates that big business spends up to $100 billion a year in corporation classrooms to develop thinking and other fundamental skills the schools have failed to teach.

IS IT REALLY POSSIBLE TO TEACH ANYONE HOW TO THINK?

The idea that it is impossible to teach people to think, which has been advanced again and again throughout this century, did not proceed from scholarly research, but from an unscholarly assumption that if thinking *was not being taught* and *had not been taught,* it therefore *could not be taught.* The most knowledgeable people have attacked that assumption, yet their arguments, though compelling, have never managed to overcome the prevailing ignorance.

In every decade of this century the teaching of thinking has had numerous champions, including such famous individuals as John Dewey, Alfred North Whitehead, and Jean Piaget. In fact, when Edward Glaser published his watershed work, *Experiment in the Teaching of Critical Thinking,* he listed over 340 important books and scholarly articles—all of them written before 1940 and all of them either documenting that thinking can be taught or demonstrating why and how to teach it.[4] The following brief quotations and explanatory notes suggest the emphases of many of those works.

- Graham Wallas, *The Art of Thought,* 1926, 288. "My whole argument . . . in this book, is that an art of thought exists, that the practice of that art is one of the most important activities of human society, that training in that art should be part of the education of the future thinker, and that in this, as in other cases, a complete separation between teaching and doing will be fatal to the art itself."
- John Dewey, *How We Think,* 1933, 78. "We state emphatically that, upon its intellectual side, education consists in the formation of wide-awake, careful, thorough habits of thinking."
- Victor H. Noll, *The Habit of Scientific Thinking: A Handbook for Teach-*

ers, 1935, 2, 17. "The school has been largely concerned with imparting information to its pupils. . . . We have always poured facts into the more or less docile pupil until he could reproduce enough of them to pass a final examination, or until he could hold no more. Now we are slowly coming to realize that this kind of education is not meeting the needs of the times." He later states, after detailing the principles that underlay his program, "Teachers who wish to develop habits of scientific thinking in their pupils must first of all set up these habits as definite goals of instruction. To assume that if we teach our subject matter well scientific thinking will result automatically, is sheer folly."

In brief, scholars have known throughout this century that thinking can be taught. Moreover, in the almost five decades since Glaser's work was published, thousands of studies have not only reconfirmed, but extended that knowledge. We now know, for example, that even those mental talents long considered almost mystical—imaginativeness and originality—can be taught effectively.[5] The problem was and continues to be not whether we can teach thinking, but whether we are willing to make the pedagogical changes necessary to do so.

DON'T SOME COURSES TEACH THINKING AUTOMATICALLY?

The misconception that certain courses teach thinking automatically has proved especially resistant to correction over the decades. Here is what Edward Glaser wrote about it in 1941:

> The studies by Curtis, Caldwell and Lundeen, Downing, Noll, Peterson, Powers, Sinclair and Tolman, and Zepf in the field of science training; by Daily, Fawcett, Hall, Lazar, Parker, Perry and Shendarker in the field of mathematics, and by Barlow, Biddle, Hill, Jewett, Jones, Salisbury, Teller, White, and Wrightstone in the fields of English, Logic, and the Social Studies, all point to the conclusion that the content alone of any subject is not likely to give general training to the mind, and is not likely to develop a generalized ability to think critically. . . .
>
> In general, the research indicates that if the objective is to develop in pupils an attitude of "reasonableness" and regard for the weight of evidence and to develop ability to think critically about controversial problems, then the component attitudes and abilities involved in thinking critically about such problems must be set up as definite goals of instruction.[6]

Why have this research and the innumerable studies that have joined it in the past half-century failed to dispel the misconception? Because many teachers confuse *telling students what to think* with *teaching students how to think.* Many science teachers, for example, believe that since a thinking process (scientific method) is at the heart of every scientific enterprise, informing students of the great scientific achievements and letting them duplicate some of those in the laboratory cannot help but develop in students scientific habits of mind. Similarly, many English teachers and others in the humanities believe that "exposing" students to the greatest thought and expression in human history plants seeds that will automatically bear fruit in students' own thinking and writing.

Such beliefs suggest a mystical conception of learning, a kind of skill-through-inspiration view akin to the conception underlying many popular books in the "self-improvement" genre. This conception is strongly rooted in western education: the word "professor," after all, derives from a Latin verb whose meaning is not to *guide* or *coach,* but to *profess.* A professor is thus by definition one who proclaims things to students and the most highly acclaimed professors are those whose eloquence renders students spellbound. Inspiration, of course, can play a valuable role in education by motivating students to strive for excellence; yet listening to inspiring speeches can no more teach students to think than listening to music can make them musicians or watching sports competition can make them athletes.

To persuade ourselves that no course teaches thinking skills automatically, we need only consider the courses in critical and creative thinking that are being instituted in colleges around the country. Surely if any subject matter were able to teach thinking in and of itself, it would be the subject matter of these courses. And yet what if such courses were taught as most other courses are taught? That is, what if the instructor merely lectured and the students dutifully took notes and later spat them back on exams? Would students be learning to think? No.

DON'T GOOD TEACHERS ALREADY TEACH STUDENTS HOW TO THINK?

Close examination of any recent major study of American education will reveal that very few teachers are doing much to develop students' thinking skills. Consider, for example, the study conducted by UCLA's John I. Goodlad, one of the most comprehensive educational studies ever completed (over 1,000 classrooms and 17,163 students). This study disclosed that, though terms like *intellectual development, scientific method, critical thinking,* and *problem solving* appear regularly in statements of educational aims, activities to realize these ideals are seldom found in classrooms in any of the major academic areas of the curriculum: English, social studies, mathematics, and science. "The data on our sample of classes," Goodlad writes, "are clear and convincing—teaching in the four basic subjects required for college admission is characterized, on the average, by a narrow range of repetitive instructional activities favoring passive student behavior."[7]

But what of the minority of teachers in those schools? Would it be safe to assume that they are teaching students how to think? No, it would not. It might be reasonable to assume that all good teachers pose interesting problems for students to ponder, and thus feed students' natural curiosity and stimulate their desire to learn. In other words, it might be reasonable to argue that all good teachers *encourage* students to think. But that is not the same as teaching students how to think. Teaching how to think means providing students first with a knowledge of the principles and techniques of creative and critical thinking, and second with regular guided practice in applying those principles and techniques to problem-solving and decision-making situations.

To say that most teachers do not teach students how to think certainly seems an insult to teachers. However, I submit that it is not, precisely because this generation of teachers, like several generations before it, was never trained to teach thinking. (Moreover, many teachers were never trained to think effectively themselves. Whatever skill they have was acquired intuitively or by fortunate accident.) There is no shame in having been denied the necessary training to meet students' cognitive needs; the only shame is in refusing to remedy the deficiency once it is discovered, and the enthusiastic response of educators to the thinking movement in recent years suggests that the great majority of teachers are eager to remedy this deficiency.

WHY HAVE EDUCATORS HISTORICALLY NEGLECTED THE TEACHING OF THINKING?

Since a full answer to this question would exceed the space available here, our discussion will be limited to brief mention of the most important reasons for the historic neglect of thinking in education. One reason is that until recently, the teaching of writing has generally excluded meaningful consideration of the *substance* of students' expression. This exclusion dates from the early sixteenth century, when Petrus Ramus, a professor at the University of Paris, moved the teaching of the classical concept of "invention" from rhetoric to logic, never realizing that logic would in time lose its important place in the curriculum and, because rhetoric was limited to considerations of style, students would receive no training in the production of ideas.

Another reason that modern education has neglected the teaching of thinking skills is western philosophy's rejection of the traditional concept of mind, a concept uniquely congenial to the teaching of thinking, and its assumption that language controls thought. The human mind, according to the traditional concept, is composed of intellect and will; thus, people can use reason to arrive at the truth and can, in most cases, freely choose their actions. That view was challenged by a number of philosophers, chiefly by Thomas Hobbes in the seventeenth century and David Hume in the eighteenth, who held that the mind is constituted by sense and imagination. The most serious consequence of their rejection of the traditional concept of mind, according to Mortimer Adler, is "the conclusion that men differ from other animals only in degree, not in kind."[8]

The assumption that language controls thought, a view espoused by Ludwig Wittgenstein, among others, constituted a reversal of the traditional view that thought controls language, and led to the conclusion that the *use* of words, and not their meaning, is the only proper object of study. Thus the attention of philosophers was diverted from the study of thought to the study of words and the various ways and contexts in which they are used.[9] (It is possible, of course, to *combine* the study of thought and the study of expression, and some contemporary approaches do so.)

A third reason for the neglect of thinking in education is the advent of Darwinism and Freudianism. Darwinism not only intensified interest in physical reality and diminished interest in the metaphysical, but also transformed Hobbes' and Hume's conception of mind into a scientific hypothesis. Even to those who still accepted the notions of intellect and will, sensory data seemed more relevant than cognition. Freudianism thrust the unconscious mind into prominence and made discussions of the conscious mind unfashionable, if not irrelevant. Later, behaviorism advanced the doctrine that human beings are conditioned in essentially the same manner as animals, a doctrine that found support among some ethologists and sociobiologists. According to this doctrine, the human mind is reactive rather than active, and incapable of independence and self-direction.

Yet another, and in some ways more significant reason for the neglect of thinking is the powerful influence of the psychometrics movement on educational practice, traces of which are still observable today. The tenets of this movement are concisely explained in this critical comment by Richard Weil, Jr.

[Members of this movement believed] that a given individual has a fixed thinking capacity; that this capacity cannot be increased; that you cannot teach a person to think any better than he *can* think; and that therefore all you can do in the educational process is to pack and cram, into a sort of mental portmanteau, as many durable items of fact as the poor, quivering, but defenseless brain of the school child can be made to carry.[10]

For the first six decades of this century, these intellectual emphases rendered ineffectual the efforts of educational reformers who labored to gain a place for thinking instruction in the curriculum. Then, for a brief time in the 1960s, there were indications that the reformers might succeed, but the inevitable reaction against behaviorism, scientism, and psychometric pessimism took an unfortunate form. The spokesmen of that reaction, apparently confusing rational*ism* with rational*ity,* attacked reason and advanced the Rousseavian idea that *feelings* are more trustworthy than thought, thereby setting the thinking movement back for almost two more decades.

WHAT HAS HAPPENED IN RECENT YEARS TO MAKE THE TEACHING OF THINKING AN EDUCATIONAL IMPERATIVE?

The extreme anti-intellectualism of the 1960s and early 1970s, with its "Don't trust anyone over 30" slogan and preference for feeling over thought (together with the permissivism in education this preference reinforced), produced millions of citizens and workers who were not only untrained in thinking, but also lacking in the mental discipline and organized approach to work and life that traditional education, for all its faults, had provided. These deficiencies became evident in the late-1970s when public attention was focused on two troubling trends: the steady decline in Scholastic Aptitude Test scores and the weakening of the U.S. place in the world market because of industry's failure to meet the challenge of foreign, notably Japanese, competition.

Numerous business and professional organizations issued statements calling for thinking to be taught in the schools. Typical of the message they conveyed is this statement from Raymond T. Schuler, president of the New York State Business Council:

Business will always prefer people who have broad-based skills—people who can think critically, who can adapt well to new situations, and who can teach themselves. A person who is taught today's skills may have obsolete skills by the time he or she reaches the workforce. But a person who is taught to *think* well will always be able to adapt.[11]

Soon a distinguished presidential commission on education and numerous business, professional, and educational organizations added their voices to the growing chorus of those calling for the teaching of thinking. Journals and magazines that had long ignored the subject began publishing articles on thinking and such related subjects as problem solving, reasoning, and decision making. Books on the right brain/left brain phenomenon appeared, gaining more attention in a few months than the work of earlier scholars had received in decades. The media spotlight was at last shining on the subject of thinking.

Media attention also gave new prominence to theories and practices not directly associated with the movement in education, but related in their underlying premises, notably the cognitive psychotherapy of such individuals as Aaron Beck and Albert Ellis. Ellis is the founder of the Institute for Rational-Emotive Therapy (RET). The Institute, through its clinicians around the country and around the world, practices a form of psychotherapy based on the following thesis: "Emotional pain or disturbance . . . usually originates in some irrational or illogical ideas. The job of the neurotic is to uncover and understand the basic unrealistic ideas with which he is disturbing himself; to see clearly the misinformation and illogic behind these ideas; and, on the basis of better information and clearer thinking, to *change* the notions which lie behind and keep creating his disturbance." Ellis suggests that "man can live the most self-fulfilling, creative, and emotionally satisfying life by intelligently organizing and disciplining his thinking."[12]

Psychologist Carol Tavris, in her seminal work *Anger: The Misunderstood Emotion,* finds that shallow thinking is a significant factor in child abuse and other forms of aggression, and argues that "the moral use of anger . . . requires an awareness of choice and an embrace of reason. It is knowing when to become angry—'this is wrong, this I will protest'—and when to make peace; when to take action, and when to be silent; knowing the likely cause of one's anger and not berating the blameless."[13]

The work of cognitive therapists and scholars like Tavris have added powerful new arguments for the teaching of thinking in schools: thinking must be taught not just because it is the fundamental academic skill, but because it is the fundamental coping mechanism, the means by which we ensure people's mental health and enable them to play a constructive role in society.

One final example of a development that has added strength to the thinking movement in education is the outspoken criticism of the computer movement by one of the founders of that movement. (While not inherently a threat to thinking instruction, the computer has been erroneously regarded by some as a machine whose very use teaches students how to think.) In a number of magazine interviews, Dr. Joseph Weizenbaum, Professor of Computer Science at MIT and pioneer in the development of the computer, has challenged the idea that computer literacy is good for the mind. Here are a few of his comments from the March 1984 issue of *Harper's Magazine.*

A new human malady has been invented, just as the makers of patent medicine in the past invented illnesses such as 'tired blood' in order to create a market for their products. Now it's computer illiteracy. The future, we are told, will belong to those familiar with the computer. What a joke this would be if only it didn't victimize so many innocent bystanders. . . . I think [the computer] inhibits children's creativity. In most cases the computer programs kids and not the other way around. Once they have started a program, the computer may leave them a few degrees of freedom, to be sure, but on the whole it will tell them what to do and when to do it. . . . The introduction of the computer into any problem area, be it medicine, education, or whatever, usually creates the impression that grievous deficiencies are being corrected, that something is being done. But often its principal effect is to push problems even further into obscurity—to avoid confrontation with the need for fundamentally critical thinking.[14]

In brief, the thinking movement in education has gained prominence and support both because people in business and the professions recognized the problem-solving and decision-making deficiencies of high school and college graduates and because informed individuals and groups have independently arrived at exactly the same conclusion the most eminent educators have proclaimed for a century—a society will have an abundance of effective thinkers only if the schools and colleges teach the skills of thinking, directly and thoroughly.

IS THINKING SUBJECT-SPECIFIC?

This question has been the focus of considerable confusion in recent years, partly because of the ambiguity of the term "subject-specific," and partly because of certain misconceptions about thinking. Let us first eliminate the ambiguity. Saying "thinking is subject-specific" can mean simply that whenever one thinks, one thinks about something, some subject—ethics, perhaps, or engineering, or medicine; in other words, that it is impossible to be thinking about nothing. (The fact that one may think about *nothingness* is not a contradiction because, in that case, *nothingness* would not be "nothing"—it would be the subject about which one is thinking.) This claim is so modest that it would be unreasonable not to grant it.

However, saying "thinking is subject-specific" can mean much more. It can mean that the process of thinking is different for every subject and therefore that thinking skills are properly taught only in the context of particular courses and not in a separate course. According to this view, the courses in critical thinking or creative thinking now being offered in numerous colleges around the country should be discontinued because they cannot achieve their objectives. This is essentially the view John McPeck, professor of philosophy at Canada's University of Western Ontario, advanced in *Critical Thinking and Education.* (The title is misleading; the book treats creative thinking as well as critical thinking.)

If McPeck's book were not so complex, it might satisfy our purpose to demonstrate its fatal flaw. However, it is complex, a curious mixture of insight and fallacy, so it demands more careful examination. First, let us note the insights. McPeck correctly argues that critical thinking can evaluate hypotheses, but cannot form them; that it is not enough to have thinking skills since one must also have the disposition to use them; that it is inconsistent and self-defeating to exclude value judgments from critical thinking instruction, as some individuals have recommended; that programs that focus narrowly on creative thinking (he specifies Edward deBono's program) do students a disservice by suggesting that there is some inherent value in novelty and originality apart from the value of what they produce; and that even the best available tests of thinking skills leave something to be desired.[15]

These observations are valuable. They identify problems that must be addressed if thinking instruction is to achieve what its proponents intend it to achieve. Unfortunately, the observations are mixed with a number of serious errors. To begin with, McPeck seems not to have probed the subject of critical thinking sufficiently; this deficiency is evident in a number of places in his book. For example, he writes, "When [Robert Ennis'] paper was published in 1962 there was a paucity of literature analysing the concept [of critical thinking] in such a manner that educators could directly teach, and psychologists accurately test, critical thinking."[16] McPeck's bibliography supports this statement, showing as it does only five books published before 1950 (and most of these of little import).

Had McPeck exercised greater diligence in researching the literature, he would have realized the error of his statement. Scores of respected scholars made significant contributions to our knowledge of critical thinking before 1962, scholars like John Dewey, Karl Duncker, Ernest Dimnet, Henry Hazlitt, Joseph Jastrow, Victor Noll, Joseph Rossman, Edward Thorndike, Jean Piaget, Graham Wallas, and Joseph Wertheimer. In fact, McPeck ignores one of the key historical works in the field, Edward Glaser's *Experiment in the Teaching of Critical Thinking.* Had McPeck read this work, he never would have written the sentence quoted above since Glaser's bibliography of important works on critical thinking published almost twenty years before 1962 (in 1941) numbered *over 340 citations!*

Numerous other errors might be cited, such as his suggestion that the fact that one researcher (Ennis) has not, in McPeck's view, changed his view of critical thinking "suggests, among other things, that *we* have not come very far in these past two decades." (Emphasis added.)[17] As if one man's progress or lack of it were the measure of hundreds or thousands of individuals in a field! The error that stands out above all the others, however, lies in the book's central premise that it is "impossible to conceive of critical thinking as a generalized skill."[18]

Richard Paul, director of the Sonoma State University's Center for Critical Thinking and Moral Critique and chairman of the annual International Conference on Critical Thinking, answers McPeck's argument by pointing out that subjects are not natural, but artificial divisions of reality created by human thought and subject to human revision, and that "even concepts and lines of reasoning that are clearly within one category are also simultaneous within others." Paul adds that many problems are multilogical, touching a number of disciplines. He cites the example of alcoholism, which has medical, legal, moral, psychological, sociological, and other dimensions.[19]

Other evidence weighs impressively against the idea that thinking skills are subject-specific. Many approaches to thinking skills have been found useful, not only in the particular discipline for which they were originally designed, but in other disciplines as well. For example, the Guided Design approach developed by Charles Wales and Robert Stager for the University of West Virginia engineering program has been used successfully in chemistry, communications, computer science, counseling, journalism, nursing, political science, and physics. Then, too, comparisons of approaches to thinking instruction designed for different subjects reveal some variations in terminology, but essentially the same cognitive skills. Finally, Reuven Feuerstein's Instrumental Enrichment program, which has proven successful with students who have significant deficiencies in thinking skills, is content-free.

But perhaps the best evidence that McPeck is mistaken lies in the fact that numerous other skills—from writing and speaking to typing and driving a car—are subject-specific and yet are taught in special courses. No reasonable person would think of arguing that because compositions are always written about a specific subject, the course in freshman composition should be abolished. Nor should any such argument be made concerning the teaching of thinking skills.

IS IT NECESSARY TO TEACH THINKING *ACROSS THE CURRICULUM?*

Not all authorities are in agreement that thinking should be taught across the curriculum, but any disagreement that exists on this question derives, I believe, from different definitions of "teaching across the curriculum" rather than from differences of viewpoint about the importance of making cognitive skills central to education.

The expression "teaching thinking across the curriculum," as used in this book, does not mean introducing alien concepts and terms into a course or substituting new course content for existing content. Nor does it necessarily mean directly pursuing every single objective in the list of objectives found in a course in thinking. Rather, it means focusing on the attitudes, habits, and intellectual skills common to all disciplines or specific to one discipline in such a way that students both understand how important contributors to the discipline reached their conclusions and solved problems, and acquire skill in reaching conclusions and solving problems themselves. In other words, it means going beyond filling students with information and admiration of other people's competencies to developing their own competencies so that they can deal with the "logically messy" situations they encounter in the particular discipline.[20]

There are two compelling reasons for teaching thinking in as many courses as possible. The first reason is that if it is taught in only one place or a few places, it is not likely to take root. Teaching thinking is analogous to teaching writing. Both thinking and writing are skills that, to be maintained, require practice. For decades every college student has been required to complete one or two semesters of Freshman English. Yet studies show that without continued writing practice in other courses, writing skills deteriorate. If such is the case with writing skills, which students study in virtually every grade from elementary school on, it is hardly reasonable to expect thinking skills, *which are less systematically taught,* to be maintained without continuing attention.

If educators want to persuade students that thinking skills are vital in every area of life, they must show students that those skills are important enough to receive regular attention in every academic discipline. Moreover, if they wish students to have the level of cognitive skill necessary to resist the shallow and specious thinking so prevalent today, they must assist students in reaching that level of skill.

The second reason for teaching thinking across the curriculum is that wherever it is taught, it tends to increase students' enthusiasm for the course. The traditional lecture approach and the traditional textbook not only deny students training in analyzing problems and issues, but also suggest to students that the subject of the course is static, inert, dead. Teaching thinking in a course emphasizes the processes that give every subject its vitality—hypothesizing, interpreting, seeking alternative views, raising questions, evaluating, discovering. That emphasis creates excitement and encourages involvement. When a curriculum produces those results, it invariably attracts students, and that is no small benefit in these days of declining enrollments.

Saying that thinking should be taught across the curriculum does not, of course, imply that it is unnecessary to have courses that deal principally or solely with thinking skills. The most desirable situation (at least in colleges) would be to have one or more courses devoted to thinking *and* to have specific thinking objectives in other courses across the curriculum.

WON'T TEACHING THINKING ACROSS THE CURRICULUM DETRACT FROM SUBJECT MATTER LEARNING?

This frequently expressed concern is a reasonable one, given the evidence of student deficiencies in other skill areas such as reading, writing, speaking, and study skills, as well as widespread student ignorance of fundamental historical information. If teaching thinking involved installing a large body of information to compete with or displace existing course material, then this concern would be sufficient cause to oppose the teaching of thinking across the curriculum. However, that is not what teaching thinking involves. Admittedly, before students can be expected to apply principles and techniques, they must first be introduced to them, so some material must be added. But that addition is minimal. The only significant change that is required is a change in teaching *methodology*.

A single example will illustrate how big a difference a small change can make. An economics professor recently gave his students two essays to read, each written by an economist, each developing a different side of the same issue. The students were required to read the essays and know what each author said. Then on the exam the professor asked the students to write an essay accurately stating the views of each person. Although he was undoubtedly unaware of the fact, he was testing little more than students' recollection of the material. Had he instead asked them to state which author's position they found more persuasive and why, he would have been testing several important thinking skills as well as testing understanding.

If such expectations were made central to his course, he would be subtly conveying the message that careful evaluation and judgment is important in economics and encouraging students to refine their thinking skills. Moreover, he would be doing these things *without in any way neglecting existing course content.* In fact, if Yale psychology professor Robert Sternberg is correct, the instructor would be *enhancing* course content. Sternberg is one of a growing number of educational psychologists who define intelligence itself in terms of thinking. "Intelligence," Sternberg suggests, "consists of a set of developed thinking and learning skills used in academic and everyday problem solving."[21]

SHOULDN'T K THROUGH 12 THINKING INSTRUCTION BE LIMITED TO THE HONORS PROGRAM?

Definitely not. Everyone needs thinking skills to meet the demands of career and citizenship. More important, everyone needs such skills to realize his or her potential as a human being. The highest of Abraham Maslow's hierarchy of human needs, self-actualization, is unachievable without the ability to think productively. Thus to deny meaningful instruction in thinking to students below a certain IQ or proficiency level is to deny them an essential part of their humanity. Similarly, the constitutional guarantees of freedom to speak, to choose one's own religion, and so on, lose much of their meaning when only some individuals are trained to evaluate and choose among competing views.

Such arguments are admittedly idealistic. But the case for teaching thinking to all students and not just to honor students can be made in practical terms as well. Harvard's Jerome Bruner has ably demonstrated that any subject, no matter how complex, can be taught to students at any level of education in a meaningful way.[22] In addition, cognitive research has documented that all thinking skills— even those most closely associated with the gifted, such as imaginativeness and originality—can be taught to virtually anyone.

Students in regular and even remedial programs not only need instruction in thinking: they need it more than students in honors classes. The latter students, in many cases, have already developed relatively effective thinking strategies of their own, intuitively. Their good fortune in that regard may, in fact, be one of the reasons they have become honor students! Classroom instruction can teach others by direct instruction what honor students have learned intuitively; and it can extend the honor students' cognitive skills beyond the limits of intuitive learning.

WON'T INSTRUCTION IN THINKING INVITE PROTESTS FROM PARENTS AND CONSERVATIVE RELIGIOUS OR POLITICAL GROUPS?

Since teaching students to think often involves consideration of controversial issues, protests from parents and from conservative religious or political groups may very well occur. But there is no reason to fear them as long as the issues to be considered are selected with sensitivity to the students' ages and levels of academic preparation, and the issues are treated objectively. When these conditions are not met, then educators have the obligation to practice the good thinking they preach, acknowledge the lapses, and take reasonable steps to ensure that they will not occur in the future.

That last sentence may seem rather hard on teachers. It should not be taken to suggest that parents and others never protest unreasonably. (They often do.) It means only that it is easy for teachers to confuse teaching students how to think with telling them what to think and thereby turn teaching into propagandizing. In selecting issues to discuss, a teacher will understandably be tempted to choose those she feels strongly about herself, but doing so may undermine the impartiality upon which effective instruction and fairness alike depend. Say, for example, she feels strongly that abortion is every woman's right and those who disagree are unreasonable, and chooses the issue of abortion for her students to discuss and write about. Her feelings may prevent her from objectively considering all pertinent evidence, as she expects her students to do. Moreover, it may lead her to unfairness in evaluating student work and leading discussion. (Note: It is not necessary to choose only those subjects about which you have no firm views— only that you be willing to set aside those views and re-examine the issue objectively. Any issue to which your commitment is so strong as to preclude such willingness should not be selected.)

Human nature being as it is, some individuals will be drawn to the teaching of thinking in their classrooms, consciously or unconsciously, not only by their commitment to students' cognitive development, but also by zeal for their own political, religious, or philosophic beliefs. And that commitment can prompt them to classify ideas as logical or illogical, reasonable or unreasonable, by the pathetic standard of whether the ideas agree with their own.

Several years ago at a conference on critical thinking, I heard a professor from a respected university, a man who had written a textbook on thinking, demonstrate his approach to teaching thinking. He spoke for more than an hour and showed a number of transparencies that revealed errors in thinking. All the examples concerned political issues, and, in every case, the error demonstrated reflected a conservative point of view. Though the speaker was undoubtedly unaware of the underlying message in his material, it was clear to his audience: the reasoning of political conservatives tends to be illogical, whereas that of liberals tends to be logical.

If such lapses can occur for experts on thinking, they surely can and do occur for nonexperts. To be aware of the dangers and learn how to avoid them, as subsequent chapters will assist you in doing, is the best approach. But it is also helpful to regard protests from parents and others with an open mind, realizing the possibility that their complaints may, on occasion, be well founded.

WILL THE ADDITION OF THINKING INSTRUCTION TO A CURRICULUM MAKE THE TEACHER'S JOB EASIER?

Like most valuable changes in curriculum, the addition of thinking objectives to a course will cost something. The cost in this case is a sacrifice of smoothness and neatness of instruction. Teaching students by the methods we will discuss in this book will be different from teaching them by lecturing. So teachers who have grown accustomed to lecturing will for a time experience the awkwardness that comes with any new approach. And even after they acquire skill in teaching thinking, they will have to contend with certain inevitable difficulties. It is more difficult, for example, to lead students in discussion than to lecture them, and more difficult to maintain classroom decorum when students are animatedly exchanging views than when they are quietly slumbering. Similarly, it is more difficult to keep precise pace with the syllabus in a dynamic situation than in a static one.

The adjustment for students may be difficult, too, at first. The methods that teachers will be instituting will not only be new to students, but will require them to become more actively involved in class discussion and struggle with perplexing problems and issues. Less proficient students will surely be apprehensive about their ability to master the skills of thought; more proficient students will very likely be upset over the realization that memorizing/regurgitating will no longer earn them As. Such reactions demand that teachers provide special guidance and encouragement until the new methods become familiar to students.

These adjustments will exist for both college and elementary/secondary teachers. But for the latter the emphasis on thinking skills will create two special challenges: making administrators realize that the loss in tidiness and measured pace with the syllabus is not a reflection of teacher inadequacy, but of the nature of the new learning process; and gaining the budgetary support necessary to make the thinking program work. Thinking instruction cannot be effective when classes are too large to permit every student to contribute to discussions or when teachers lack the time to evaluate student work and provide individual consultations. (Chapter 9 will discuss these matters at greater length.)

Revising courses to include thinking instruction thus does not make the job of teaching any easier; in fact, by demanding adjustments in teaching methodology and in some cases creating new challenges, it makes that job more difficult. Nevertheless, such revision can make teaching considerably more satisfying by transforming passive, bored observers into vital, enthusiastic learners. And that is no small achievement.

APPLICATION

Which of your prior views about thinking, if any, does this chapter reinforce? Which, if any, does it challenge? In light of this chapter, what modifications might be made in your approach to teaching?

chapter 2

A HOLISTIC APPROACH TO THE TEACHING OF THINKING

Because the teaching of thinking has developed through two separate disciplines, philosophy and psychology, each of which has remained insulated from the other, thinking instruction has tended to reflect two very different models—the creative thinking model and the critical thinking model. Each has both strengths and weaknesses.

The creative thinking model focuses principally on the production of ideas, the aspect of thinking many authorities, including Harvard's David Perkins, have found to be most seriously lacking in students. Moreover, because this model views creativity as a dynamic process, courses based on it have tended to treat thinking as a skill and thus have organized lessons sequentially and coherently. On the other hand, the creative thinking model seldom treats logic in any significant way and so is less effective in dealing with the evaluation of ideas. It sometimes fosters the false notions that creative ideas need no refinement and that creative people needn't (or shouldn't) be logical, thereby failing to prepare students to overcome imperfections in their ideas and to cope effectively with the rejection that often greets creative ideas.

The critical thinking model, historically much older than the creative model, is the model most often referred to by people in business, the professions, and education when they argue that the schools should teach students to think. Its great strength is that it covers in depth the requirements of logic and the analysis of ideas. Perhaps because of the thoroughness of its treatment of complex matters, or perhaps because of its Lockean conception of mind, the critical thinking model has tended to ignore creative thinking and to encourage a topical, rather than sequential organization of course material. In addition, the critical model often makes students see thinking as a negative and reactive enterprise, thereby limiting their competency to finding fault with existing ideas rather than producing better ideas, and savaging other people's arguments while ignoring the flaws in their own.

The importance of addressing one's own thinking errors has long been recognized by scholars. For example, Alfred Binet, the developer of intelligence testing, believed self-criticism to be a central factor in intelligence, a factor that is not inborn but must be developed. And Victor Noll, in his handbook on scientific thinking, wrote: "Criticizing one's own behavior is perhaps even more fundamental than criticizing that of others."[1] Nevertheless, despite the diligent efforts of textbook authors and instructors, the critical thinking model has not proved very effective in promoting such self-criticism in students. Although many students become adept at finding fallacies in other people's arguments—sometimes so much so that their approach has been termed a "fallacy frenzy"—they usually regard their own arguments as above criticism.

Not only have creative thinking advocates and critical thinking advocates tolerated the gulf between their approaches; they have often widened it by attacking each other's approaches. Some creative thinking advocates blame the neglect of creativity on society's emphasis on reasoning, and critical thinking advocates respond by likening creative thinking instruction to game playing. This unfortunate squabbling among scholars and educators has its counterpart in popular literature, with its side-show terminology of "left-brain *people*" and "right-brain *people.*" (The use of such terms suggests the need for pressing an older term back into service—"brainless people.")

The larger truths lost in this squabble are that both creative thinking and critical thinking have been neglected, that both are needed for solving problems and resolving issues, and that each benefits from the other—critical thinking saves creative from pursuing novelty for its own sake; creative thinking prevents critical from being merely reactive and negative.

These truths are further underscored by research. As Jerre Levy of the University of Chicago notes in reviewing studies of the brain, "The creations of human culture derive from the fully integrated actions of the whole brain, and any further advances will require an intimate and brilliant collaborative synthesis of the special skills of both sides of the brain. All of the available data point to the validity of this conclusion; none supports the idea that normal people function like split-brain patients, using only one hemisphere at a time." She argues further that the very structure of the brain, with the *corpus callosum* interconnecting the two hemispheres and facilitating their arousal, implies profound integration.[2]

TEACHING THINKING HOLISTICALLY

An alternative to choosing between the creative model and the critical model for teaching thinking is to use a holistic model which incorporates the principles and strategies of both. Such a model, if well-designed, offers at least two important advantages:

- *A holistic model embraces both the production and the evaluation of ideas and presents students with one coherent, sequential approach to productive thinking.* Thus such a model retains the strengths of the individual models, yet eliminates, or at least significantly reduces, their weaknesses. In addition, it helps students understand the interplay that occurs between creative and critical thinking in real-life thinking situations.
- *A holistic thinking model fits a broader range of thinking situations than does a creative model or a critical model.* There are three main thinking activities: making decisions, solving problems, and analyzing issues. Given the existence of different thinking models, it is not surprising that each of these situations has generated a separate research literature and separate teaching approaches, and has not unlikely created the impression that the three situations have little in common. In fact, though the terminology may differ from one situation to another, the essential skills in all three situations are nearly identical. All three require imagination: decision making, in generating alternative courses of action and likely scenarios that might develop in the implementation of decisions; problem solving, in producing ingenious solutions; issue analysis, in identifying possible objections to a line of thought. All three also require open-mindedness, reflectiveness, resourcefulness in obtaining information, careful interpretation, and logical reasoning.*

The comprehensiveness of a holistic model provides an additional benefit. "The most vexing and significant 'real life' problems," philosopher Richard Paul explains, "are logically messy. They span multiple categories and disciplines. They are typically not 'in' any one of them." Unfortunately, Paul observes, most textbook and classroom problems have tended to be one-system problems.[3] A holistic model, drawing as it does on creative as well as critical thinking, and therefore inviting associations outside the particular discipline, will encourage instructors to assign problems that touch not one, but several disciplines.

Before turning to our holistic model, let us examine creative thinking and critical thinking more closely, exposing misconceptions and identifying the important facts and principles that any holistic model must reflect.

---

*Since decision making tends to concern either a problem or an issue—"What should I do about this situation?" or "What is the best view to take of this issue?"—throughout this book decision making will be subsumed under those headings.

MISCONCEPTIONS ABOUT CREATIVE THINKING

In the mid-1950s, J. P. Guilford of the University of Southern California, curious about the extent of psychologists' neglect of the subject of creativity, examined *Psychological Abstracts.* He found that of approximately 121,000 titles listed in the previous 23 years, only 186 had any direct bearing on creativity. That is less than two-tenths of one percent![4] Little wonder that misconceptions about creativity abound. Here are the most serious ones:

> *The misconception that creativity is found in some fields, but not in others; that the arts, for example, demand imaginativeness and originality, whereas science, business, and the professions demand only logical thinking.*

This misconception has been widely accepted for decades. Noted psychologist Abraham Maslow describes how he came to realize the error of this notion. After assuming for years that *"any* painter was leading a creative live, *any* poet, *any* composer" because creativity was "the sole prerogative of certain professionals," he found through his experiments, especially one with a poor uneducated housewife, that he was mistaken. "I learned from her and others like her," he explains, "that a first-rate soup is more creative than a second-rate painting, and that generally, cooking or parenthood or making a home could be creative whereas poetry need not be; it could be uncreative."[5]

But what of science? Is the traditional notion that science is a matter of meticulous logic "untainted" by intuition or inspiration also inaccurate? According to many of the most knowledgeable individuals, yes. Karl Popper, for example, writes that "there is no such thing as a logical method of having new ideas, or a logical reconstruction of this process"; instead, "every discovery contains 'an irrational element,' or 'a creative intuition,' in Bergson's sense."[6]

Albert Einstein agreed. "The mere formulation of a problem," he noted, "is often far more essential than its solution which may be merely a matter of mathematical or experimental skill. To raise new questions, new possibilities, to regard old problems from a new angle requires creative imagination and marks real advances in science."[7] And philosopher of science Jacob Bronowski observes that "the discoveries of science, the works of art are explorations—more, are explosions, of a hidden likeness. The discoverer or artist presents in them two aspects of nature and fuses them into one. This is the act of creation, in which an original thought is born, and it is the same act in original science and original art."[8]

In light of these clarifications, how might we reasonably explain the role creativity plays in the various disciplines and the relationship of that role to critical (logical) thinking? Eliot Hutchinson's answer is as follows:

> The arts and science, I believe, roughly classify themselves from the creative aspect, not on the basis of content and method, as so many aestheticians have vainly tried to show, but rather according to the demands they make upon the intuitive faculty. It is not a question of separating the arts from the sciences

because one is imaginative and emotional and the other is logical and technical. Each discipline contains a range of all these elements. It is rather a question of grouping together all forms of either art or science which are created under the same conditions of insight, and then of asking what these have in common. If a careful analysis is made, they will be found to have much. *The identity of great disciplines of thought has its roots ultimately in the intuitive faculty, no matter how many poles they are apart in superficial content.* [Emphasis added.][9]

The misconception that creativity is synonymous with defying convention.

If this notion did not arise from the "doing your own thing" fixation of the 1960s, it nevertheless was reinforced by it. That fixation made it easier to equate creativity with the kind of bizarre, self-indulgent behavior many rock musicians consider creative expression. "For many people," George Kneller writes, "being creative seems to imply nothing more than releasing impulses or relaxing tensions. . . . Yet uninhibited swiveling at the hips is hardly creative dancing, nor is hurling colors at a canvas creative painting."[10]

It is true that to be creative a person must escape slavish conformity to the status quo and be willing to entertain new ideas, but that is not the same as defying convention. It is, rather, suspending the influence of convention on one's mind (and thereby being open to new ideas) while dealing with problems and issues.

The misconception that creativity requires a special talent or a high IQ.

It has been fashionable for generations to believe that highly creative people enjoy special intellectual abilities denied to others and that the higher people's IQ scores, the greater their chances for creative achievement. However, when such beliefs have been tested, they have been found to have no basis in fact. Creativity requires no special talents, only the application of talents virtually everyone has. Furthermore, a high IQ score is not an indication of creative ability, nor a low score an indication of its absence. The great majority of creative achievers fall below the genius level score of 135. (This will come as no surprise to anyone familiar with the IQ test's origin: the test was never designed to measure creativity.)[11]

The misconception that creative people can achieve without effort.

This idea no doubt arises from the fact that achievements themselves receive headlines, whereas the years of work that made them possible are lost in finer newsprint. "Genius is 99 percent perspiration and 1 percent inspiration," wrote one of this century's most creative people, Thomas Edison, and his life bore out the message. The more than 1100 patents he held did not come without effort. It was his habit to work twenty or more hours a day, often wrestling with a troublesome problem for years before achieving a breakthrough—thirteen years in the case of the phonograph.

A close look at lives of other creative achievers reveals similar perseverance. Lester Pfister, one of the developers of hybrid corn, began with 50,000 stalks and worked by hand for five years; by the time he had perfected the strain, he had but four stalks left and he was impoverished. Astronomer Johannes Kepler spent seven years working out his first and second laws of planetary motion. Before Alexander Graham Bell could invent the telephone, he had to learn a subject entirely new to him (electricity). In the process of inventing the tractor, Henry Ford worked up 871 models before creating one he was satisfied with. As these few examples indicate, creative people are not less hardworking than others, but more so.

The misconception that the use of drugs enhances creativity.

Brewster Ghiselin explains the error of this view.

A certain amount of eccentricity, some excess, taint, or 'tykeishness' is often prized by creative minds as a guarantee of ability to move apart or outside [formalist thought]. Drugs or alcohol are sometimes used to produce abnormal states [of mind] to the same end of disrupting the habitual set of the mind, but they are of dubious value, apart from the dangers of addiction, since their action reduces judgment, and the activities they provoke are hallucinatory rather than illuminating. What is needed is control and direction. . . . In short the creative discipline when successful may generate a trancelike state, but one does not throw oneself into a trance in order to create.[12]

The misconception that creative people are mentally unstable.

Some people consider "creative person" and "lunatic" to be near-synonyms. Unfortunately, from time to time a study is published that on the surface seems to lend credibility to this belief. On closer inspection, however, the data in many of these studies yield a different conclusion. For example, Frank Barron conducted a study of writers in which the most creative of his subjects scored higher on psychopathology, yet that was not all; they also scored exceptionally high on ego strength, which indicated that they possessed the psychological resources to balance the otherwise dangerous tendencies.[13]

In comparisons between creative people and emotionally disturbed people, the significant facts are usually not the similarities, but the differences. In one unusual study, for instance, creative thinking tests were administered to schizophrenics. The subjects showed "an astonishingly impoverished imagination, inflexibility, lack of originality, and inability to summon any kind of response to new problems. Their answers gave no evidence of the rich fantasy and wild imagination popularly attributed to schizophrenics. There was only an impoverished, stifled, frozen creativity."[14]

A great many authorities not only reject the idea that creativity and mental instability are in any way linked; they also affirm a positive connection between creativity and mental health. In the following quotation, psychologist Harold Anderson summarizes the view of such respected authorities as Erich Fromm, Rollo May, Carl Rogers, Abraham Maslow, J. P. Guilford, and Ernest Hilgard:

> The consensus of these authors is that creativity is an expression of a mentally or psychologically healthy person, that creativity is associated with wholeness, unity, honesty, integrity, personal involvement, enthusiasm, high motivation, and action.

> There is also agreement that neurosis either accompanies or causes a degraded quality of one's creativity. For neurotic persons and persons with other forms of mental disease [who are, at the same time, creative] such assumptions as the following are offered: that these persons are creative in spite of their disease; that they are producing below the achievements they would show without the disease; that they are on the downgrade, or that they are pseudo creative, that is, they may have brilliant original ideas which, because of the neurosis, they do not communicate.[15]

"CREATIVE IDEA" DEFINED

What exactly is a creative idea? How can a creative idea be differentiated from an uncreative one? To begin with, a creative idea is original, imaginative, uncommon. That does not mean that the object of the creative act must itself always be new. The creativity may lie in improving an existing thing. In fact, according to one estimate, 80 percent of the patents issued by the U.S. patent office are reportedly issued for improvements in existing things, rather than for new things.[16] Nor does it mean the object of the creative act must be something of great importance. A new way of teaching a dog to do tricks or discouraging a little brother from being a pest is no less creative because it is solving a relatively minor problem.

However, something more than originality is required for an idea to be classified as creative; otherwise, the most bizarre idea would be the most creative. The idea must not only be uncommon, but *uncommonly good* as well, solving the problem or resolving the issue in an ingenious way.

Creative ideas may be found in any field. There are creative concepts and theories, many of which we no longer recognize as such because they are so familiar to us; for example, the concept of a library, Galileo's concept of the solar system, and Einstein's theory of relativity. There are also creative experiments in science and social science, like psychologist Wolfgang Kohler's "stick problem," now famous for establishing that higher animals can solve problems through insight. The idea involved putting a small stick and a large stick in an ape's cage and placing a piece of fruit outside, just beyond the reach of the animal's arm when holding the larger stick. To reach the fruit, the animal had to first achieve the insight of inserting one stick inside the other.

Creative ideas can be found, as well, in courtrooms and in executive suites. The sentence Veronica Simmons, a Los Angeles judge, imposed on a landlord was creative. After finding him guilty of violating probation by refusing to improve the rat-infested apartment he had rented to a family of seven, she sentenced him to live in a similar apartment for 30 days.[17] And the "You meet the nicest people on a Honda" advertising campaign Soichiro Honda designed in the early 1960s was a creative way of increasing the market for his motorcycles by overcoming the motorcycle's previous tough-guy image.

Ralph Nader's idea of broadening the measure of our country's economic health to include the condition of the consumer is a creative idea. Nader argues that the standard measures of Gross National Product—increases or decreases in housing starts and production of food and goods—need to be balanced by measures of how many people are housed and fed and properly nourished.[18]

Also creative are Harvard educator James Q. Wilson's idea for using the classroom to teach parenting techniques and his proposed method for teaching them. His suggestions involve replacing classroom lectures with videotapes of actual families and teaching students to evaluate the parental techniques they observe. This approach, which presents factual dramas in a medium (TV) with which teenagers are comfortable will, Wilson hopes, help the youngsters escape the "vicious cycle of nagging, exasperation, appeasement, and random hitting" they might otherwise fall prey to as parents.[19]

The need for creative ideas never diminishes—every day new situations arise to pose new problems or aggravate old ones. The Sahara desert continues to expand southward at a rate of 60 feet a day, leaving more and more people malnourished and susceptible to disease. The prison system in this country grows increasingly overcrowded and its inmates more likely to become, upon release, an even greater threat to society than before incarceration. Pollution in its various forms—most notably, hazardous waste and acid precipitation—poison our air and underground water supplies. Weapons escalation increases the danger of nuclear holocaust.

Often one problem challenges many fields. The scourge of AIDS, for example, a disease previously unknown to mankind, has researchers searching for a cure, public health authorities challenged to devise means of halting its spread, lawyers and ethicists wrestling with new issues ("Is it legally or morally right to bar AIDS-stricken children from school?"), and friends and relatives of victims challenged to find ways to comfort them. These problems and thousands of other problems and issues pose powerful challenges to human creativity.

IMPORTANT FACTS ABOUT CREATIVITY

Creative ideas often come from associating things not commonly associated or from actively bringing together antithetical elements.

Johann Gutenberg's insight for the printing press occurred to him after watching a wine-press in operation. The idea for the forklift truck reportedly came to its inventor while he watched donuts being lifted out of a bakery oven on steel "fingers." More recent examples of creative ideas achieved from unusual associations include the Hearing Dog programs for the deaf (inspired by the Seeing Eye Dog programs for the blind); the planned use of sea lions as lifeguards in Laguna Beach, California, by the Friends of the Sea Lion rehabilitation center; and the Homework Hotline, an afternoon TV program offered by Los Angeles station KLCS-TV, undoubtedly patterned after drug and suicide hotlines.

What possible association can the concept of cloning have with the toy industry? None, most of us would answer. And yet Mary Curran of El Cerrito, California, has forced an association that promises to be as profitable as it is creative. Working from front and profile photographs, she makes and sells almost-life-size dolls of people.[20]

Actively bringing together opposites or antitheses is termed "Janusian thinking," after the Roman god Janus, whose many faces were turned in different directions. Psychiatrist Albert Rothenberg, who has done extensive research on creativity, coined the term. He cites a letter written by Einstein in 1919, but unpublished for more than fifty years, which demonstrates that Janusian thinking was responsible for the insight that led to Einstein's formulation of the theory of relativity.[21]

The trigger mechanism for creative thinking is the disposition to be curious, to wonder, to inquire.

Asking "What's wrong here?" and/or "Why is this the way it is, and how did it come to be that way?" leads to the identification of problems and challenges. If Alexander Fleming had not wondered about his observation of the inhibiting effect of molds on staphylococcus colony growth, he would never have made the discoveries that led to the development of penicillin. (Other researchers had made the same observation, but had been uncurious about it.) Curiosity was similarly responsible for Charles Nicolle's discovery of the cause of typhus, Walter Reed's discovery of the cause of yellow fever, and Wilhelm Roentgen's discovery of X-rays.

Walter Chrysler, the automobile manufacturer, was an insatiably curious person. When he was a young railroad mechanic, he saved up his pay and bought a Pierce-Arrow automobile for $5000, a substantial sum at that time. His purpose was not to drive about and impress people, but to take it apart and put it together again, to see how it worked, to stimulate his own creativity, and to decide how he might improve the machine. The questions prompted by his curiosity—"Why couldn't this be done that way instead?" and "Wouldn't the addition of _____ improve its performance?"—led to the manufacture of the automobiles that bear his name.

The importance of curiosity is stressed in the training of industrial engineers, who are often taught to walk through a company and question everything, even things whose purpose seems obvious, asking, for example, "Is this operation necessary at all? What would we lose if we eliminated it? If it is essential, how can we improve it?" In doing so, they open their minds to the insights that are available to anyone who is willing to wonder.

A more recent example of the importance of curiosity for creativity is found in the work of psychological researcher Jack Hokanson, who has researched catharsis theories for over 20 years. Hokanson noticed that women did not respond to insults belligerently, as men did; for women, aggression was apparently not a cathartic for anger. (As it turned out, friendliness was!) His curiosity led him to wonder whether aggression was really instinctive, as the prevailing belief asserted, or a learned reaction; and his wondering helped to set the stage for the contemporary view of anger explained in detail in Carol Tavris's *Anger: The Misunderstood Emotion.* [22]

Unconscious assumptions undermine curiosity.

The more people take for granted, the less curiosity they have; and familiarity tends to make people take many things for granted. Take, for example, the subject of bathing. In our culture we are taught that bathing is a private act whose sole purpose is cleanliness. That, we assume, is the way it always was, and indeed, always should be. As a result of that assumption, many of us are repulsed by the oriental practice of family bathing. And our assumption prevents us from wondering about the origins of our bathing customs.

Only when we succeed in breaking through that assumption are we able to entertain the questions, "Was it always so in western culture? What are the historical facts?" The answer that awaits us is that in the time of the ancient Romans bathing was public and served to promote not only cleanliness, but also regeneration and social communication. This view of bathing continued into the Middle Ages, when, contrary to common belief, bathing conditions were better than in New York tenements at the turn of the twentieth century. It was only with the Protestant Reformation and the Catholic Counter-Reformation that nakedness became sinful and public bathing was discontinued. [23]

The production of ideas is stimulated by deferring judgment.

The human mind moves back and forth between producing and judging ideas with ease, so it is understandable that many people have developed the habit of producing an idea, evaluating it, then producing another, and so on. But a number of studies have shown that people produce more and better ideas when they postpone making a judgment until they have produced many ideas. Moreover, studies indicate that early ideas tend to be common ideas and so by extending the effort to produce ideas—pressing, say, beyond five or six to thirty or forty—people are more likely to achieve a greater proportion of good ideas. [24] As Alfred North Whitehead advises, "The probability is that nine hundred and ninety-nine of [our ideas] will come to nothing . . . but we had better entertain them all, however skeptically, for the thousandth idea may be the one that will change the world." [25]

Flexibility of mind is essential for creativity.

Most people have their minds made up about many matters. As a result, their thinking is often constricted, and they are blinded to new and promising possibilities. Being flexible means being willing to let go of certainties and approach situations openly, without twisting them to fit preconceived notions. It means refusing to be controlled by tradition or fashion. Above all, being flexible means being ready to *challenge the obvious.*

For thousands of years it was obvious that a heavier object falls faster than a lighter one . . . until Galileo entertained the possibility that the truth might be otherwise. For centuries it was obvious that the center of consciousness was the human heart rather than the brain . . . until someone had the courage to challenge that view. And the time-honored wisdom of the medical profession made it obvious that people who suffered and died from severe pains in the chest had succumbed to "acute indigestion" . . . until William Herrick questioned that diagnosis and discovered the condition known as heart attack.

"Every new and good thing," writes Brewster Ghiselin, "is liable to seem eccentric and dangerous at first glance"[26] Indeed, many of the truest and most useful ideas seem positively absurd. To become flexible, we must overcome prejudice, dogmatism, and resistance to change. Prejudice makes us see the world in neat categories, precisely labeled, and not admitting of variation; it also makes us explain away or ignore whatever does not conform to stereotyped notions. Dogmatism prompts us to regard issues as clear-cut, settled, and indisputable and thus prevents us from dealing with complexity and ambiguity and from doing what flexibility demands—changing our minds about matters, quickly and ungrudgingly, whenever the facts warrant doing so. Resistance to change is responsible for our clinging to old beliefs even after they have been disproved.

Fear of failure can block creativity.

The risk of failure is always present in two forms—failure to achieve what we set out to achieve, and failure to persuade others that our solution or decision is worthy of acceptance and application. The latter kind, often the more painful to bear, is much more common than is realized, even in the case of ideas we would think would be greeted most enthusiastically.

For example, Galileo was threatened with excommunication and death for suggesting that the sun is the center of the solar system. When Charles Newbold invented the cast-iron plow, farmers spurned it on the grounds that the iron would pollute the soil. When Dr. Horace Wells first used gas as an anesthetic in pulling teeth, the medical profession scorned him. Joseph Lister and Ignaz Semmelweiss were scoffed for their advocacy of antiseptic conditions in hospitals. Elias Howe's sewing machine was rejected in the United States; he was forced to market it in England. And Sylvester Graham's warnings about the effects of mechanization on foods and his advocacy of natural eating habits and organic foods were largely unheeded until a century after his death.

People who wish to realize their creative potential need to learn how to deal not only with the risk of failure, but also with the fear of failure. Researcher Sheila Mumford has demonstrated that such fear can block creativity by influencing the approaches people take to problems and causing them to make mistakes.[27]

THE ROLE OF CRITICAL THINKING

Chapter 1 presented this holistic definition of thinking: "Thinking . . . is any mental activity that helps formulate or solve a problem, make a decision, or fulfill a desire to understand; it is a searching for answers, a reaching for meaning." Creative thinking, as we have seen, *produces* ideas. Critical thinking *evaluates* those ideas, as well as the ideas we encounter in such activities as reading and listening, testing them for usefulness and/or soundness, and refining them as necessary. The importance of critical thinking in solving problems and resolving issues is suggested by the following facts:

Solutions that seem practical or efficacious are sometimes not.

Soviet military researchers reportedly had the creative idea of training dogs to run under attacking tanks with bombs strapped to their backs. They employed the Pavlovian method of training the dogs to associate food with the bottoms of tanks. The only problem was that the dogs associated food with Russian tanks and so carried their deadly burdens back to the Russian army instead of to the enemy. To cite another example, the idea of appointing tough prison inmates as "building tenders" in Texas prisons seemed to be an ingenious way of maintaining control both of the prisons and of the prisons' budgets. Unfortunately, the practice resulted in loss of control over prisoners, a fact dramatized by forty murders and five hundred stabbings in one 18-month period.[28]

A more widely publicized example of a solution with unexpected results is the Coca Cola gaffe of 1985, in which the manufacturer abandoned its own formula in favor of a new one, only to be forced by declining profits and angry consumer reaction to reinstate the old version. In all three cases, if the originators of the ideas had examined them critically (or done so more effectively), the unfortunate results that followed could have been avoided.

Human perception is often flawed and memory distorted.

Studies of perception reveal how inaccurate it can be even while people are trying to be accurate. Before Taster's Choice coffee was first introduced, marketing tests were conducted to determine which color label would be best for the product. The *very same coffee* was put in jars with three different labels and people were asked to try the coffee and give their reactions; the majority found the coffee in the jar with the yellow label watery, the coffee in the jar with the brown label strong (many said it had kept them up at night), and the coffee in the jar with the red label just right, even delicious.[29]

More searching studies of human perception and its relationship with memory have been conducted, among the most interesting of them the studies of Harvard professor Elizabeth Loftus on eyewitness testimony. Remembering is not a passive process, she notes, but a constructive, integrative one. Similarly, perceptions are not recorded in the manner of videotape recordings; rather, they occur in three stages: the acquisition stage, the retention stage, and the retrieval stage. At each of these stages events can occur that distort the perceptions without the person's awareness. Examples of events that commonly occur are allowing attention to lapse while perceiving and thereby missing important details, perceiving things the way they usually are rather than the way they are on the particular occasion, having post-event information such as news reports and suggestions by other people mix with the original perception, and unconsciously transferring details from the memory of one situation to the memory of another.[30]

Guessing and unconscious assuming often masquerade as knowing.

Knowing consists of being in possession of the facts about something and realizing that we possess them. (It usually implies, as well, being able to express what is known and how we came to know it.) Unfortunately, it is possible to experience the feeling of conviction that accompanies knowing and yet not know, as when we confidently call someone "Ed" for years, certain that his name is Ed, only to find out that his name is Arthur. Such "false knowing" has its root in assuming—that is, taking something for granted—or in guessing and then later remembering what was guessed as if we had learned it from a reliable source.

Knowledge is seldom (if ever) complete.

No field of study can claim knowledge that is fixed and final. When discoveries occur, old ideas must be reevaluated and sometimes revised or abandoned. Complicating this reevaluation process further is the fact that there is often considerable lag time in a culture's replacement of disproved ideas. Consider, for example, the popular (Freudian) idea that ventilating anger reduces anger. Studies refuting that idea date back at least to 1956 (Seymour Feshbach) and continued on through the 1960s and 1970s (Jack Hokanson, among others). These studies showed that in many cases ventilating anger not only fails to reduce anger, *it often increases it.* [31] Yet during that time period, therapy groups advocating the expression of hostility continued to proliferate. In fact, articles and books citing the therapeutic benefits of watching "professional" wrestling and other exhibitions of real or mock violence are *still being published.*

The fact that today's knowledge may be overturned or at least revised tomorrow (or may have already been overturned without our realizing it) could lead us to the kind of skepticism that refuses to embrace any idea. That would be foolish because, in the practical sense, it is impossible to build a life on that view. Besides, it is not the embracing of an idea that causes problems—it is the refusal to relax that embrace when good sense dictates doing so. It is enough to form convictions with care and carry them lightly, being willing to reconsider them whenever new evidence calls them into question.

Bias is a natural phenomenon and affects judgment, sometimes profoundly.

The notion that people are automatically objective is a myth. In normal circumstances people approach situations under the influence of their experiences and their beliefs. At times this influence will be blatantly biased, as in cases where stereotyped notions cause people to have their minds made up in advance. A person, let us say, picks up the newspaper and reads this headline: " 'Noah's Ark Remnants to Be Tested," which appeared over a story explaining that an expedition had taken bags of rock and chunks of decayed wood from Mount Ararat and would have them tested to determine whether they were from the ark described in the Bible.[32] Now if the person is an atheist who rejects the Bible as a fairy tale, or a believer who accepts the biblical account literally, then her reaction to the news story may well be already determined before she reads it.

At other times, the influence of experience and belief will be subtle, amounting to no more than a preference or prejudice so slight as to be unrecognized. In some ways this subtle form is more dangerous to sound thinking. Hearing Richard Nixon talking on television, for instance, a person may oppose his ideas for no reason other than a vague dislike for the man.

Although objectivity does not come automatically, however, it can in large measure be achieved. The key to achieving it is to become sensitive to both the blatant and subtle influence of experience and belief and to make allowances for them. Critical thinking provides the means for doing so.

Reasoning is often confused with rationalizing or is otherwise flawed.

In reasoning the conclusion is reached after examining and weighing the evidence; in rationalizing the conclusion is reached first and the evidence is then carefully selected to support it. Rationalizing, in other words, is a dishonest substitute for reasoning that serves to support prejudices and shield people from unpleasant realities. As this explanation suggests, it is impossible to judge the soundness of an argument solely on the basis of whether evidence is offered in its behalf; it is necessary to determine whether the evidence presented represents a fair survey of the evidence available.

The other flaws that commonly occur in reasoning are classified under the general term "fallacies." Fallacies may be either formal—errors in which the conclusion does not follow from the premises of an argument—or informal— errors that commonly occur because of a faulty perspective or the careless expression of an idea. When a person *deliberately* flaws an argument in order to deceive the other person, he has not committed a fallacy, but "sophistry." Examples of fallacies are attacking the other person instead of addressing the issue, overgeneralizing, and oversimplifying. (These and other fallacies are discussed in Chapter 4.) Because reasoning can be confused with rationalizing or flawed by fallacies, it should never be presumed correct, but *proved* so through careful and critical examination.

Opinions, even those of experts, can be mistaken.

There is a great deal of confusion today about opinion. The fact that everyone living in a democracy has a right to his opinion is often taken to mean that everyone's opinion is right. The confusion lies mainly in the fact that the word "opinion" is used to express two very different things: matters of taste, on the one hand, and matters of judgment, on the other. It is true that there is little point in disputing matters of taste; that is, matters such as whether one prefers a large car to a small car or the color blue to the color red or husky brunettes to slender blondes. Though people do argue over whether someone is attractive or homely, such arguments are seldom very productive because, as the saying goes, "Beauty lies in the eye of the beholder" and, more importantly, *there is no satisfactory way to determine who is right.*

In matters of judgment, on the other hand, it is appropriate to speak of an opinion being right or wrong because there is a way to make such a determination—by examining the evidence and finding which view best reflects it. That determination is not always easy to make: often years, even centuries, must pass before the means are available to accumulate the necessary evidence. Nevertheless, it is possible (theoretically, if not practically) to make. Accordingly, if in 2000 B.C. two people were arguing about whether the earth revolves around the sun, the one who argued in the negative was right and the other wrong, irrespective of the fact that confirmation would not be possible for several thousand years. Critical thinking is the means by which assertions and arguments are evaluated in light of available evidence.

> *Even when solutions are eminently practical, reasoning flawless, and opinions enlightened, other people will not necessarily perceive that they are.*

That many people are fearful of change and therefore resist it is a fact found on every page of human history. Inventions whose usefulness would seem to have been all too obvious were at first rejected. The baby carriage, the umbrella, the bathtub, and razors, for example, were all considered too radical, and the railroad was regarded as a creation of Satan "to lead immortal souls down to Hell."[33] The list of ideas that met similar scorn—from the notion of air travel to the concept of zero—is long indeed.

Anyone who would persuade others of the merit of a new idea, however obvious that merit may seem to him or her, must first identify and work out the imperfections in the idea and the complications that are likely to arise in implementing it, and then anticipate and prepare to answer the objections of the people that must be persuaded. These important mental tasks are classified under critical thinking.

A HOLISTIC MODEL

The holistic model presented here is a general one that covers both problem solving and issue analysis. The two activities have much in common, most importantly their basic stages. Both begin with the realization that a challenge exists (a problem or issue) that needs to be addressed. Both proceed to define the challenge, compile relevant information that will be useful in responding to it, and formulate one or more possible responses to the challenge. Finally, both analyze the possible responses to determine the best one, then elaborate or refine that one, as necessary.*

Although their basic stages are the same, however, problem solving and issue analysis differ in their essential focus. Issues, unlike problems, concern matters which not only challenge people, but tend to cause controversy, a condition characterized by the division of intelligent, informed people into two or more opposing camps, each certain that it is right and the opposition wrong. Therefore, whereas problem solving addresses the question "What is the most effective *course of action?*" issue analysis addresses the question "What is the most reasonable *belief?*" The ways in which these questions affect activity within the stages of the holistic process will be addressed at appropriate places in our discussion.

For decades thinking instruction researchers have noted that though textbook and classroom problems are neatly formulated for students, real-life problems are not. As a result, even proficient students are often stymied when they enter business and the professions. The experts have therefore argued that thinking instruction should include practice in *formulating* problems. Moreover, in recent years more and more researchers have cautioned that thinking instruction can be effective only if it emphasizes *dispositions* as well as skills. If students lack the willingness or inclination to think creatively and critically, the argument goes, they will not do so regardless of the level of skill they possess.

Both arguments are sound, but they have yielded relatively little progress in teaching students to formulate problems or develop the desired dispositions. One difficulty has been that the formulation of problems fits well in a process approach, but not very well in a topical approach, and most textbooks adopt the latter. Another has been the difficulty of finding an effective means of developing dispositions. How, teachers and authors have wondered, can we make someone WANT to think well?

The holistic approach detailed below overcomes the first difficulty by focusing on the *process* of thinking and addressing problem formulation as a specific stage. It overcomes the second, considerably more formidable, difficulty by treating the indisposition to think creatively and critically as largely a *perceptual problem.* In other words, it asserts that students not only lack experience in producing and evaluating ideas; they also lack the perspective from which problems and issues are regarded as intellectual challenges.† This perceptual problem cound be addressed outside the holistic process, but treating it in various places within the process, most importantly as the first stage of the process, gives it the prominence it deserves.

The holistic approach to the teaching of thinking has five stages: *Exploration, Expression, Investigation, Idea Production, and Evaluation/Refinement.* Let us look closely at each.

*Researchers do not always agree about the number of stages, particularly in creative thinking; however, their disagreement has never been substantive, but merely over whether to combine activities under one heading or several. The key question to ask about any holistic description of thinking, including the description that will be offered here, is, "Does it cover both the production and evaluation of ideas and account for all important activities in each?"

†The lack of enthusiasm many students display toward the discussion of ideas is surely related to the views that "everyone is entitled to his opinion" and that "everything depends on how you look at it." Chapter 3 deals with these and other obstacles to cognitive development.

Stage 1: Exploration

It is axiomatic that we must perceive that a problem (issue) exists before we can make a conscious effort to deal with it. Moreover, it is well-established that good thinkers have a heightened perception of problems and issues. Unfortunately, educators have tended to view perception as a "gift" conferred by divine providence or beneficent genes rather than as an ability that everyone has the capacity to develop. Hence they have seldom tried to cultivate it. Indeed, they have often inadvertently stifled it by giving students ready-made problems instead of having them find their own.[34] (Ready-made problems are not without merit, of course; it would be grossly inefficient to have students find *all* their own problems.) Since the perception of problems and issues is intimately related to curiosity and discontentment, those characteristics are the key to its development.

Problem solving and issue analysis may be said to begin when a person experiences one or both of these states of mind: (1) wondering about why something is as it is, or whether it is as people say it is; and/or (2) a feeling of frustration and irritation because something is not what it should/might be or has gone wrong and should be set right. Such a state of mind may be thrust upon a person by life, as it was upon Viktor Frankl when he was sent to a concentration camp and the manuscript he had worked on for years destroyed. (His creative response was to use the years of suffering to study the human mind and spirit, an effort which resulted in the publication of *Man's Search for Meaning* and other books, as well as the development of his unique system of psychotherapy, "logotherapy.")

Yet such a state of wonder or discontentment need not be passively awaited—it can be stimulated. There are a number of ways of doing so. One is to seek out problems and issues by reading and listening and observing for (a) the products and procedures and processes people complain need to be improved, and (b) the ideas people argue about. Here are just a few subjects, each of which suggests one or more problems or issues: the quality of political leadership, pollution, the federal bureaucracy, the criminal justice system, highway safety, inflation, violence in the media, unemployment, health care costs, teenage sex, international terrorism, nuclear disarmament. The list could, of course, be extended to include the innumerable problems and issues of local or personal concern.

Once we develop a list of problematic products, procedures, and processes, we can ask questions about each as a further means of stimulating wonder. Alex Osborn devised a comprehensive checklist of questions for products. Similar checklists could be developed for procedures and processes. Here, slightly adapted, is Osborn's list:

Can the object be put to other uses in its present form?

Can it be modified so as to serve additional uses?

How might it be adapted? What else is it like? (Could that thing provide a model for adapting this?)

Can it be changed in color, motion, smell, form, shape, or some other way?

Can it be magnified? If so, in what way? What can be added? (Time? Frequency?) Can it be made stronger? Larger? Thicker? Of extra value? Can it be made in duplicate? Can it be exaggerated in some way?

Can it be reduced? How? By making it smaller? Condensing it? Streamlining it? Shortening it? Understating it? Omitting some part of it? Breaking into components?

Can something be substituted for it? What else? A different ingredient? Material? Process? Power? Place? Approach?

Can it be rearranged? Can components be interchanged into a different pattern? A different layout? A different sequence? Can the pace or schedule be modified?

Can anything be reversed? For example, can positive and negative be transposed? Can opposites be found? Can it be turned backward? Upside down?

Can something be combined with it? Is any other blend, alloy, assortment, or ensemble possible?[35]

Another way to stimulate wonder or discontentment is to look for unmet needs. Every new product or service and most new concepts have been created in response to some need (or desire) that was not being met by existing products, services, or concepts. Travelers' dissatisfaction with public transportation, for example, led to the invention of the car-rental-service concept; later, the dissatisfaction of many travelers with the high prices being charged for rental cars led to the invention of the "Rent-a-Wreck" and "Rent-a-Heap" concept of providing older cars in good mechanical condition for those wishing cheap yet dependable transportation. Tracing the history of any modern product, service, or concept from lamps, beds, and watches to restaurants and newspapers (an interesting assignment for students) will reveal a series of responses to previously unmet needs. And searching for today's unmet needs is a powerful stimulus to meeting them.

Yet another way to stimulate wonder (though not, in this case, discontentment) is to notice other people's creative ideas and consider their implications. In such cases, it is not, strictly speaking, a problem that is sought, but an *opportunity.* Every creative idea carries within it the seeds for other creative ideas, if it is responded to in the right way. Most people, on seeing others' creative ideas, say to themselves, "I wish I had thought of that" and quietly envy the other person. A better way to respond is to ask, "How might these ideas be extended or applied in different areas?"

When the idea of extending automobile financing was introduced in the late 1950s, Lee Iacocca, then a junior executive at Ford, wondered how he could build upon that idea and devised the "56 for '56" campaign that enabled buyers to purchase a new Ford and take 56 months to pay. Similarly, Gutenberg's printing press was a creative extension of the wine press idea; and the Hearing Dog concept is a creative extension of the Seeing Eye dog concept.

By stimulating their own wonder and discontentment, students will not only find problems and issues (and opportunities) to serve as the focus of the other stages of the holistic process; they will also develop greater sensitivity to experience. As a result, they will be more likely to perceive interesting possibilities in what others see as mere information. Let's say, for example, they are reading a passage like the following in their weekly newsmagazine:

> Other scholars would encourage judges to strengthen their efforts at negotiating pretrial settlements. Some even propose diverting libel cases out of the court system to arbitration, where the emphasis would be on retractions or other statements to correct the record.[36]

Whereas others would regard this matter-of-factly, perceptive students might think "Arbitration in libel cases . . . hmmm . . . Where else might this approach be used?" Using this thought as a springboard, the students might, at a later stage of the holistic process, produce the intriguing idea of using arbitration in certain kinds of civil suits as a way of lightening the court load and thereby improving the justice system.

Stage 2: Expression

The formal beginning of this stage is the moment when we realize that something is wrong, that a problem or issue or opportunity exists and challenges us. The purpose of this stage is to find the best expression of the problem or issue. In the case of problems, the best expression is the one that will produce the most creative, constructive idea. In the case of issues, the best expression is the one that captures the essence of the controversy.

Many people ignore this stage completely in their efforts to be creative. They assume the problem is self-evident and begin at once to search for solutions. Such an approach is a mistake for several reasons. First, the feeling that a problem is self-evident usually arises from unconscious assumptions about what the solution should be. Those assumptions are, as a rule, intimately bound up with the common, the familiar, the preconceived notion of what is appropriate, the expected—in short, with the very forces that tend to militate *against* creativity! Similarly, the feeling that an issue is self-evident is often synonymous with commitment to one side of the issue; hence, it is not likely to encourage an objective consideration of the evidence.

Another reason it is a mistake to begin solving a problem without first expressing it (a reason that does not apply to issues) is that most problems can be expressed in a number of ways and there is no way of telling how good any expression is except by comparing it with other expressions.

A third important reason for taking the time to express both problems and issues carefully and, whenever possible, to make them visual by writing them down is that clear wording can dispel vagueness and confusion and the act of writing can help focus our attention and stimulate the flow of ideas. As Henry Hazlitt observed, "A problem properly stated is partly solved."

So far in our discussion of this stage most of what has been said applies to both problems and issues. At this point, however, we encounter a significant difference. Because problem solving is a search for the best action to take and issue analysis is a search for the most reasonable belief, the form used for expressing problems is not the same as that used for expressing issues. The following easy steps, presented here as you might present them to students, should eliminate any confusion.

1. *Decide whether you are dealing with a problem or an issue.* Consider whether the specific subject involved tends to arouse partisan feelings and to divide informed, intelligent people. It it doesn't, treat it as a problem. If it does, treat it as an issue. Here are some sample *problems:* a student trying to study in a noisy dormitory, a child frightened at the prospect of making a first trip to the hospital, an advertising executive given the assignment of creating television commercials to combat drunken driving, a businesswoman dealing with subtle sexual harassment from her boss. Here are some sample *issues:* a congressman writing legislation to lower the age of sexual consent, a public school teacher selecting a nondenominational prayer for her classroom, an anthropologist claiming that human beings are by nature violent, a human rights organization spokeswoman urging that products from South Africa be boycotted.

Each of the situations in the first group is properly considered a problem because there is nothing about the situation which is likely to divide informed, intelligent people. Of course, someone, somewhere, might conceivably take a different view of a situation than most people take—for example, challenging the right of a student to a quiet dormitory atmosphere—but that is likely to be an infrequent reaction. Each of the situations in the second group, however, is likely to provoke considerable disagreement because each involves a matter that is controversial.*

2. *If you are dealing with a problem, proceed as follows.* Express the problem in writing, as clearly as possible, and in as many ways as you can, using the "How can . . . ?" form. To demonstrate how this form is used, let us consider this timely problem: in the 1970s and early 1980s in the United States, over 7000 schools closed their doors because of declining enrollments, budget cuts, and inflation.[37] Here are various ways this problem might be expressed:

How can school enrollments be increased?

How can school budgets be reduced?

How can the impact of inflation on education be lessened?

How can school buildings best be used after the schools are closed down?

*The following situation will occur on occasion: a problem without a trace of controversy will generate a controversial solution; for example, the advertising executive might decide to do a commercial that shows gory film footage of real accidents. Such a situation would be handled as follows: the problem would be approached as a problem until the point at which the controversial solution was decided upon, when it would be treated as an issue until a decision was reached concerning the reasonableness of using such a commercial.

How can the unused space in school buildings be used to generate income so the school will not have to be closed?

How can school buildings be used in evenings and on weekends to generate income?

The "How can . . . ?" form is preferred because it is simple and it invites answers in the form of solutions. Other forms of questions tend not to invite such answers. The benefits of expressing the problem in so many different ways include being encouraged to move beyond familiar and habitual perspectives, increasing our opportunities to avoid narrowness and maintaining flexibility, opening numerous lines of thought (it is unlikely that we'll think of ways to reduce the school budget or to generate income in the evenings if our focus is limited to how to increase enrollment), and providing approaches to fall back on should one expression prove unproductive.

The "How can . . . ?" expression can be used for any kind of problem. A cotton farmer, for example, might ask "How can I increase my cotton-crop profits?" A person confined to a wheelchair might ask, "How can I get from my car to the beach for a swim without bothering my friends and relatives to carry me down and back?" A winemaker might ask "How can I help in the effort to curb drunken driving?" And a beef distributor might ask "How can I continue selling beef to people who have turned to chicken and fish out of concern for their health?"

3. *If you are dealing with an issue, proceed as follows.* Determine the essential elements of dispute in the issue and express them in writing, as clearly as possible, in the form of questions using the "Is (are) . . .?" "Does (do) . . .?" or "Should . . .?" format. If, for example, the issue concerned abortion, two of the essential elements would undoubtedly be "Is the fetus a human being?" and "Should a woman have the right to decide the fate of her fetus?" If the issue concerned capital punishment, two of the essential elements of dispute would be "Is it within the rights of government to decide matters of life and death?" and "Does capital punishment constitute cruel and unusual treatment?"

The key to determining the essential elements of dispute is the arguments each side of the issue emphasizes in its presentations. Generally the points each side believes essential will be plainly expressed and reinforced in any presentation. On occasion, however, they will be found implied rather than expressed. It is your job to express all important elements and not just the ones on the side of the issue you tend to agree with. (It is important here to acknowledge and transcend your biases.) Anything less than full and objective consideration of all essential elements renders analysis mere pretense.

4. *If you are dealing with a problem, choose the best expression you have produced, if such a choice is possible.* Sometimes one expression will stand out so clearly from the others and immediately suggest such good ideas that this choice will be easy. At other times, however, you will be unsure which expression is best. In that case, it is advisable to defer choosing until after the investigation (or even the production) stage of the holistic process.

Stage 3: Investigation

The purpose of this stage is to determine what information will be necessary or helpful in solving the problem or what evidence is relevant to the issue and then to obtain that information or evidence. Some guides to thinking seem to imply that knowledge is unimportant, that creative and critical thinking skills will suffice. This is not so. Without knowledge, the exercise of skills will be unproductive or, worse, productive of error.

Those who counsel child abusers or spouse beaters are unlikely to be very effective if they are ignorant of the fact that most such individuals were victims of this behavior in childhood. Someone analyzing the issue of tariffs on foreign goods is unlikely to grasp its full import unless he or she knows that in the first half of the decade of the 1980s, almost two million production jobs were lost. And anyone considering the issue of whether the criminally insane should be held accountable for their crimes is more likely to deal meaningfully with the issue if he is acquainted with the argument that assigning some degree of responsibility has therapeutic value both for the individual and the community.[38]

Investigation is especially important in dealing with complex and controversial issues. Unless we know the historical background, the various viewpoints involved, and the different lines of reasoning that have been or could be advanced, our efforts are not likely to be very meaningful. A. E. Mander makes the point vividly:

> The fewer the facts [one] possesses, the simpler the problem seems to him. If we know only a dozen facts, it is not difficult to find a theory to fit them. But suppose there are five hundred thousand facts known—but not known to us! Of what value then is our poor little theory which has been designed to fit, and which perhaps fits, only about a dozen of the five hundred thousand facts!"[39]

Some students will find it strange to consider investigation a part of the creative process because they are used to associating it with dull, mechanical activity involving little if any thought. They will need to be shown that it does not have to be that way.

There are three sources of information we can consult in investigating a problem or issue—ourselves, the people around us, and authorities. Most people (especially students) do a poor job with all three sources.

Ourselves   Each of us is a veritable knowledge factory. We have been receiving sense impressions since birth (indeed, before birth). These include innumerable experiences and observations. In addition to all this information, we have all the ideas we have ever generated, consciously and unconsciously. The problem is seldom that we don't know anything about a subject—it is that we have classified our experiences, observations, and thoughts so narrowly that we miss many helpful associations, associations that could be a source of insights.

Let's say that while in college we had a setback to our love life when our girl(boy)friend whom our parents never cared for threw us over for someone else, causing us to neglect our studies and very nearly fail out of school were it not for the counseling of a sensitive professor. We may have that experience filed in our memories under the heading "Love life, painful experience in." But consider just a few of the other possible headings: "Emotional factors in learning," "Value of personal counseling by faculty," "Important qualities in a mate," and so on.

One of the most useful things to do in investigating is to reopen our file of experiences and observations, asking, "What have I learned that can help me solve this problem or issue," and establish as many cross-references as we can, remembering that the uncommon associations are often most valuable. Doing so multiplies our store of useful information and increases our skill in using it.

But what should we do when our experience and observation is too limited to be very helpful in addressing a problem or issue? Wherever possible and practical, we should set up and conduct our own experiments and make our own observations, following whatever protocols—statistical, scientific, and so on—are applicable.

People Around Us   By tapping other people's knowledge and experience we increase our store of valuable information considerably. Not all people are equally helpful, of course; the best type of person is a careful thinker who is reasonably knowledgeable about our subject and willing to share ideas. (I am not referring to authorities here; we will discuss them separately.) Not all of us know many such people, but most of us know at least a few. Their views can often be helpful, especially in subjects that do not demand highly specialized knowledge.

Investigating other people's views calls for little talking and a lot of careful listening. We do well, in such cases, to ask questions rather than make statements; for example, if we were analyzing the issue of whether cigarette advertising should be banned, we might begin by asking, "What effects do you think cigarette ads have on people's smoking habits?" Later we might ask the person's view of banning cigarette advertising and other relevant questions. Our principal interest, however, should not be in people's views, but the reasons they offer for them and the evidence that supports them. One of the greatest benefits of such discussions with others is that they often provide valuable leads—the titles of worthwhile books and articles and the names of knowledgeable people.

Authorities   Authorities are commonly thought of as people who live far away and are inaccessible. That, of course, is a mistaken view. Unless we live on a mountaintop or in the middle of a desert, there are authorities of various kinds all around us, not all of them at the same level of expertise, to be sure, but authorities nonetheless. With a little imagination, we can find them quite easily. College professors are experts in their subject areas. Physicians are experts in medicine, lawyers in law, engineers in engineering, corporation executives in one or more specialties in business. And if the particular questions we have in mind exceed their expertise, they can usually refer us to someone else. (If they can't, we can always call a local or state agency, like the county medical association, and ask them to recommend an authority; or we can look in the yellow pages of the telephone directory.)

If the authorities are within easy travelling distance, we can arrange to interview them in person; if they are not, we can arrange a telephone interview. The usual courtesies, naturally, apply here: calling or writing ahead for an appointment; carefully preparing questions in advance, including follow-up questions; arriving on time; asking permission to tape the interview; and not overstaying our welcome. When dealing with an issue, rather than a problem, among the most important questions to ask authorities, tactfully of course, is how they respond to other authorities who oppose their position. Their answers to such questions are likely to reveal the strengths or weaknesses of their positions more clearly than any other questions we might ask.

If the authorities we wish or need to consult are unavailable or deceased, we must turn to the library. Knowing where to look for what we need (or, if we don't know, finding out from a librarian) is essential, as is a systematic approach to looking. A good general approach, subject to variation depending upon the problem or issue, is as follows: developing an appropriate list of "descriptors" (subject headings) by consulting the index volume of *Encyclopedia Americana* or a specialized reference work such as the *Thesaurus of Psychological Terms;* reading articles in general and/or specialized encyclopedias; consulting almanacs, magazine/journal indexes, *Books in Print,* and the card catalog; and obtaining and reading promising books and articles. Many students will need instruction in how to read selectively, using a book's index or table of contents to determine which parts of the book are relevant to their concerns, and consulting only those sections.

In consulting authorities in person or through their works, we may be tempted to surrender our judgment to them. That temptation must be resisted. However eminent they may be, authorities are human and therefore subject to error; moreover, in the case of issues, thorough research will produce *conflicting testimony* from authorities, leaving us with the responsibility of deciding which position is most reasonable.

Stage 4: Idea Production

For problems, this stage consists of producing possible solutions from which the best one may be chosen. Thus if the problem were, "How can the criminal justice system be improved to save the taxpayers money?" the solutions might range from ideas for handling cases more expeditiously in the courts, to alternatives to incarceration; from new cellblock designs that reduce the need for guards, to turning over the running of prisons to private corporations (a solution already implemented in some places) and to converting prisons to public benefit corporations (an idea recently proposed[40]), among other ideas.

For issues, this stage is somewhat more complex, though the overall general aim is the same as with problems—to force our thinking out of the molds which conditioning and habit have created and consider many possible responses before embracing any. The ideas we produce will include not only direct answers to our expressions of the issue ("Is (are) . . . ?" "Does (did) . . . ?" and "Should . . . ?") but any other ideas that help us construct answers.

One type of idea of special importance in dealing with issues is definitions of terms. When developed with care, definitions can dispel much of the confusion and misunderstanding that surrounds issues. If, for example, the issue were expressed as "Is pornography emotionally harmful to those who read it or view it?" we would first consider exactly what we, and others, mean by pornography. Depiction of homosexual or sado-masochistic acts? Graphic depiction of heterosexual acts? Suggestively posed nudes? Next we would consider what we and others mean by emotional harm. The formation of socially disapproved sexual habits? The development of distorted attitudes toward sex? A propensity to criminality (for example, rape)? The acceptance of misconceptions about the opposite sex? A tendency to promiscuity? A general blunting of sensitivity toward others? Increased tolerance for brutality and coercion? A devaluing of the rights of individuals?

Finally, we would consider who, specifically, we mean when we refer to the readers/viewers of pornography. Children? Adolescents? Adults? Women? Men? People of normal or above–normal intelligence? People of subnormal intelligence? The emotionally healthy? The emotionally disturbed? Each of these categories of people would have characteristics that distinguish it from the others, and some of those characteristics might be more relevant than others to the issue in question.

The quality and quantity of the ideas we produce in response to problems and issues depends not only upon our willingness to postpone evaluation and judgment, but also upon our ability to stimulate our imagination. At first most students will have difficulty producing more than a few solutions or definitions or interpretations, and for precisely the same reason that few students can do more than one or two chin-ups in a gym class—they have never practiced doing so. Practicing the following techniques, and receiving your continuing encouragement to press for a greater number and variety of ideas, will help them overcome that difficulty. (For your convenience, the techniques are presented here as you would present them to students.)

Force Uncommon Responses   Studies have shown that early ideas are more common and therefore less creative than later ideas.[41] Exactly why this is so is not known, but one plausible hypothesis is that familiar, safe responses lie closest to the surface of consciousness and therefore are thought of first. Since it is difficult, perhaps impossible, to leap over such ideas, the best approach is to suffer them, listing all ideas that first come to mind, reminding yourself that they probably won't count for much, and then, when they are exhausted, to say to yourself, "So much for the ideas anyone could produce; now I will think of a large number of ideas that few, if any, others would think of" and force yourself to produce some uncommon ones, refusing to concern yourself about whether they are good or bad, appropriate or inappropriate. That can be decided later.

It is often the uncommon idea that provides the best solution to a problem. In the 1860s, for example, an inventor named Faber invented a crude talking machine with a bellows that imitated the function of the human lungs and an artificial throat, larynx, and lips. Edison's phonograph was more successful because he addressed the problem in an uncommon way. Similarly, hundreds of inventors constructed flying machines on the flapping principle they observed in birds; but it was the Wright brothers' uncommon approach that succeeded.

In striving for uncommon ideas, people often unconsciously stay within the boundaries of their own discipline. This is a mistake. Explains Peter A. Carruthers, head of the theoretical physics division at the Los Alamos National Laboratory, "You'd be surprised how many times just posing a problem to a colleague in a different field will give an important lead. It's because each field has become so developed and so dug in that you can't see into the next trough. *It's at the intersections that you get the nice overviews.*" (Emphasis added.)[42]

Use Free Association   This technique consists of looking at the ideas you have already produced and letting those ideas suggest others. It is important to give your mind free rein when using this approach, and not attempt to screen out any ideas that occur. (Sometimes an idea that seems totally irrelevant at the moment it occurs will later prove valuable.) Note that this technique can easily slide into aimless daydreaming; it is therefore best used sparingly, as a variation on other techniques rather than as a substitute for them.

Use Analogy   An analogy is a reference to one or more similarities between two otherwise very different things; for example, a ballerina's graceful movements might be compared to the movement of a swan in the water or to a gazelle. To use analogy as a technique for stimulating ideas, ask yourself what the problem is like, what it reminds you of; or, if appropriate, ask more specific questions, such as "What does this *look* like (or sound, taste, smell, or feel like)?" or "What does this *function* like?"

Look for Unusual Combinations   Sometimes the best solution to a problem will be to combine things not previously combined. A miner's cap, for example, combines a flashlight and a protective helmet; a new recipe combines ingredients differently. This technique works well not only with products but with systems and services, as well. For example, punishment and rehabilitation might be combined by having prisoners learn skills and do productive work for private industry. They could be paid for their efforts and use part of the money to repay the state for the expense of housing and feeding them. (This idea might even come by way of analogy, by noting that prisons sometimes resemble large factory complexes.)

Visualize the Solution   This technique consists of imagining the problem solved and visualizing what it would look like then. For example, before chains and snow tires were invented, someone lamenting the way his tires slipped and slid on snowy, icy roads could have pictured in his mind the condition he wished for—tires turning smoothly, biting the snow, clinging surely to the ice—and could have asked himself how the tires would have to be modified in oder to perform that way. Thus stimulated, he might have conceived of pieces of chain wrapped around the tires, or deeper treads, or protruding steel spikes.

Construct Pro and Con Arguments   This strategy, an essential one in dealing with issues, consists of listing all conceivable arguments that might be advanced on either side of the issue. To use it, we simply address our expression(s) of the issue—"Is . . . ?" "Does (did) . . . ?" and/or "Should . . . ?"—and list as many *yes* and *no* responses as we can, together with the reasoning that supports each response.

A warning is necessary here. We should expect ourselves to be biased and expect that bias to affect our efforts to construct arguments. Unless we are perfectly neutral about the issue (an unlikely circumstance), our preference for one side of the issue may blind us to the existence of arguments for the other side. For the strategy of listing arguments to work to our advantage, we must discipline ourselves to set aside preferences, and even *convictions,* long enough to identify all relevant arguments.

Construct Relevant Scenarios   We often tend to think of ideas exclusively as *assertions*—claims about what is or should be—such as "Respect for the rights of others is being eroded in our society," and "Ethics instruction belongs in the nation's schools." Those are ideas, to be sure, but so are *scenarios,* imaginatively conceived examples of situations and events that are relevant to the issue under consideration. In fact, well-constructed scenarios have a special value that assertions lack—they represent reality itself and not just conclusions about reality.

Let's say that the issue we are analyzing concerns whether a woman must have offered "earnest resistance" to a man's sexual advances in order for a rape charge to be filed in the courts. (This was still a legal requirement in some states as recently as 1982.) Here are three scenarios we might construct:

A woman has just returned from a date with a young man whom she has known for some time, has dated previously, and has had sexual intercourse with on several occasions. She invites him into her apartment and proceeds to engage in sexual foreplay with him. When he proposes that they have intercourse, she says "No" several times, but does not stop him from performing the act.

A woman is lying in a hospital bed, heavily sedated after experiencing a nervous breakdown. A male nurse realizes she is unable to resist his advances and so assaults her sexually.

Walking from the campus library to her dormitory one evening, a college student passes through a dimly lighted wooded area. Suddenly, two men jump out at her, one brandishing a knife and warning that if she resists having sexual intercourse with them, he will kill her. Fearing for her life, she submits.

A close reading of these scenarios will reveal the importance of constructing more than a single scenario, and of taking care that those constructed cover the broad range of possibilities. All of these, like every good scenario, are believable. However, they do not all shed equal light on the issue of whether "earnest resistance" is a reasonable legal requirement. Taken alone, the first scenario might lead us to an affirmative answer. Yet as the other two make clear, such an answer is shallow. Under the very plausible circumstances they present, the requirement of "earnest resistance" is quite unreasonable.

Using any of the above techniques skillfully requires practice. Students will have to learn not only how to move from one technique to another without becoming distracted, but also how to steer their minds without stopping the flow of thought. The difficulty is analogous to that involved in learning to drive a car. Beginners often have trouble keeping the car in their own lane without braking; eventually they learn (most of them at least) how to steer the car even at relatively high speeds. It is similar with producing ideas; with experience students will learn to allow their minds considerable leeway in producing ideas while avoiding any veering off into irrelevancy.

In the literature on creativity, particularly popular literature, much is made of the phenomenon of insight, the sudden illumination that solves the problem or resolves the issue. This phenomenon is sometimes termed the "Ahah!" reaction, symbolized by a light bulb suddenly flashing above a cartoon character's head; it has also been compared to the moment when one finds the missing part of a picture puzzle. There is abundant evidence that insight does occur: one of the most-often cited examples is Archimedes' reaction when he sat down in a tub of water, noticed the displacement of the water by the mass of his body, and instantly conceptualized the principle of specific gravity; another is August von Kekule's dream of snakelike atoms, one of which seized its own tail and thereby suggested to the famous chemist that the molecules of certain organic compounds are ring-shaped; a third is Wolfgang Kohler's ape Sultan's triumphant realization, after failing to reach bananas outside his cage, that he could fit two sticks together and pull them to him.

Such reports, unfortunately, can create false impressions. Though insights often occur during moments of leisure, authorities are in agreement that it is not the leisure that brings them about (otherwise the village loafer would be, simultaneously, the village genius)—it is the exhausting, at times unbearably frustrating, work that precedes leisure. The most generally accepted speculation is that when one turns away from a project after having labored over it to a point physicist Peter Carruthers terms "the brink of confusion," the conscious mind turns the problem over to the unconscious, which in some unexplained way continues working on it, sometimes producing an insight.[43]

Another, perhaps more serious, false impression is that hard work necessarily produces a dramatic insight for every problem or issue. In many cases (perhaps most), the solutions we produce arrive modestly in the course of our conscious activity. And they are no less valuable for that fact.

Stage 5: Evaluation and Refinement

As we noted earlier, it is important to defer judgment during the production of ideas because it interrupts the flow of ideas and, when unfamiliarity is mistaken for inferiority, results in the discarding of valuable ideas. Yet judgment is crucial because our ideas are often flawed, sometimes seriously so. Therefore in this, the final stage of the holistic process, judgment dominates. Because the ideas being judged in problem solving are rather different from those in issue analysis, we will consider each separately.

Problem Solving   For problem solving, we first examine the solutions we produced earlier and decide which one(s) constitute the most satisfactory response to the problem. If two or more ideas are satisfactory, we consider how they might be combined. Next we work out the details of the solution by asking and answering appropriate questions. If the solution involves *doing* something, those questions are:

> How exactly is it to be done, step by step?
>
> By whom is it to be done?
>
> When is it to be done? (According to what timetable?)
>
> Where is it to be done?
>
> Who will finance it?
>
> What tools or materials, if any, are to be used?
>
> From what source will they be obtained?
>
> How and by whom will they be transported?
>
> Where will they be stored?
>
> What special conditions, if any, will be required for the solution to be carried out?

If the solution involves *making* something, a new product, for example, the appropriate questions are:

> How will it work? (Be specific.)
>
> What will it look like? (Be specific as to size, shape, color, texture, and any other relevant descriptive details.)
>
> What material will it be made of?
>
> What will the product cost to make?
>
> Who will pay for it?
>
> How exactly will it be used?
>
> Who will use it? When? Where?
>
> How will it be packaged? Delivered? Stored?

Then we look for imperfections and complications. This can be done in four different ways. First, we can check for common kinds of imperfections; that is, imperfections that occur in clarity (in the sense of explaining the idea), safety, convenience, efficiency, economy, simplicity, comfort, durability, beauty, and compatibility. Secondly, we can compare our solution with competing products, processes, or services and determine whether it is inferior in any respect. Thirdly, we can consider what changes our solution will cause in existing procedures and what complications those changes may create. Finally, we can consider the effects our solution will have on people's physical, moral, emotional, intellectual, and financial well-being and determine whether any of those effects will be undesirable.

In addition, we should anticipate, as well as we can, the negative reactions other people are likely to have to our solution, in particular people whose endorsement of the idea will be important to its success. Among the most common negative reactions are these: the solution is impractical, too expensive, illegal, immoral, inefficient, unworkable, disruptive of existing procedures, unaesthetic, too radical, unappealing to others, and unfair. Any negative reaction that may be *reasonably* raised to our idea indicates an imperfection or complication that should be addressed.

The final step in the evaluation/refinement of solutions to problems is to devise improvements that overcome whatever imperfections and complications we identified. If a particular imperfection or complication resists improvement, we can treat it as a problem, expressing it in a number of ways (Stage 2) and applying the techniques used to produce possible solutions (Stage 4).

If the foregoing explanation of evaluation/refinement of solutions to problems makes it seem an arduous activity, be assured that it is so. As Eliot Hutchinson explains:

> There is nothing trifling, incidental or dilettantish about this business of [refining solutions]. It is work, days and nights of it, months and years of it, the perspiration that is nine-tenths genius. And it tires, discourages, exhausts. . . . The history both of art and of science is largely the history of man's personal endurance, his acceptance of labor as the price of success. To be sure some [people] dash off a brilliant piece of work, spread themselves for a time. But 90 percent of reputable authors, no matter how sure their technique, and well-nigh all reputable scientists revamp their work until what was given in insight is so overlaid with secondary material that it is hardly to be recognized. Elaboration is for the mature only; it is for the rigorous, the exacting, the profound.[44]

Issue Analysis Evaluating/refining responses to issues is no less demanding than evaluating/refining solutions to problems. We begin this stage by examining the ideas generated in the production stage and identify those that seem most reasonable. Next, using the ideas we have decided are most reasonable, we frame our response to the essential elements of dispute. That response should include an answer to the questions framed earlier (Stage 2) and a statement of the reasoning underlying that answer. In other words, if the question were "Does capital punishment constitute cruel and unusual treatment?" we would answer the question and explain why, in our view, our answer is the most reasonable one. (Since controversial issues are by definition matters that divide intelligent, informed people, the most reasonable answer will seldom be a simple "yes" or "no," or merely express unqualified endorsement of one side's view.) This answer would constitute our essential argument.*

The next step is to evaluate our argument for soundness by applying two tests. The first is for truth and relevance and is performed by examining *each sentence* (or major part of a sentence) in the argument in light of our investigation of the issue. The errors we must be alert for in this examination, in addition to simple factual inaccuracy, are the various kinds of informal fallacy, the most common of which are the following: either-or thinking, stereotyping, attacking the person, straw man, shifting the burden of proof, contradiction, faulty analogy, faulty causation, irrelevant or irrational appeal, hasty conclusion, overgeneralization, and oversimplification. (These errors are discussed more fully in Chapter 4.)

Evaluating the sentences against a checklist of fallacies is not the only way to conduct the test for truth and relevance. Another effective way is to anticipate the objections people who oppose our idea might raise to it. We can do this by brainstorming possible objections, listing every one we can think of, refusing to screen out even the seemingly outlandish ones, or by conducting an imaginary dialogue with someone who objects to our argument, preferably someone we know and whose reactions we can, to some extent, predict. This approach calls for role-playing, an activity some people may at first feel awkward doing, but one that can easily be mastered. It consists of making an assertion that expresses our view, then putting ourselves in the other person's frame of mind and answering for her, then responding from our point of view, and so on.

Ideally, our expression of the other person's point of view would contain not only assertions, but evidence, as well—for example, the situations the person might describe to show the inadequacy of our ideas. Not all of the objections these approaches would produce would be valid, of course. People sometimes react negatively not because of real flaws in a position, but because of jealousy or lack of understanding or bad thinking habits or fear of the new. Nevertheless, in most cases we would discover some objections worthy of our consideration.

The second test to be applied in the evaluation of an argument is the test of validity; that is, the test of whether the reasons offered are sufficient to support the position we have taken on the issue. Any time the reasons can be shown to support another position, one that differs from ours, as well as or better than they do ours, they must be considered insufficient and our argument invalid.† (The errors affecting the truth, relevancy, and validity of arguments are discussed at length in Chapter 4.)

If the tests for truth, relevancy and validity reveal flaws in our argument, we should revise it to eliminate those flaws, *even if that means radically changing, even reversing, our position on the issue.*

---

*So defined, an argument does not meet the exacting standards of a formal syllogism. It does, however, reveal the conclusion reached and the reasoning process by which it was reached; thus any error in logic will usually be evident.

†In *formal* logic an argument is valid when the conclusion follows logically from the premises. There are a number of specific formal errors that invalidate an argument.

USING THE HOLISTIC APPROACH EFFECTIVELY

The above holistic approach (the formal designation for which is a *heuristic*), like all approaches, can be a useful tool for problem solving and issue analysis. However, like any tool, it can be inappropriately or ineffectively used. To use it well, students should be taught, and from time to time reminded, of the following facts:

Some problems and issues will require fewer than five stages to solve.

Though the first stage of the holistic process—exploration—is a necessary one in most situations, occasionally the process will start with the second stage—expression. Such is the case, for example, when an engineer or scientific researcher is *assigned* a particular problem or issue. Also, many simple problems that occur in a familiar context can be solved without the third stage—investigation—and sometimes the solutions produced will require little or no refinement.

On occasion the stages may occur in a different order.

For example, if an issue is unfamiliar or unusually complex, we may have to do some investigating before being able to express it. In other situations, the effort to articulate a problem or issue may trigger a flow of possible solutions before investigation takes place. Similarly, the evaluation of a solution may suggest a new and better expression of the problem or prompt additional ideas for its solution.

The mind will produce ideas, not just when directed to, but also at unexpected times.

Once we have become intensely interested in a problem or issue, useful ideas are likely to occur to us at any time; an unusual expression of the problem, for example, may occur while showering, the design of a creative experiment while sleeping, several possible solutions while walking down the street or working on something entirely unrelated. Moreover, ideas that arrive unexpectedly often never return, and if they are not recorded at once (or as soon as feasible), they may be forgotten and thus lost. Students should therefore be encouraged to develop the habit of writing ideas down immediately. Doing so needn't interfere with what they are doing at the time: they need pause only long enough to make a brief note for future reference. In such situations, of course, as in situations where idea production is directed, judgment should be deferred.

The length of time necessary to solve a problem or resolve an issue may vary greatly.

Both teachers and students are victimized by time constraints. Teachers are usually forced to choose homework assignments that can be completed within the time between class periods and exam questions that can be completed in one hour. And students, as a result of years of meeting those demands, come to expect real-life problems to be solvable in similar time frames. That expectation is unfortunate, for in real life the process of solving problems and analyzing issues is often protracted, lasting for weeks, months, sometimes years. Teachers should do all they can to overcome unrealistic expectations. One effective approach is to give on occasion a homework assignment or exam problem that requires extending effort beyond the usual time period; that is, an assignment or problem for which students will submit only two or three stages of the holistic process and complete the other stages in subsequent days or weeks.

Many times the stages of the holistic thinking process overlap.

For clarity's sake and ease of learning, the process detailed in this chapter, like all heuristics, is presented in distinct stages. In some thinking situations the stages will not be as neatly separated as the model suggests; they will overlap. Students should be made aware of this fact, not at the outset of their work with the holistic model (too much complexity too early can make some students fearful), but after they have become familiar with it and gained some confidence using it.

Once people become skilled in applying the holistic process, they will sometimes modify it in useful ways.

Because there are differences in the protocols of the various disciplines, and because creativity applies to people's intellectual *styles* as well as to the products of their thinking, proficient thinkers may develop shortcuts in the holistic process or special strategies that facilitate problem solving and issue analysis, at least for them. This fact should not be taken to mean that students ought to attempt to modify the process before they master it: most of the "improvements" likely to occur to students—like skipping the expression of the problem or combining idea production and judgment—will have the effect of hindering it. Genuine mastery, it should be noted, takes more than a few months or even years to achieve.

In light of the foregoing facts, the holistic approach detailed in this chapter should not be used slavishly.

The holistic approach is a means to an end, nothing more. The end it serves is effective problem solving and issue analysis. Does this qualification suggest that students would be better off without a general approach to problem solving and issue analysis? Far from it. As Benjamin Bloom and Lois Broder, among others, have documented, confusion and the lack of confidence it breeds are considerably greater obstacles to effective thinking than slavishness of approach.[45] Moreover, problem solving and issue analysis are undeniably two-phased activities, involving the production and the evaluation of ideas, and any attempt to improve students' skills in these activities necessarily entails answering, "How can one produce better ideas and do so more reliably?" and "How does one go about evaluating ideas?" In other words, anyone who discards general thinking models will be driven by the demands of the learning situation to create just such a model.

One final note. Some authorities believe that the thinking models held up to students should mirror as nearly as possible the actual practices of expert thinkers in the various disciplines.[46] This belief can be challenged on the basis that the studies of expert thinkers' thought processes are unreliable. K. A. Ericcson and H. A. Simon, for example, have found that when experts are asked to verbalize information that would not normally be verbalized, the instruction may affect the process, so that what they subsequently report may be inaccurate.[47]

Yet quite aside from that challenge, the belief that the expert model is best for students rests on two unwarranted assumptions. The first is that expert thinkers proceed in the most efficacious manner. Given the fact that thinking skills have been sadly neglected in the majority of schools and colleges for almost a century, and, therefore, that experts have acquired their skills by trial and error, it would seem more reasonable to believe that few experts have achieved anything approaching maximum efficiency and effectiveness. Their intellectual and practical achievements may thus have been realized *despite* many of their habits of mind rather than *because* of them.

The second unwarranted assumption is that what works best for experts will work best for novices. Even on the face of the matter it would seem that the mastery of such complex skills as creative and critical thinking depends on certain *enabling activities,* activities that are almost essential in the novice stage but unnecessary once mastery is achieved. A noteworthy example is pressing for a large quantity of ideas, postponing all judgment about their relative quality until later. When viewed as an enabling activity, this approach makes sense even if, as some studies reveal, experts are occasionally able to mix idea production and judgment without sacrificing fluency. (By way of analogy, novice basketball players spend innumerable hours in elementary dribbling, passing, shooting, and defensive footwork drills, many of which are not necessary for professionals.)

Nor do we need to rely on reasoning alone to support the idea that the best model for novices is not mirrored on professional practice. G. Fischer and others have shown that it is often appropriate to use approaches that are different from those they will ultimately be required to use.[48] In addition, Mike U. Smith of Southeast Missouri State University and Ron Good of Florida State University have found that there are more significant differences between successful novices and unsuccessful novices than between experts and novices in general.[49] The former differences are surely more readily understandable to students, and therefore a better basis of instruction, than the latter.

APPLICATIONS

1. Review stage 1 of the holistic process and apply the techniques detailed there for the next few days, keeping a record of the challenges you discover. Then select one of those challenges and apply the rest of the holistic process to it.
2. Begin keeping a journal record of challenges that you find interesting and that your students would find interesting. If you wish, list general challenges separately from challenges within your field. (As later chapters will explain, this journal can provide excellent material for classwork and homework.)

chapter 3

OBSTACLES TO COGNITIVE DEVELOPMENT

Anyone who approaches the teaching of thinking skills with the idea that students will be well disposed to learn, or will learn easily and apply their learning consistently, is likely to be quickly disillusioned. Two broad types of obstacles to effective learning exist. The first arises from the human condition itself; that is, from tendencies that exist apparently quite apart from any cultural influences (though they may be intensified or diminished to some extent by such influences). The following quotations identify some of the most troublesome of these tendencies:

> The most interesting and astounding contradiction in life is to me the constant insistence by nearly all people upon "logic," "logical reasoning," "sound reasoning" on the one hand, and on the other their inability to display it, and their unwillingness to accept it when displayed by others.[1]

> A candid examination of our own minds convinces us that the average man, in by far the majority of cases, does not determine his actions by reasoning, but that he first acts, and then justifies or explains his acts.[2]

> When we have once adopted an opinion, our pride makes us loth to admit that we are wrong. When objections are made to our views, we are more concerned with discovering how to combat them than how much truth or sound sense there may be in them; we are at pains rather to find fresh support for our own views, than to face frankly any new facts that appear to contradict them. We

all know how easy it is to become annoyed at the suggestion that we have made a mistake; that our first feeling is that we would rather do anything than admit it, and our first thought is "How can I explain it away?"[3]

Most men and women die vague about life and death, religion or morals, politics or art. Even about purely practical issues we are far from being clear. We imagine that other people know definitely their own minds about their children's education, about their own careers, or about the use they should make of their money. The notion helps us to imagine that we ourselves are only separated from decision on these important issues by the lightest curtain of uncertainty. But it is not so. Other people, like ourselves, live in perpetual vagueness. Like us they foolishly imagine they are thinking of some important subject when they are merely thinking of thinking about it.[4]

The most recent of these quotations was written almost fifty years ago. That they still ring true today is certainly due in part to education's neglect of thinking skills, but it is also due to the fact that these tendencies are an inevitable part of being human. Therefore, it would be naive to expect to eliminate them; the goal of thinking skills instruction is rather to help students recognize and control them.

The second type of obstacle arises not from the imperfections of our humanity, but from the attitudes and values of the culture we live in. This type of obstacle varies from culture to culture; indeed, it often varies within a culture from one historical period to another. Such was apparently the case in ancient China. Ancient Chinese civilization, one of the most creative in recorded history, is credited with many inventions, among them the following: metallic coins, between 2800 and 2700 B.C.; the compass, by at least 1122 B.C.; paper—from trees, rags, and hemp in the early first century A.D.; glass and anesthetics in the early second century A.D.; and printing from wooden plates by 593 A.D. (almost a thousand years before Gutenberg). The list could go on, from the well-known invention of gunpowder to the less recognized invention of the taxicab.

Yet the inventiveness of the ancient Chinese was not continued by their descendants and over the centuries western civilization not only caught up, but eventually surpassed Chinese civilization. Perhaps there were a number of causes of this phenomenon, but historians believe one was especially prominent—ancestor worship. As that practice became more and more common, the Chinese focused their attention more on the past than on the future, and so ultimately lost, not their creative potential, but the *inclination to use that potential.*

A culture, of course, can provide positive reinforcement instead of negative. Just before the first World War, Rollo Walter Brown, an American college professor, took a leave from his university duties and travelled to France to find an answer to the question, "How is it that while even educated Americans abuse the English language, the French—from educated people to relatively uneducated pushcart peddlers—write and speak French precisely, even lovingly?" The answers he found and published in *How the French Boy Learns to Write* revealed a coalition of factors, including schools teaching language skills faithfully and well; parents, other adults, newspapers, books, and magazines reinforcing the

lessons of the schools; and communities holding speaking and writing competi-
tions and honoring those who performed well. In short, Brown found that French
students learned to write and speak well because virtually everything in French
culture supported that objective. (Brown's book is available in a 1948 edition
published by the National Council of Teachers of English.)

The influence of modern American culture on young people's cognitive
development is unfortunately more negative than positive; moreover, the advanced state of modern communication, as we will see, compounds that influence.

NEGATIVE ELEMENTS OF MODERN AMERICAN CULTURE

It has been estimated that by the time a young person graduates from high school,
he or she has spent 11,000 hours in the classroom and 22,000 hours watching
television.[5] All things being equal, television would have twice as much impact
on students' minds than education. However, all things are not equal. Television
producers have more means at their disposal to maintain the attention of their
audience than do teachers (means such as the use of music to manipulate emotions, the device of cutting from one scene to another, and the use of laugh tracks
and applause tracks to cue responses), so it would not be unreasonable to conclude that the impact of television is even greater than the statistics suggest.

Most of the criticism of television published over the last 30 years focuses
on its obvious effects, which include keeping young people away from books and
thereby denying them opportunities to develop their imaginations, depriving
them of intellectual challenges by keying programming to the lowest common
intellectual denominator, and retarding their use of language by feeding them a
steady diet of slang and clichés. Each of these is a serious effect and plays a part
in obstructing students' cognitive development. But there are other, more serious
effects.

Television invites passivity in viewers and discourages them from using
their critical faculties. This is not a necessary effect; it derives from the *kind of
programming* that has come to dominate the medium. The main options in
television programming, like those in any medium of communication, are three:
to narrate, to inform, to analyze. The overwhelming majority of programming,
however, is narrative, telling stories (usually fictional) in dramatic format and
employing the devices of plot, character, setting, action, and theme used in
literature, but in a stereotypical, contrived manner, and lacking literature's effect
of enlarging one's experience and stimulating reflection. Soap operas, situation
comedies, movies, and dramatic series are examples of narrative programming,
as are most commercials.

Except for occasional documentaries, informative programming is confined
to newscasts and talk shows. The former bombard viewers with discrete factual
"segments" of recent vintage and some shock value, each one typically presented
in a matter of seconds and without commentary. ("In-depth" treatments last a
few minutes; occasionally, in the case of programs like "60 Minutes" and "20/
20," fifteen or twenty minutes.) Talk shows typically consist of a series of five-
minute discussions, separated, and often interrupted, by commercials. These
discussions feature a host and guests drawn, as a rule, from a roster of "celebri-

ties" with some product or endeavor to promote. Conversation usually covers a wide range of topics, the guests' role being to make provocative pronouncements without regard for their own expertise or lack thereof. The unspoken messages of informative programming are that superficiality is acceptable, a smattering of information makes a person informed, and expertise is not a requirement for having and expressing opinions.

A fourth kind of program, not classifiable under any of the above headings, is the game show, whose aim is merely to entertain. Game shows serve to reinforce the misconceptions that knowledge is a collection of unrelated items of information, that the worthwhile questions are Who? What? Where? and When? (How? is seldom asked, and Why? never), and that intelligence is the ability to answer such questions on cue. In brief, game shows suggest that being a good thinker means nothing more than having a command of trivia.

The most neglected mode of communication on television is analysis. This is really not surprising; as Neil Postman has observed, "Thinking is not a performing art, so it doesn't play well on television." That fact, he points out, is responsible for a change in the popular conception of *knowing*. Today *knowing* has come to mean having pictures, not sentences, in our heads. It is also responsible for the fact that in politics, education, and commerce, discourse has given way to show business formats with their focus on images.[6]

The negative effects of television may be the principal negative effects on young people's cognitive development, but they are not the only ones. The movie, music, and publishing industries are responsible for others. The overemphasis on box office receipts has resulted in a subgenre of films that pander to the spirit of rebelliousness in teenagers by presenting teachers, parents, and other authority figures as morons and glorifying rude and disruptive behavior, especially that occurring in school. In addition, this overemphasis has produced a focus on the sensational that frequently substitutes gratuitous sexual material or gore for coherence of plot and character development and thus leads young people to confuse glitter with substance.

Rock music has filled the lives of young people with a din that distracts them from reflection. Moreover, the penchant of many rock performers for bizarre dress and behavior has conveyed the message that style is more important than substance (or, in extreme cases, that style *is* substance), just as the unintelligibility and/or incoherence of their song lyrics has suggested that undisciplined thought and expression are somehow more creative than disciplined.

Negative elements in magazine publishing include playing to people's morbid curiosity about celebrities; in book publishing, giving inordinate attention to fiction rather than nonfiction and to physical well-being rather than intellectual and spiritual well-being. Diet and bodybuilding books are marketed with an enthusiasm that used to be reserved for the great books of the western world, and self-improvement books all too often offer techniques for advertising the self or inflicting it on others instead of guidelines for improving it. The defense frequently offered by publishers, that they merely give the public what it wants, neatly sidesteps the fact that the market dictates reading habits as well as the reverse.

One additional negative element in contemporary American culture is of special importance in that it touches all the elements mentioned above. That element is advertising. Advertising is so much a part of every day (indeed, almost every waking hour) of our lives that we sometimes lose sight of the most significant fact about it, that it is, in essence, self-congratulation of the worst kind, the kind disguised as altruism. The fact that advertising of the right kind, used in the right manner, provides an irreplaceable service in no way lessens the fact that *advertisements aim to make us suspend critical judgment and accept biased testimony at face value.* If Neil Postman is correct in estimating that teenagers view, on the average, 800–900 television commercials per week (not to mention print and other kinds of advertisements), then it is clear that advertising represents a truly formidable obstacle to thinking instruction.[7]

Several shallow themes run through all the expressions of popular culture mentioned above and are often used as appeals in advertising. One is that the possession of material goods and the leisure to enjoy them not only constitutes success but unfailingly produces happiness, a theme unctuously advanced on the popular television show, *Lifestyles of the Rich and Famous.* This view has even infected unlikely individuals; some television evangelists, for example, promise true believers not only God's pleasure, but an enviable investment portfolio as well.

Another theme is that activities that are highly dramatic, fast-paced, and exciting to the senses are more worthwhile than other activities. Most thinking activities and serious discussion, alas, fail to meet this unrealistic standard. Yet another theme is that celebrity carries with it some vague, mysterious validation of one's opinions and values; in other words, that there is no other way to judge an idea than by the popularity of those who embrace it. Not all of these themes were originally fashioned by popular culture. Some are merely reflections of faulty ideas unwisely embraced by scholars, ideas whose correction has not yet been effected or has not yet had an influence on popular culture.

RESULTING OBSTACLES TO COGNITIVE DEVELOPMENT

To trace all the obvious and subtle effects of these elements would be impossible. Nevertheless, we can identify the most formidable obstacles to students' cognitive development, the obstacles that educators must recognize and combat if thinking skills instruction is to be effective. There are six such obstacles: disdain for intellectual rigor, a misconception about self, a misconception about truth, confusion about values, the habit of basing beliefs on feelings, and intellectual insecurity.

Disdain for Intellectual Rigor

Solving problems, making decisions, and evaluating issues is hard work and requires an active approach, perseverance in the face of difficulty and confusion, and refusal to settle for easy answers. Yet many students are deficient in all these areas. To begin with, they are so conditioned to being spectators rather than active participants that they do not know how to attack a problem or issue and are therefore distressed when asked to do so. Passivity, after all, is as John Dewey warned, "the opposite of thought" and not only prevents a person from expressing judgment and understanding, but also "dulls curiosity, generates mind-wandering, and causes learning to be a task instead of a delight."[8]

In addition, many students demonstrate an indisposition and/or inability to deal with complexity. This characteristic is hardly surprising: dealing with complexity demands that one have a mature attention span and be able to concentrate, yet commercial television does not permit viewers to extend their attention span longer than ten minutes, often forcing them to shift attention four or five times within a period of two minutes. After years of such conditioning, it is highly unlikely that students will be able to achieve the intense concentration—becoming completely absorbed in a problem, screening out irrelevancies and distractions, and maintaining a sense of direction while moving from one aspect to another—that difficult problems or issues require. As if this deficiency were not enough, constant exposure to television and loud music has made many students uneasy in the very atmosphere most conducive to reflective thought, the atmosphere of silence.

The negative elements in our culture have also created in many students the unrealistic demand that school subjects be "interesting." That demand is not, in itself, unreasonable; however, two fallacies accompany it. One is that things are properly classified as either inherently interesting or inherently uninteresting. In reality, though treatments of a subject may vary in quality, there are no interest*ing* subjects—only interest*ed* people. The other fallacy is that only presentations that assault our senses with the fury of the latest MTV (music television) videodisk and provide instant gratification are deserving of attention. Burdened with such false notions, students are unlikely to greet rigorous courses hospitably.

Yet another aspect of disdain for intellectual rigor is the tolerance many students have of mediocrity. Where mediocrity carries no stigma, there can be no motivation to excellence. Accordingly, relatively few students will aspire to more than the lowest levels of proficiency and fewer will actually achieve those levels. Tolerance of mediocrity helps to explain the laziness many students display toward schoolwork and the casualness with which they regard poor grades. It also accounts in part for the lack of basic skills and the disappointing level of effectiveness of many efforts at remediation.

A Misconception About Self

Socrates' direction, "know thyself," is one of the cornerstones of western philosophy and remains an imperative for the teaching of thinking skills. Unless students have an accurate sense of self and are aware of the inherited and acquired strengths and weaknesses they bring to the enterprise of thinking, they can hardly be expected to master the skills of thinking. Unfortunately, a serious misconception about self is prevalent today—the romantic notion that the self is effectively insulated from the influences of society.

Being one's self, according to this false notion, involves merely looking within and apprehending the ideas, inclinations, desires, and ideas found there.

Expressing one's self means "doing your own thing"—that is, articulating in word or action what is within one's mind and heart *as opposed to* what other people want one to do and say. Popular self-improvement books typically build on this theme, urging people to accept themselves and assert their individuality and independence from others. Interestingly, books concerned with the *physical* self—diet and exercise books—take the opposite approach, urging people to take a good look at their flabby, unappealing bodies and set about changing them!

The thought that every person is automatically his or her own unique person is both pleasant and popular. Yet it is essentially mistaken. The influences of others on people's intellectual development precede by years their ability to control such influences. In childhood people hear literally thousands of discussions, see thousands of events before they are able to interpret them. They digest innumerable ideas, some reasonable, some unreasonable or even absurd: for example, that democracy is a blessing and should be cherished; that the rich have a moral obligation to help the poor; that a woman's place is in the home; that blacks are lazy, Italians violent, Jews cheap, and atheists immoral. What parents tell children and the way they treat them influences their image of self and others. Parental kindness or abusiveness, attention or neglect, coldness or warmth shape individuals in ways that can be altered only with great difficulty in later years.

Even when people are able to screen out false ideas from parents and others, they do not always do so because on many occasions their intellectual defenses are down. Most important of all, people internalize all the ideas and attitudes they absorb uncritically and traces of them remain indefinitely. Illusions aside, much of what is in people's minds and hearts—their hopes, dreams, aspirations, expectations—arrived there without their awareness and consent.

Ironically, those who counsel people to accept themselves uncritically lead them into the very trap they claim to be helping them avoid, the trap of dependence on others. The only way for people to become individuals is to give up the illusion of automatic uniqueness and carefully examine the self they have taken for granted, identifying the influences society has had on them, evaluating those influences against some reasonably objective standard, and deciding which ones they will strengthen and which they will combat. That is the way of all self-improvement (and, interestingly, the way of psychotherapy, as well).

People's failure to acknowledge their conditioning not only makes them victims of that conditioning, it also robs them of the motivation to learn, especially the motivation to learn how to think more effectively. If a person believes he is unalterably unique, he is not likely to be concerned about conformity. If he believes individuality and independence are conferred automatically at conception, he is not likely to strive to achieve them. If he believes all knowledge and wisdom derive from within the individual self, he is not likely to value the experiences conveyed in books and lectures.

Misconceptions About Truth

Almost 400 years ago English philosopher and essayist Francis Bacon made this observation about human beliefs:

For what a man had rather were true, that he more readily believes. Therefore he rejects difficult things from impatience of research; sober things, because they narrow hope; the deeper things of nature, from superstition; the light of experience, from arrogance and pride, lest his mind should seem to be occupied with things mean and transitory; things not commonly believed, out of deference to the opinion of the vulgar. Numberless in short are the ways, and sometimes imperceptible, in which the affections color and infect the understanding.[9]

The observation makes as much sense today as the day it was written because the tendencies it describes remain the same. Yet our culture has come to reject the view of truth it is based on. At that time truth was considered to be an objective matter, quite apart from individual belief and unaffected by it. Today that sensible view has been replaced by the absurd view that truth is entirely subjective; in other words, that people create their own truth and whatever they accept as true is "true for them." This view is widespread and appears even in serious and well-intentioned discourse. Here is an example from a book that in certain other respects is interesting and useful: "This is 'education' in the root sense of the word—drawing out the learners' truth."[10] Other common expressions of this view are "one idea is as good as another," "it all depends on how you look at it," "different strokes for different folks," and "truth is relative."

The last expression, "truth is relative," reflects the modern source of the misconception. Though the notion of the relativity of truth can be traced, in part, to Rousseauvianism in the eighteenth century and to Romanticism in the nineteenth, it owes its present vigor to the uncritical acceptance of Einstein's theory of relativity in disciplines other than physics, notably history, anthropology, and ethics. Peggy Rosenthal documents this uncritical acceptance in her brilliant *Words and Values,* a highly readable examination of the way a number of concepts have bedeviled our intellectual life. And she goes on to point out how the idea of the relativity of truth lingers in popular works, even though scholars in many of the fields that embraced it have since rejected it, at least in its strong form.[11]

To understand the absurdity of the notion that truth is relative, we need only consider how often everyday reality challenges it. Here, for example, are four Associated Press news headlines together with summaries of the accompanying stories:

ILLUSIONS ABOUT RAPE PERSIST A researcher from The Urban Institute reports between one-third and two-thirds of people she surveyed continue to believe such erroneous ideas as that the majority of rape victims are promiscuous and that most reported rapes are not really rapes but acts of vengeance or attempts to preserve one's reputation.[12]

PAIR BELIEVES WRIGHTS WEREN'T FIRST IN FLIGHT Two Connecticut researchers have uncovered evidence they believe will establish that Gustave Whitehead flew his "model No. 21" two years before the Wright brothers' famous flight.[13]

FAMILY TIES CLOSER THAN EVER A survey conducted by the National Opinion Research Center of the University of Chicago concluded that the disintegration of the American family is a myth and that more modern families fit the image of "The Waltons" than ever before.[14]

FLU, TOXIC SHOCK SYNDROME CAUSES OF ATHENS PLAGUE A retired chief of epidemiology at the U.S. Centers for Disease Control has advanced the theory that the mysterious plague that caused the downfall of Athens 2400 years ago was caused by a combination of influenza and toxic shock syndrome. Past theories have suggested that the epidemic was caused by smallpox, bubonic plague, scarlet fever, measles, typhus, and other diseases.[15]

If everyone creates his or her own truth, then how can there be "illusions?" If a person believes rape victims are mostly promiscuous women, that must be the case. Similarly, if one idea is as good as another, then it doesn't matter what one believes about who flew first or whether family ties are closer than ever or what caused the plague of Athens. Everybody must be right; nobody *can* be wrong. More important, if truth lies within the individual, then research of any kind is fool's work because the proper direction of inquiry is not at what lies under the microscope or is hidden in historical documents or in any other external realities; it is inward, at what one is *inclined* or *wishes* to believe.

Carried to its logical extension, this kind of relativism obliterates the distinctions upon which rational thought depends, renders useless such words as "logic," "insight," "evidence," "probability," "plausibility," and "consistency," and reduces to near-meaninglessness such passages as the Francis Bacon observation quoted earlier.

If "one idea is as good as another," then on what grounds shall we condemn genocide or prefer modern treatments of mental disturbance over such past treatments as incantation and the administering of laxatives or, in extreme cases, flogging, starving, and stoning to death? How shall we answer those who argue that enslavement is no worse than liberty, that murdering the elderly is as humane as caring for them, or that the choice between capitalism and communism is merely a matter of personal taste?

If truth is relative, then what is the point in parents trying to determine which of the children broke the antique chair? Why should scientists attempt to determine the cause of the dinosaurs' sudden extinction millions of years ago, or NASA engineers assemble and study the wreckage of the Challenger space launch? What sense does it make for psychotherapists to probe the personal histories of their patients? Why take citizens from their occupations to serve on juries?

Before students can become excited about ideas, they must first believe that ideas are worth becoming excited about. Relativism denies them that belief. It undermines curiosity and wonder, robs students of sensitivity to problems, and makes relevant data indistinguishable from irrelevant and promising approaches indistinguishable from unpromising, thereby paralyzing creativity and leaving students mired in subjectivity. If one idea is as good as another, there is no good reason for students to subject their ideas to critical scrutiny and no purpose in the discussion of issues other than to stroke one's vanity.

Accordingly, before students can be expected to profit from thinking skills instruction, they must first learn to distinguish between assertions and truths. The former are merely attempts to express truths and, since human beings are imperfect, are therefore subject to error. Further, students must realize that the fact that beliefs change does not mean that the truth has changed. For example, if the speculation of some scientists that our solar system has a tenth planet should be proved correct, the explanation is not likely to be that a new planet was somehow added while no one was looking, but that scientists had somehow failed to notice it in the past. Finally, students must grasp the importance of basing beliefs on evidence and testing the accuracy of their judgments against norms that offer greater objectivity than intellectual habit or desire.

Confusion About Values

The widespread confusion over values, especially moral values, in modern American culture is traceable to the prevailing misconception about truth. In other words, because truth is seen as relative and one idea is considered as good as another, people perceive no basis for comparing values. Thus, the modern ethical school known as metaethical relativism declares that "there are no objectively sound procedures for justifying one moral code or one set of moral judgments as against another."[16] This view has come to be accepted even in such unlikely quarters as religion; for example, in the writings of Joseph Fletcher and Harvey Cox, among others.[17]

That this view of moral values has penetrated deep into contemporary thinking is shown in the frequency with which we hear people deliver such lines as, "Morality is a personal matter," "Who are we to say what's right for other people?" and "It's wrong to make value judgments." It is also shown in the fact that for the past couple of decades books on ethics have gathered dust on library shelves while books (and workshops and seminars) on "values clarification" have become fashionable. The term "values clarification" reflects clearly the relativistic and subjectivistic view of morality—values are not to be learned or discovered by analysis; they already exist within the individual and need only to be brought forth and clarified. The implication of this view is inescapable: there is no such thing as immorality; there are only different moralities for different people ("different strokes," as it were, "for different folks").

If followed consistently, moral relativism makes it logically impossible to evaluate any issue in which morality plays a part. If there is no basis for judging a moral code, then there is no basis for judging a particular moral action. What, then, can we say of the following situations: the case of the Chicago pupil who slipped LSD into the coffee cup of his 61-year-old teacher because she had reprimanded him for throwing paper airplanes in class; the case of the Brooklyn, N.Y., passersby who tried to smother the flames that engulfed a young man after he doused himself with motor oil and struck a match; the number of murders around the country in recent years with clear links to Satanic rituals? The answers necessitated by moral relativism—that what the student did was morally acceptable *for him,* that the passersby had no business imposing their moral code on the burning young man, and that Satanists are entitled to practice their beliefs— provide irrefutable testimony to the intellectual poverty of moral relativism.

Because the popular view of morality indisposes students to learn or discover relevant moral principles, they often fall back upon other bases of judgment. Two such bases are custom and majoritarianism, but these are exposed as inadequate the moment someone remembers that there have been some horrible customs in human history—such as infanticide, the sacrifice of humans to ensure a good harvest, and child prostitution—and that majorities have endorsed reprehensible practices, such as slavery. Another basis often used in place of moral principles is the law, but that too is revealed to be inadequate as soon as someone points out that laws are subject to change. If abortion is deemed morally acceptable because it is now legal, what do we make of the fact that it was previously illegal, and on what basis can this or any other present law be re-examined for validity in the future?

To overcome their confusion about values, students need to learn not only that it is proper to judge values, but that such judgment is inescapable because *not judging is a form of judgment.* Those who refused to judge Hitler's attempts to exterminate the Jews by that very refusal gave his actions their tacit approval. Moreover, students need to learn that the proper basis for judging moral values is neither custom nor majoritarianism nor law—it is ethical principles. Most important, they must understand that their rejection of moral relativism need not constitute an affirmation of moral absolutism. *Both* relativism and absolutism are extreme positions and both should be rejected.

Though space limitations do not permit detailed discussion of the moral principles to be used in evaluating moral issues, it is possible to state the most important ones. One that underlies almost all ethical systems is the principle of *respect for persons,* which Errol E. Harris explains as follows:

> First, that each and every person should be regarded as worthy of sympathetic consideration, and should be so treated; secondly, that no person should be regarded by another as a mere possession, or used as a mere instrument, or treated as a mere obstacle, to another's satisfaction; and thirdly, that persons are not and ought never to be treated in any undertaking as mere expendables.[18]

Two other important principles are the following: that the moral quality of an act is affected by the degree to which relevant obligations are observed and ideals honored, as well as by the consequences it produces; and that circumstances alter cases. (Relativists, by the way, did not invent the principle that "circumstances alter cases"; ethicists employed it as an operating principle and a safeguard against absolutism centuries earlier.)

The Habit of Basing Beliefs on Feelings

It would be a mistake to dismiss feelings as having no place in cognitive enterprise. They have a very important place, bridging the gap between noticing problems and issues and addressing them confidently. The confusion, frustration, and risk of failure that attend difficult endeavors are insurmountable without uncommon motivation. Such motivation is found only in those with a passion for finding answers to problems and issues and for putting those answers to work. That kind of passion is, at its best, synonymous with love of truth and is characterized by regard for evidence and a willingness to revise any idea, any belief, no matter how pleasant it may be, the moment evidence points to the need for revision.

The popular conception of feelings is very different from the foregoing description; the popular conception proceeds from the notions that individuals create their own truth and that whatever is *felt* is therefore true. This habit, much in evidence today, represents a self-indulgence in which first impressions and visceral reactions are considered the infallible products of a unique mind and are therefore trusted rather than examined. Accordingly, the habit of basing beliefs on feelings is not a different style of thinking, but a *rejection* of thinking.

One obvious reason that the habit of basing beliefs on feelings has become epidemic today is that responding according to feelings is easy—all people need do is let one of the ideas floating around in their minds rise to the surface and then express it. Since no special screening is required, it can be totally unreflective and impulsive, even capricious. Thinking, on the other hand, requires some special effort.

A less obvious reason that feelings are in the ascendancy even among intelligent people today is the fact that the words "feeling" and "thought" are often used interchangeably, making responding by feelings seem respectable. "That's what I think" and "that's what I feel" can mean about the same thing. Consider, for example, this question, which appeared in the "Voices from Across the USA" section in *USA Today:* "Do you think trade barriers are good for the USA?" Though the word "think" was used, anyone who has been the victim of an inquiring reporter's request knows that there is little time to construct a careful response. Anyone who responded "Let me think about that for a few hours, and perhaps do a little background reading to be sure I have all the facts necessary to make an informed judgment" (a reasonable enough approach to controversial issues) would surely find the reporter had moved on to another victim before the sentence was completed. No, even when the word "think" is used in such a question, what is expected is a "gut reaction."

A related word that enjoys special status in the vocabulary of people who feel rather than think is the word "opinion." This status is owed largely to the phenomenon of the "opinion poll," in which, with careful attention to the principles and approaches of statistics, people are asked their views of anything from the morality of capital punishment to the imminence of nuclear holocaust and the results are tabulated for dissemination to a presumably eager public (for the purpose, one is tempted to suppose, of "clarifying their values"). The key fact about this process is that no distinction is made between informed and uninformed opinions. All are lumped together in the final statistics. The unstated yet nevertheless clear message in opinion polls is that the feelings of the unread, fired quickly from the hip, are every bit as valid and valuable as the meticulously constructed thoughts of scholars. Little wonder that fewer and fewer young people elect to become scholars.

As if the bombardment by opinion polls, by large and small newspapers' inquiring reporter interviews, and by the expression of opinions in newspaper and magazine letters-to-editor columns were not a great enough obstacle to students' cognitive development, an experiment called "Involvision" is now underway. The experiment uses two-way cable television systems to permit home viewers to participate via touch voting "a/b/c/d/e" or "yes/no/undecided" to request product information, buy products, *or cast views on issues.* [19]

Basing beliefs on feelings rather than thought is undesirable for two reasons. The first is that feelings come so easily, so automatically, that they tend to reflect what is most prominent in people's memories, including all the clichés and vogue ideas and the slogans repeated endlessly by the legions of hucksters and demagogues who manipulate desires, needs, and emotions for personal gain. Because they are so prominent in memory, such words are readily, though incorrectly, assumed to be one's own. Psychiatrist Erich Fromm had this kind of situation in mind when he suggested that when people say "I think [or feel] this or that," it would be more accurate to say "It thinks in me." Fromm likens such situations to a phonograph saying "I am now playing a Mozart symphony" when it is really just reproducing the sound on a record someone else put on its turntable.

The second reason it is undesirable to base beliefs on feelings is that feelings express attitudes and desires, both of which can be irrational. If people have been strongly conditioned to a political philosophy, their disposition will be to approve compatible ideas without question. If they have been conditioned to a religious perspective, their disposition will be to welcome views that reinforce that belief and oppose those that challenge it. If people merely endorse their first reactions to issues, rather than going on to consider evidence for and against those reactions, they will never be able to overcome irrationality when it arises.

A single example will demonstrate how such irrational reactions can occur. In 1985 a group of concerned citizens formed Parents Music Resource Center (PMRC) and, with the National Parent-Teachers Organization (PTA), protested what they regarded as the increasing offensiveness of rock music lyrics. The news media carried a number of stories about the testimony the protestors and the music industry presented to the Senate Commerce Committee. Because the issues involved were numerous and complex, including questions of free speech and the possible relationship of song lyrics to the incidence of rape, incest, sadomasochism, and suicide, no responsible judgment about the reasonableness of the protest could possibly be made without thorough examination of the evidence presented.

Of course, many young people are extremely defensive about the music they listen to, regarding it as "our" music as opposed to "their" [adult] music, an understandable reaction given the frequency of parental outbursts against it. So the immediate response of many young people to news of the PMRC/PTA protest was, predictably, defensive in this manner: "There they go again, criticizing our music—the Senate Committee should throw them and their nonsense out." Precisely at this point, where good sense demands that the response be tested against the evidence to determine its reasonableness, the habit of basing beliefs on feelings urges that it be embraced uncritically.

To overcome the habit of basing beliefs on feelings rather than thoughts, students need to be made aware of how easily their feelings are influenced by others and how prone they (like all other humans) are to irrational responses. Moreover, they need to develop a preference for informed over uninformed opinion and the habit of responding to problems and issues thoughtfully, regardless of any internal or external pressure to do otherwise.

Intellectual Insecurity

The final obstacle to cognitive development we will consider, intellectual insecurity, is a consequence of the other five obstacles. Because of their disdain for intellectual rigor, many students are uncomfortable when problems and issues are not solved quickly and easily. Because they harbor a misconception about self, they are unprepared to deal with positions that differ from their own and so are ill at ease with dialogue. Because they harbor a misconception about truth, they are not ready to support their views and are nervous and sometimes belligerent when asked to do so. Because they are confused about values, they are defensive when discussions about values arise. Because they are in the habit of basing their belief on feelings, accepted uncritically, they can do little more than assert their views and thus are intimidated by reasoned discourse.

These unfortunate reactions, taken together, constitute a pervasive insecurity that not only obstructs students' development as thinkers, but also prevents them from becoming the kinds of believers who can learn from those with whom they disagree. C. Wright Mills classifies believers into three groups. First there are "vulgar believers," who use slogans and platitudes as weapons, frequently get angry, and verbally assault those who do not share their views. Then there are "sophisticated believers," those intellectually talented individuals who usually end up believing as they previously believed and defend the authorities they accept, point by point. When sophisticated believers do change their beliefs, they tend to do so wholly. Finally, there are "critical believers," whose arguments are developed using reason. These believers know that they are fallible and so know the importance of listening to and learning from others. Critical believers, Mills suggests, have more in common with other critical believers who differ with them than they do with vulgar or sophisticated believers who share their beliefs.[20]

To summarize the essential points made in this chapter: it would be naive to expect students to become effective thinkers without difficulty because their conditioning has created a number of obstacles to their cognitive development. For thinking instruction to succeed, teachers must do more than present the principles and techniques of holistic thinking and give regular assignments. They must help students replace irrational and negative perspectives with rational, positive ones. More specifically, they must demonstrate, wherever possible, the validity of the following ideas:

That human beings, being imperfect creatures, have certain natural tendencies that prevent them from thinking well, tendencies that must be acknowledged and combated.

That all people's thinking is to some extent influenced both by the general attitudes and values of their culture and by the specific attitudes and values of their families and friends.

That contemporary American culture has a number of negative elements that undermine young people's cognitive development.

That to be an effective thinker, a person must learn to deal patiently with complexity, develop the ability to defer gratification and concentrate for extended periods of time, and aim for excellence.

That no one is automatically unique; rather, that uniqueness of mind and manner must be developed, and such development begins in the recognition of the specific ways in which one has been conditioned.

That truth is neither created by individuals nor altered by their beliefs; that one therefore has an obligation to be scrupulously honest in considering evidence and uncompromisingly just in constructing assertions and arguments.

That the moral quality of an action is not determined by custom or consensus, but by examination of the circumstances in light of ethical principles.

That feelings can be a valuable ally to thought, but cannot substitute for thought.

APPLICATIONS

1. Think of as many situations as you can in which you have encountered someone ignorant of, or confused about, one or more of the eight important ideas listed above. Consider how you would correct or clarify that person's thinking based on what you read in the chapter.
2. For each of the eight important ideas listed above, think of a problem or issue in your academic discipline to which the idea applies in some significant way. Explain that application.

chapter 4

INSTRUCTIONAL OBJECTIVES

Some educators have an aversion to instructional objectives because much talk of objectives for the past couple of decades has used the term *behavioral* objectives, and "behavioral" is associated with behavior*ism*. Behaviorism, of course, has historically undermined philosophy and the humanities, and especially the teaching of thinking, by denying that human beings have intellects and wills and by regarding people as little different from rats and pigeons. Thus behaviorism is, at least in part, responsible for reducing education to a form of conditioning. Educators who view human beings as possessing an inherent dignity not shared by other creatures rightly resist aiding and abetting behavior*ism*.

Others oppose the idea of educational objectives for an entirely different reason, because they believe that the focus on objectives robs education of its human dimension. If classroom education is to have any spontaneity and warmth, they reason, then educators should think and speak solely in terms related to content, not in "educationese." In addition, such opponents of objectives often regard any concept relating to education in general, as distinguished from concepts relating to particular disciplines, as undermining the integrity of education. This view derives from a time when education courses were looked upon, not always without justification, as substantively inferior.

Though both of these views are understandable, both are mistaken. To damn "behavioral" because it reminds one of "behaviorism" is to practice guilt by association (accidental association, at that). If having a special interest in human behavior and endeavoring to improve that behavior makes one a behaviorist, then all the philosophers and saints revered in western civilization are suspect,

67

an absurd proposition. Further, to regard the setting of classroom objectives as destructive of spontaneity and warmth or as foreign to the spirit of one's discipline (any discipline) is capricious. No practitioner of a discipline is likely to achieve distinction unless she has a clear and coherent understanding of her short- and long-term goals. Blind groping breeds failure. Moreover, in an activity like teaching, where success depends on dispelling not only one's own confusion, but also students' confusion, clarity and coherence are imperative.

The argument for setting instructional objectives may thus be expressed quite simply: in teaching as in traveling, people are likely to have less difficulty reaching their destination if they decide where they are going before setting out and keep their destination in mind as they travel. There are a number of specific objectives important to thinking instruction. In the discussion that follows they are grouped under three general headings: dispositions, creative thinking skills, and critical thinking skills.

OBJECTIVE I: DEVELOPING OR REINFORCING THE DISPOSITIONS ASSOCIATED WITH EFFECTIVE THINKING

Historically, thinking instruction has tended to ignore the matter of dispositions to thinking. That has been a mistake because, as we have seen, human nature includes a strong disposition to irrationality, and many of the appeals in popular culture reinforce that disposition. All the understanding of creative and critical thinking and all the skill in applying that understanding to problems and issues will profit students little if they lack the *motivation* to think well.

But there is another reason for educators across the curriculum to attend more carefully to students' attitudes: the relative effectiveness of students' problem-solving efforts is strongly influenced by their attitudes. In their examination of students' problem-solving processes, Benjamin Bloom and Lois Broder list among their findings the fact that many unsuccessful problem solvers did poorly because they had negative attitudes toward reasoning, lacked faith in their ability to solve problems, and let their personal opinions interfere with their objectivity.[1]

Here, then, are the important dispositions that thinking instruction should cultivate in students.

Interest in the Sources of Their Attitudes, Beliefs, and Values

It seems, as Dostoyevsky suggested, that the second half of people's lives consists of nothing more than the habits they accumulated during the first half. One of the great challenges facing you as a thinking skills instructor is to get students to change unworthy habits of mind. Whatever approach you may devise to meet the challenge, this much is clear—it must begin with students regarding their attitudes, beliefs, and values differently, no longer taking them for granted, but seeing them as matters of interest and probing their origin and development.

**Curiosity About Their Mental Processes and Eagerness
to Develop Them Further**

Most students—indeed, people in general—know very little about their own mental processes because they have never been curious enough to ask such questions as these:

> What is my first reaction when a problem or issue arises unexpectedly? (Excited anticipation of a challenge? Panic?)
>
> What happens when I address a problem or issue? Does an image come to mind first? Words? Do I consciously employ any particular thinking strategies?
>
> What mental activities have I been engaged in when I received insights about problems or issues?
>
> How careful am I about separating hearsay from fact?
>
> In what areas do I tend to make unwarranted assumptions?
>
> How serious a problem is self-centeredness or group-centeredness (for example, *ethnic* group) for me?
>
> In what matters am I most resistant to change and what has caused me to be this way?
>
> To what or whom do I feel the strongest urge to conform?
>
> In what situations does the need to save face tend to corrupt my thinking?
>
> What is my characteristic reaction to complexity? (Nervousness? Oversimplification in order to have a neat, tidy answer?)
>
> In what ways and with what effects do stereotyped notions invade my thinking?
>
> In what situations do I tend to jump to conclusions? Why do I do so? (To sound authoritative and impress others?)
>
> What circumstances pose for me the strongest temptations to irrationality?

Self-knowledge depends upon curiosity about our own mental processes. In addition, curiosity provides innumerable insights that lead to more effective use of the mind (as well as to self-mastery)—insights like Graham Wallas' observation that often certain ideas appear on the "unfocussed fringe" of consciousness and that it is possible to be alert to these "fringe-thoughts" without diverting attention from what we are doing.[2]

**Confidence in Their Abilities and a Healthy Attitude
About Failure**

Research on "learned helplessness" has demonstrated that success is not merely a matter of having and using skills effectively: it also depends on people's *beliefs about their chances of succeeding.* Whereas some people take an optimistic view of their chance for success, gain confidence from prior successes, and take failure in stride without being daunted, other people take a pessimistic view, draw no confidence from prior successes (tending to view them as accidental and not predictive of future performance), and take even occasional failure as confirmation of their incompetency. Of the latter group, researchers have observed, "If there is a way to devalue one's present performance or to be pessimistic about one's future performance, the helpless [individuals] are likely to make use of it. Indeed, they do not even have to experience a negative outcome for this tendency to display itself."[3]

Unfortunately, as William J. J. Gordon has noted, "All problems present themselves to the mind as threats of failure."[4] So for "helpless" individuals, problems and issues, the very essence of thinking instruction, can appear frightening and produce a self-fulfilling prophecy of failure. You should be aware of this danger, seize every opportunity to bolster students' confidence in their ability, and provide guidance and encouragement whenever possible.

In addition, you should help students develop a healthy attitude toward failure, an attitude that acknowledges it as an inevitable aspect of life not just for the ungifted few, but for everyone. One way in which you can contribute to the formation of such an attitude is to inform students, from time to time, of how common failure has been in the lives of successful people. All their lives students have seen finished products and not the false starts and imperfect models that paved the way for those products. They have heard songs and read books and viewed works of art, but always in polished form, so it is understandable that they are unaware of the hours and years of frustrating labor the creators endured. Learning of the failures of successful people in your discipline and the ways in which they reacted to those failures (as a springboard for new and ultimately successful efforts rather than as irrevocable defeat) can thus help students gain a more realistic perspective.

Another way you can help students form a healthy attitude toward failure is to demonstrate that the failure of an idea often reflects not on the originator of the idea, but on the limitations of those to whom it is presented. For example, you can tell students that Dr. Seuss' first book was turned down by so many publishers that he was strongly tempted to burn it; that the perennially best-selling game *Scrabble,* invented by Alfred Butts, was labeled "worthless" and rejected by the game companies when it was first submitted to them; and that between 1939 and 1944 Chester Carlson's invention, the copying machine, was rejected by more than twenty companies before a small photo paper maker in Rochester, New York, bought it and marketed it under the name Xerox.

You might also tell students the revealing (and amusing) story of the judgment test Chuck Ross "administered" to 217 literary agents in the early 1980s. He submitted to each the original screenplay of *Casablanca,* changing only the title and the name of one character—184 rejected it, some offering criticisms of the style and others suggesting that a number of the now-famous lines in the film be changed or deleted.[5]

Willingness to Make Mistakes

"Panic of error," Alfred North Whitehead observed, "is the death of progress." The all-too-common notions that it is shameful to make mistakes and that gifted people's efforts are error-free seriously handicap students' thinking effectiveness. No one is likely to accept the challenges posed by difficult problems and issues when high priority is assigned to avoiding mistakes. And if life (or a teacher) forces such problems and issues on a person, he or she will almost certainly produce, not adventurous solutions, but common, familiar, *safe* solutions.

It is therefore important that students learn to regard mistakes as an inevitable part of meaningful thought and action, whether committed by an expert or a novice; and to realize that what counts is not how many mistakes we make, but how fully we profit from them.

Sensitivity to Problems and Issues

Sensitivity to problems and issues means a heightened awareness of problems and issues, an awareness that extends to keeping them in the backs of our minds and, more important, *being constantly ready to make worthwhile connections between them and everyday experiences.* Here is an actual case to illustrate the value of making such connections. Donald Pevsner, a consumer activist, proposes "a program to systematically donate all unused [airline] meals to the poor upon arrival at destination airports. Legal problems could be forestalled by the signing of releases-of-liability by the donees, on a legal theory analogous to 'good-samaritan' laws in tort."[6] (Pevsner estimates that the number of meals and snacks involved—that is, the number being destroyed at present—is roughly 20 million per year.)

An interesting idea, and *one that was waiting to be thought of by any one of the millions of people who have traveled by air.* The connection was not a difficult one to make, the association between food and hunger being obvious. Why, then, did not many other people make it? Simply because they were not in a state of readiness to make it. Tens of thousands of similarly fortuitous connections lie waiting to be made by those with the requisite sensitivity.

A Positive Attitude Toward Novelty

Creative ideas are, by definition, novel ideas. It has long been hypothesized that people with negative attitudes toward novelty are likely to feel uncomfortable in situations challenging their creativity. Now the brain-wave research of Colin Martindale of the University of Maine offers physiological support for the hypothesis. He has found, not surprisingly, that while resting, highly creative people are more aroused, aware of their surroundings, and apt to be disturbed by sudden noises than relatively uncreative people. But he has also found that when assigned a creative task, highly creative people immediately become calmer, less aroused, whereas uncreative people's brain wave patterns remain unaltered. Martindale terms this result "stunning" and suggests that, "confronted with novelty, whether in design, music or ideas, creative people get excited and involved, while less creative people turn suspicious or even hostile."[7]

Certainly it is not an easy assignment to change students' long-standing characteristic attitudes toward novelty, nor are there any special techniques for doing so. The best prescription is to demonstrate your interest in novelty and reward students' attempts to produce novel ideas. Be especially careful not to stifle the adventurousness of young students with warnings about "carrying novelty too far." As a general rule, you should present such cautions in careful explanations to individual students and not in remarks to entire classes.

Interest in Widening Their Experience

The wider their experience, the more knowledge students can bring to bear on problems and issues. Unfortunately, many students' experience is disturbingly narrow; moreover, they have little interest in widening it. One important objective of thinking instruction, therefore, must be to stimulate that interest.

One way to stimulate students' interest in widening their experience is to demonstrate that because good ideas can be found in unlikely places, even cultures that have been regarded as primitive should not be presumed to have nothing to offer. For example, throughout most of this century the medical practices of African (or American Indian) tribes have been dismissed as sheer superstition. Tribal doctors were termed, derisively, "witch doctors." Today's view of tribal medicine is considerably more respectful. We know know that some of the lessons western medicine has learned only in the past ten or twenty years, like the fact that sickness is often preceded by stress, were understood by tribal doctors for centuries. And the medical establishment's overdue willingness to learn from tribal doctors is paying dividends—for example, in the identification of natural (herbal) remedies for disease.[8]

Another way to simulate students' interest is to demonstrate that old-fashioned approaches can sometimes offer solutions to modern problems. An interesting example concerns the agricultural methods of the Amish people of Pennsylvania. Most people have regarded the Amish as quaint curiosities because of their old-fashioned dress and way of life. Not long ago the idea of studying their methods of farming as a means of aiding the modern agriculture industry or studying their community structure to learn how to cope with modern social problems would have been dismissed as ludicrous. Yet there is now evidence that the Amish have insights that could help our more "advanced" society. For example, they are able to minimize crop erosion and achieve acceptable crop yields without commercial fertilizers; and problems of abandoned children, criminals, welfare cheaters, and the homeless, indigent elderly are for them virtually nonexistent.[9]

A third way to stimulate students' interest in widening their experience is to break down the notion that each academic discipline is separate, disconnected from all others. The compartmentalization of knowledge that results from this notion keeps students from applying what they learn in one subject to other subjects. Whenever possible, illustrate how the interaction between academic fields has produced desirable results; in addition, encourage students to explore such interactions.

Respect for and Willingness to Use Intuition When Appropriate

Harvard professor Jerome Bruner defines *intuition* as "the intellectual technique of arriving at plausible but tentative formulations without going through the analytic steps by which such formulations would be found to be valid or invalid conclusions."[10] In popular writing, intuition is often treated as a mystical process, but Bruner and other scholars regard it as a kind of hunch or educated guess. Intuition can play a useful role in problem-solving and issue analysis, for example by suggesting avenues for investigation or interesting hypotheses. Indeed, those who lack intuition or refuse to use it often find themselves intellectually paralyzed, unable to attack a problem or issue because of the bewildering number of possible approaches or the sheer bulk of their data.

Intuition, however, has a serious limitation: even the most educated hunches and guesses can prove wrong. For this reason, intuition should never be taken as the measure of its own worth; when later investigation or analysis shows it to be deficient, it should be rejected. It will have served a valuable purpose by stimulating or expediting one's thinking.

Perhaps because of this limitation of intuition, or because of educators' admonitions about guessing, many students are wary of intuition. Therefore, any effort to help them develop their intuition will have to be patiently sustained before it is likely to bear fruit.

The Desire to Reason Well and to Base Judgments on Evidence

Perhaps at some deep level everyone wants to reason well and base judgments on evidence, in the same way that everyone (in the view of many philosophers) is oriented toward doing good and avoiding evil. But at another level a very different dynamic is at work. It is that level psychologist Carol Tavris is referring to when she observes that "the very organization of our mental faculties seems designed to screen out information we don't want to hear, information that is at odds with our basic beliefs." The many theories of cognitive consistency that have been advanced, she explains, tie this phenomenon to human beings' "fundamental need to find meaning and order in life's experiences."[11]

To make students *desire* to reason well and to be willing to exert the effort to do so, you will have to demonstrate that right reasoning makes a difference, that errors in reasoning lead to faulty solutions and unreasonable beliefs, both of which can generate frustration, disappointment, and anguish. Thus you should try to persuade students (not merely verbally, of course, but by classroom experiences) that it is in their own best interests to reason well.

Willingness to Subject Their Ideas to Scrutiny

The mark of a critical thinker is not the readiness to subject other people's ideas to scrutiny; it is the readiness to subject one's own ideas to scrutiny. The latter readiness is much more difficult to develop because people naturally tend to regard their own ideas as extensions of themselves. Doubting one's own ideas seems tantamount to doubting one's self. Thus the greatest challenge in pursuing this objective is to guide students to discover that the process of evaluating and approving or disapproving one's own ideas is perfectly natural and that honest self-criticism ultimately strengthens the self.

Another challenge this objective poses for you is to help students understand that there is no contradiction between having convictions and being open-minded. On the one hand, many students have been taught that convictions are good, that lacking convictions is bad, and that compromising convictions is even worse. On the other hand, they have been taught to be open-minded. "How can I do both?" they wonder. The difficulty arises from their misunderstanding of both terms.

"Having convictions," as the term is most often used, does not mean being closed-minded and refusing to examine beliefs in light of new evidence. It merely means having the courage to stand by beliefs in the face of temptations to violate them *for insufficient reason.* Similarly, "being open-minded" does not mean being spineless or indecisive. It merely means being willing to give all new evidence a fair and impartial hearing. Thus being open-minded does not threaten one's integrity—it merely provides a means of examining one's convictions on a regular basis to ensure that they are worthy.

Willingness to Entertain Opposing Views Without Reacting Defensively

Closely related to the objective of subjecting one's own ideas to scrutiny is the objective of entertaining opposing views without reacting defensively. That people should react defensively to opposing views is understandable; after all, such views proclaim that they are in error. Nevertheless, that reaction is unjustifiable because it hinders the search for the best solutions and the most reasonable beliefs. However unpleasant it may be to learn that we are wrong, it is nevertheless helpful; and it is preferable to gain that knowledge privately through our own honest analysis of opposing views than to have it forced upon us publicly while presenting our flawed views.

This objective is best achieved through exercises and activities that demonstrate to students the practical value of considering opposing views and revising their own ideas, as necessary, before making those ideas public. One of the best activities is to have students make formal oral presentations, stating their views on controversial issues and defending those views in response to challenges from the class. Frequent experience on the receiving end of such challenges will usually persuade even stubborn students of the wisdom of evaluating their ideas in advance.

Curiosity About the Relationships Among Ideas

Many critics of American education have lamented the fact that curiosity has traditionally been discouraged, not only directly ("Don't ask so many questions," "Curiosity killed the cat"), but also indirectly in the subtle signs of the teacher's impatience or annoyance with questions ("Let's try to keep on track now," or "We've got a lot more material to cover"). If students are to overcome the effects of such experiences and regain their curiosity, you must provide considerable stimulation—prompting and encouraging students to wonder and ask lots of questions, taking time to answer or guide them to discover answers. In addition, you must reward their progress.

Of particular importance to thinking skills are questions that probe cause-effect relationships: What (force or agent) caused this to be as it is? What effects have occurred as a result of its being as it is? Such questions underline the reality of change and the almost infinite opportunities to make the world better and thereby add a dimension to one's life.

A Passion for Truth

The expression "philosophic attitude" is common in the humanities; the expression "scientific attitude" is common in the sciences, social sciences, and technologies. "Passion for truth" is intended to convey what is essential to both those attitudes—a restlessness to know more accurately or more fully, coupled with the disposition to test what one has always thought or what has been traditionally believed. Where others regard assertions (at least those assertions that flatter habitual ways of thinking) as a kind of evidence, good thinkers recognize them as *claims* to be examined in light of evidence. And their characteristic reaction to assertions is less often "I agree," or "I disagree," than "Let's find out."

A wealth of new ideas lies beyond "Let's find out." For example, for millennia it was thought that human learning begins at birth—then a researcher investigated, and found that fetuses can hear, and so learn, a great deal through the walls of the uterus. Similarly, for generations it was assumed that fields used for such crops as soybeans and corn must be plowed every year to maintain production levels. Then University of Illinois researchers decided to find out for sure if that was the case, and discovered that such fields can be left unplowed (and therefore safer from erosion) for three years before any loss in productivity occurs.[12]

To develop a passion for truth in students, you must provide frequent experiences designed to break down the erroneous notions that each person makes his own truth and that uninformed opinions are as good as informed ones. Because popular culture tends to reinforce these notions, this challenge is formidable.

A Healthy Attitude Toward Argumentation

Many people confuse argumentation with quarreling, but the two are very different: whereas argumentation is reasoned discourse, quarreling is verbal contention;

whereas argumentation generates light, quarreling generates only heat; whereas the purpose of argumentation is to discover the truth, the purpose of quarreling is to indulge the ego. Compounding the confusion is our society's extreme competitiveness and the new end-justifies-means ("win at all costs") philosophy it has spawned, a philosophy that has invaded the intellectual, as well as the athletic, arena.

To overcome such confusion and help students develop a healthy attitude toward argumentation, you should provide regular opportunities to practice the skills of creative and critical thinking in an atmosphere that reduces competitiveness to reasonable dimensions, penalizes sophistry, and puts reason at the service of truth instead of vanity.

OBJECTIVE II: DEVELOPING OR REINFORCING HABITS AND SKILLS THAT ENHANCE THE PRODUCTION OF IDEAS

The habits and skills that enhance the production of ideas comprise creative thinking. Training in these habits and skills is, as noted in Chapter 2, an essential part of thinking instruction (albeit one that some *critical* thinking courses and materials overlook). Both classroom experience and research document that students who lack these skills are unlikely to be successful in meeting the challenges of real-life problems and issues.[13] The habits and skills that enhance the production of ideas are as follows:

Skill in Defining Problems and Issues

The perspectives we take on problems or issues can significantly affect the conclusions we reach. The way a psychologist regards conflict, for example, can make a difference in her approach with patients for whom conflict is a problem. If she regards conflict as a real problem, her focus will be on how to deal with it. If, on the other hand, she regards conflict as only a *symptom* of an underlying problem, she will pay little attention to the conflict and concentrate on whatever she believes lies deeper. Carol Tavris cites the example of a therapist dealing with a patient whose habit of saving money created a conflict with her spendthrift husband; believing that the underlying problem was the woman's unconscious desire to withhold intimacy, the therapist focused on that and ignored the money conflict.[14] If the latter was the actual problem, the therapist's approach surely did little good.

Consider also the school problem discussed in Chapter 2; namely, the closing of over 7000 schools because of declining enrollments, budget cuts, and inflation. If we define that problem as "How can school enrollments be increased?" it is unlikely that we will produce any ideas for reducing school budgets. Or if we define it as "How can school buildings best be used after the schools are closed down?" it is unlikely that we will produce any ideas for generating income from unused space so that the school will not have to be closed down.

Ideas for reducing school budgets are likely to occur to us only if we define the problem as "How can school budgets be reduced?" Ideas for generating income from unused space are likely to occur to us only if we define the problem as "How can the unused space in school buildings be used to generate income so that the school will not have to be closed down?"

To develop students' skills in defining problems and issues, you must give students frequent opportunities to construct definitions, as well as guidance in ranging out many alternatives before deciding on any one.

The Ability to Defer Judgment

A number of studies have demonstrated the value of deferring judgment while producing ideas. As Sidney Parnes' explains, "extended effort in producing ideas on a creative thinking problem tends to reward problem-solvers with a greater proportion of good ideas among the later ones on their lists." Parnes speculates that the reason for this effect is twofold. To begin with, "a subject's associative hierarchy will call forth the most dominant responses first, which will be the most habitual or usual ones. After he has purged these, he will shift to weaker responses in his repertoire; that is, ones that he has not habitually associated with the given task, and hence, he will tend to become more original." Secondly, "as a subject considers ideas that do come to his mind, he will list the safest ones first—the ones he is more certain will be accepted. These will obviously be the less original, the more tried and true ones."[15]

The ability to defer judgment may seem achievable simply by resolving not to evaluate ideas as they are being produced, but it is not, for there are two kinds of judgment. One is the kind that occurs slowly, after evaluation and reflection. The other is so swift that we are barely aware it is taking place. In the latter, ideas are screened at the very instant they are produced and either approved or disapproved; if disapproved, they are discarded before we can begin to evaluate them. Thus in guiding students' development of this ability, you must ensure that students break the screening habit and record every idea that occurs to them.

The Ability to Produce Many Ideas with Facility

This ability, also known as idea fluency, is related to the ability to defer judgment. To acquire it, students must first break the common habit of prematurely terminating idea-production and turning to judgment. In other words, they must learn to resist settling for the first few ideas that come to mind. Next they must break the start/stop habit—that is, the habit of producing an idea and then pondering/judging it before producing another. That habit creates a series of interruptions that retards the flow of ideas and creates mental blocks that would otherwise not have occurred.

Of course, even when judgment is deferred, ideas will seldom flow without interruption, so it is unrealistic to expect students (or anyone else) to be able to produce an unbroken string of ideas. Thus one important aspect of idea fluency is skill in dealing with mental blocks—that is, skill in restarting the flow of ideas, with a minimum of delay, once it has been stopped.

Among the strategies useful in dealing with mental blocks are looking back at the ideas already produced and letting one of those ideas suggest a new one: employing one of the strategies for stimulating imagination (see pages 41–44); copying our list of ideas over again, being alert to new ideas on the fringe of consciousness; and walking away from the problem for a time. In the case of problems, when all else fails, we can select a different expression of the problem and produce a different list of ideas.

How many ideas must a person produce before being considered idea-fluent? Since the number of ideas capable of being produced varies from problem to problem, it is impossible to set a meaningful number. Moreover, quantity of ideas by itself is not a reliable measure of idea fluency in the larger sense; quality must also be considered. Nevertheless, research makes clear that the most productive people are generous in producing ideas. Ernest Hemingway produced more than thirty titles before settling on *For Whom the Bell Tolls*. Alex Osborn once saw an editor write down over 100 possible captions for a short editorial. And in the process of inventing the tractor, Henry Ford produced 871 models before selecting one.

The Ability to Shift Perspectives While Producing Ideas

This ability, also known as flexibility, is especially important in dealing with complex problems and controversial issues. It permits a person to see the same detail from different angles, the same question from different points of view. Inflexible people are commonly considered unable to *embrace* different views. The more significant fact is that they are unable to *conceive* different views, a much greater deficiency because it blocks imaginativeness.

Flexibility is important not only in the production of ideas, but also in manipulating the information derived from investigating a problem or issue. In their well-known study of college students, Benjamin Bloom and Lois Broder found that poor problem solvers did not lack any important information that good problem solvers possessed. Instead, they lacked the ability to bring their information to bear on the problem. "It seemed, then," the researchers concluded, "that the ideas which the nonsuccessful problem solvers possessed were huge, unwieldy things, figuratively capable of fitting into only one particular space—that in which they had originally been framed. The ideas of the successful problem solver, in contrast, were many-faceted things which could be turned this way and that, expanded or contracted, and made to fit the space in which they were needed."[16]

To help your students achieve flexibility in their thinking, give them frequent practice in considering viewpoints other than their own and in arranging data in various ways. One way to do this is to create exercises that challenge them to present the same data to a number of different audiences, first studying the particular characteristics of the audience and their probable needs and expectations, and then arranging the material effectively. Another way is to have students engage in debates and defend, not their own position, but the opposing position.

The Habit of Seeking Imaginative Ideas

Imaginativeness is one of the distinguishing characteristics of creative ideas and one of the most important traits of highly creative people. It is imaginativeness that suggests the daring hypothesis, the new and promising area of investigation, the ingenious experiment, the novel interpretation. Contrary to popular belief, however, imagination is not a special inborn talent some individuals possess and others irremediably lack. Rather, it is a skill that is acquired through practice. Those who are unimaginative have simply not *learned* to be imaginative.

The habit of deferring judgment and pressing idea production beyond common responses will provide a start to being imaginative, as will the habit of viewing problems and issues from varied perspectives. But students also need to overcome their fear of being different and to develop the habit of consciously seeking imaginative ideas. The following six strategies for producing ideas can stimulate imagination: (1) forcing uncommon responses; (2) using free association; (3) using analogy; (4) looking for unusual combinations; (5) visualizing the solution; (6) constructing pro and con arguments; and (6) constructing relevant scenarios. (See Chapter 2 for a detailed discussion of these techniques.)

OBJECTIVE III: DEVELOPING OR REINFORCING HABITS AND SKILLS THAT ENHANCE THE EVALUATION OF IDEAS

The habits and skills that enhance the evaluation of ideas comprise critical thinking. Those habits and skills are as follows:

Fairmindedness in Evaluating Issues

In practical terms, fairmindedness means granting to other points of view the same consideration we desire for our own— testing them against the evidence rather than against our preconceived notions, refusing to magnify their flaws, acknowledging insights even when they challenge our thinking, and interpreting generously where there is no good reason for interpreting otherwise.

Lamentably, fairmindedness is most essential at the very time when it is most difficult to practice, in the consideration of controversial issues when our own values and beliefs are at issue and we feel threatened. That is the time when special effort must be made to treat the other side fairly.

The Ability to Select and Apply Criteria of Evaluation

The criteria of evaluation to be used in evaluating data will vary from field to field. If the problem or issue involves statistics, statistical criteria should be used; if it is legal, then legal precedents and the rules governing their use are appropriate;

if it concerns morality, then the principles of ethics should be consulted. Not infrequently, a problem or issue will touch several disciplines; in such cases, several different sets of criteria should be applied. (Note that before students can be expected to apply any criteria, whether general criteria or subject-specific ones, they must be *trained* to apply them. Simply knowing what the criteria are is no guarantee that they can apply them properly.)

Skill in Determining the Structure of a Piece of Discourse

This skill, particularly as applied to argumentative (analytical) discourse, is essential—students must understand both what an argument says and how it says it before they can deal effectively with it. Teachers all too often assume that because students are proficient readers, they are therefore able to recognize structure. That assumption is unwarranted, particularly in the case of long, complex articles or books. To determine the structure of an argument students must:

1. Distinguish between statements of fact and statements of opinion (interpretation or judgment).
2. Identify the central assertion (in the case of argumentative discourse, an opinion), the main supporting assertions, and the evidence on which the argument rests.
3. Determine the relationships among all major statements in the piece of discourse. The principal relationships are "and" relationships, signifying that an assertion or item of evidence is being *added* to what preceded; "but" relationships, signifying that what follows is being *contrasted* with what preceded; and "therefore" relationships, signifying that what follows is a *conclusion* drawn from what has preceded.* Simple arguments often take the form _____, AND _____, THEREFORE _____; or _____, BUT _____, THEREFORE _____. Complex arguments contain networks of such relationships.

To deal effectively with extended arguments, students must be able to reduce them to manageable proportions. This is most easily done by writing a *précis,* a concise restatement of the original that preserves its essential structure and tone. Unfortunately, précis writing has for decades been neglected in American education. If thinking instruction is to be maximally effective, précis writing must be be taught early and reinforced often at all levels of education. (Though few contemporary composition textbooks provide detailed coverage of this skill, many older ones do.)

Skill in Evaluating the Reliability of Sources

If they have never been shown that sources can differ considerably in their reliability and have never been guided to understand the reasons for such differences, many students are likely to assume that everything that is published or

---

*Other words and phrases, of course, are often used in place of "and," "but," and "therefore."

broadcast is equally reliable. To displace that assumption, you must provide frequent opportunities for students to evaluate sources and discuss their findings.

Among the questions you should direct students to ask of their sources are these: Does the author or reporter have any special expertise in the matter? Is his report based on personal observation or experience (as opposed to second- or third-hand reporting)? If it is, were the conditions conducive to accuracy? Was there independent confirmation of the author/reporter's findings? How consistent is the report with other evidence? How reputable is the magazine, journal, publishing house, or other agency (such as a television program) in which the report appeared? Is it given to the sensational? How careful does the author/reporter seem to be about avoiding unsupported assertions? How impartial is he? If the report refers to specific research, does the author provide important details, including the original source of publication?

Skill in Interpreting Factual Data

It is easy to read too much into data, particularly data which confirms a previously-held belief. Consider this case: A Nashville, Tennessee, resident who strongly advocates the teaching of sex education in the schools reads that 78 percent of 2100 Nashville residents polled believe that the schools should teach sex education.[17] She is justified in concluding that, if the poll was done properly, a majority of the residents of Nashville favor sex education. However, without further evidence she is not justified in making any judgment on their views regarding what exactly is to be taught or how or by whom. However tempted she may be to conclude that those polled share her views about specific aspects of a sex education program, she has no warrant to do so. They may, for example, favor a sex education program radically different than the one she has in mind.

Headlines and very brief news accounts can easily lead to misinterpretation. Suppose, for example, a headline reads, "Pay Raises for Local Teachers Triple National Average," and the accompanying story says little more than that local raises were 10.5 percent in comparison with the 3.5 percent national average. Despite the fact that the article presents no judgment, readers might be very tempted to believe that the teachers' raise was unreasonably high, especially if those readers were biased against teachers to begin with. Yet without knowing at least what the teachers were paid before (or after) the raise, it would be impossible to interpret the statistics fairly. It could be they were so underpaid that after the raise their salaries were well below the national average.

Skill in Testing Hypotheses

One important task of critical thinking is to evaluate the credibility of hypotheses; that is, to determine how believable they are in light of the evidence. Few students are likely to be able to conduct such evaluations without instruction: *tens of thousands of true/false questions will have created in their minds the impression that statements are either absolutely true or absolutely false.* Specifically, they will need to learn both to use the following scale in evaluating hypotheses and to defend their evaluations:[18]

Certainly true

True beyond reasonable doubt

Highly probable

Probable

Indifferent

Improbable

Highly improbable

False beyond reasonable doubt

Certainly false

The Ability to Make Important Distinctions

Sound reasoning often depends upon one's ability to make important distinctions. It would be impossible to list all the distinctions that students should learn to make; they are simply too numerous, and in many cases their form changes with the situation. (For example, the distinction between *seldom* and *never* is essentially the same as that between *often* and *always,* yet the form is different.) Still, it is possible to identify the most crucial distinctions, the ones that arise again and again in critical thinking situations. They are as follows:

- *The distinction between preference and judgment.* Many people confuse preference and judgment, partly because the popular word *opinion* is used to cover both. It is important to distinguish between these terms because preferences do not need to be defended, but judgments do. An opinion is properly considered a preference in matters of *taste,* such as whether redheads are more attractive than brunettes, about which there can be no objective measure. However, it is considered a judgment in matters of *fact,* about which there is an objective measure—how well the opinion fits the evidence.
- *The distinction between the degree of emotion in one's expression and the reasonableness of his or her idea.* Many people commit the error of assuming that because someone speaks excitedly, the message is therefore extreme; conversely, that if someone speaks calmly, the message is rational. It is possible to deliver the most insane nonsense in a calm manner and a penetrating insight in a frenzied manner.
- *The distinction between the appearance and the reality.* Appearances can deceive: the person who seems to be a snob may simply be shy; a product that seems well made may fall apart after it is used a few times; and ideas that on the surface appear profound may on closer consideration prove shallow. Therefore, first impressions should always be tested before being accepted as accurate.
- *The distinction between the person and the idea.* Why do advertisers pay famous spokespeople large sums of money to promote their products?

Because they know that the favorable feelings many people have for the spokespeople will unconsciously be transferred to the products. Such confusion of person and idea is also common in argument; uncritical people tend to accept the ideas of those they like and to reject the ideas of those they dislike. Critical thinkers keep people and ideas separated in their minds. Knowing that the most admirable person can occasionally be wrong, and the least admirable can be right, they judge ideas on their merits, regardless of who expresses them.

- *The distinction between why a person thinks as he does and whether what he thinks is correct.* Interest in why people think (and act) as they do is certainly legitimate; after all, that interest is one of the foundations of psychology. But many people falsely assume that worthy reasons and motives validate an idea and unworthy reasons and motives invalidate it. The fact that a member of congress supports the construction of a nuclear power plant in a neighboring district because his relatives stand to gain financially does not mean that the idea of building the power plant is a bad one. It may be good *in spite of* that official's personal motives for supporting it. Ideas should be judged on their merits and not on the vices or virtues of their supporters.

So far our examples of distinctions have been general ones—that is, distinctions that have wide general application. Narrower, more specific distinctions, of course, are also important. An example of this kind is psychiatrist John Bowlby's distinction between children's "anger of hope" and "anger of despair," the latter often being produced by neglect and abuse.[19]

Skill in Recognizing and Evaluating Unstated Assumptions

Unstated assumptions are ideas not reached by conscious thought but merely taken for granted without thinking. It is natural to make assumptions; by doing so we save time and energy. We begin our day assuming the car will be in the garage and will start when we want it to. Then we assume the office will be open, we have not been fired without being notified, and that our work will be compensated at the end of the week. And so on. Without assumptions, we would have to ponder every word we utter, every move we make every moment of every day. Very little would get accomplished.

The examples noted above are all warranted assumptions; that is, what they take for granted is justified by past experience or conditions known to exist. (If the unexpected happens and, let us say, a car that has shown no signs of "ill health" fails to start one day, the assumption that it would start would still have been warranted.) Unfortunately, many other assumptions are unwarranted—they take *too much* for granted. It is impossible to list all the particular unwarranted assumptions that we might make, but the following general ones occur often enough to be noteworthy:

- *The assumption that others will share our enthusiasm for our solutions.* People tend to have their own preferred solutions, and the more creative our solutions are, the less likely they are to be similar to others'.

- *The assumption that small imperfections in our solutions will not affect people's acceptance of them.* When people have their own preferred solutions, they are apt to magnify imperfections in other people's solutions because they are unconsciously seeking an excuse to reject those solutions.
- *The assumption that if our thinking is clear to us, it will be clear to others.* Anyone who has sat in a class listening to a professor who serenely delivered a lecture transparently clear to him or her but a perfect muddle to everyone else should understand the error here. Ideas are clear to others only if they are painstakingly constructed to be clear.
- *The assumption that those who stand to benefit from our ideas will accept them automatically.* The history of invention is littered with evidence to the contrary. Acceptance follows people's *perceiving* an idea's worth. If the perception is lacking, the acceptance will be also.
- *The assumption that people's senses are always trustworthy.* The literature on eyewitness testimony underlines the fact that many things can go wrong with people's perception, a number of them quite outside the person's control. (See Elizabeth F. Loftus' interesting book, *Eyewitness Testimony,* Harvard University Press, 1979, for a detailed treatment of the subject.)
- *The assumption that having reasons provides assurance that reasoning has taken place.* This assumption is no more warranted than the assumption that having money proves that it has been earned. (Money can be begged, borrowed, or stolen, as well as earned.) Reasons may be developed by careful analysis or simply lifted mindlessly from the stream of other people's statements that floods our waking moments every day.
- *The assumption that conviction constitutes proof.* Error is no respecter of convictions. People can be passionately committed to ideas that are silly, shallow, even absurd. In fact, it is often strength of conviction that blinds people to the foolishness of ideas.
- *The assumption that if one event closely follows another in time, it must have been caused by the other.* This assumption is a common one, occurring even in the thinking of people committed to careful analysis. For example, political analysts sometimes blame a president for developments that occur shortly after he took office when the real causes are to be found in previous administrations.
- *The assumption that if the majority believes something, it must be so.* The number of people who endorse an idea is not a good measure of its soundness. If it were, there would have been no basis to condemn slavery, infanticide, the castration of choir boys to preserve their high-pitched voices, and the execution of witches, all practices that were at one time approved by majorities. No, the measure of an idea is the quality of the arguments for and against it, irrespective of the number of people who support those arguments.
- *The assumption that the way things are is the way they must be or should be.* The fact that a condition or state of affairs exists or has existed for a long time cannot be taken as a justification for its existence. If it could, then doctors would have no business fighting disease, the colonists were wrong in declaring their independence, and the efforts of human rights organizations to abolish torture and end war are improper. The fact is that life is filled with both good and bad states of affairs, many of human

creation, and it is the job of responsible, thinking people to reinforce the former and overcome the latter.

- *The assumption that if an idea is flawed it is worthless.* Humans are imperfect creatures and their ideas necessarily reflect that imperfection. But the imperfections in ideas vary considerably in significance; not all imperfections are serious enough to render an idea worthless. An important part of a thinker's job is to determine how significant each imperfection is and, if possible, to find ways to overcome it.

The Ability to Detect Fallacies

Fallacies are errors in thinking; they occur because, to borrow a phrase from Richard Paul, people are naturally "mired in bias."[20] Psychologists call that bias *egocentrism* (self-centeredness), a condition of intellectual immaturity that prevents one from viewing the world objectively. Vestiges of egocentrism linger even in the intellectually mature and are manifested in mine-is-better thinking, which inclines people to favor those ideas that are compatible with their beliefs and values and to approach problems and issues predisposed, if not positively committed, to the side that permits them to go on thinking as they do. Thus inclined, they may easily substitute rationalizing for reasoning, employ the devices of sophistry, or commit one of the fallacies detailed below.*

Illogical Conclusion   In formal logic, this fallacy is known as *non sequitur,* a Latin term meaning that the conclusion does not follow logically from the premises of the syllogism (the formal statement of the argument). A syllogism is a kind of verbal mathematics: $a + b = c$ (or $1 + 2 = 3$). It is composed of three statements: the *major premise,* the *minor premise,* and the *conclusion.* Often one of the premises in an argument is not stated, but merely implied.

A number of rules govern formal argument and the violation of any of those rules invalidates an argument. Since the thinking instruction that takes place in the great majority of classrooms does not involve formal logic, we will not discuss it here. Readers who wish to pursue the subject in depth should consult a formal logic text, such as Frederick Copi's *Introduction to Logic* (Macmillan). Here are two examples of illogical conclusions, with an explanation of the error in each:

> ARGUMENT: People who frequently miss Western Civilization class are in jeopardy of failing. Bert never misses Western Civilization class. Therefore, Bert is not in jeopardy of failing.
> COMMENT: The conclusion is invalid because the first premise does not say missing class is the *only* reason for failing. There may be other reasons as well, such as failing to do the assigned work. Bert may be in jeopardy of failing for one of those reasons.
> ARGUMENT: If one's parents have influence, one can get an executive posi-

---

*In rationalizing, the conclusion is drawn to fit one's existing beliefs and then evidence is found to support it; in reasoning, all relevant evidence is considered and then the most reasonable conclusion is drawn. Sophistry is a defense mechanism that puts thought at the service of ego rather than of truth, typically by finding some real or imagined minor flaw in the reasoning of one's opponent and using that flaw as the basis of dismissing her entire argument, good points as well as bad.

tion immediately on graduation from college. Jill got an executive position immediately on graduation from college. Therefore, her parents have influence.

COMMENT: The conclusion is invalid because the first premise does not rule out the possibility of someone getting an executive position because she is unusually able. Since Jill could be such a person, it does not follow that her parents necessarily have influence.

Either-Or Thinking   Either-or thinking (also known as polar thinking) consists of falsely believing that rejecting one extreme position on an issue necessitates embracing the other extreme. That is, it denies the possibility of moderate positions on issues. A classic case of either-or thinking is found in the evolution/creation debate that has continued for more than a century. Ironically, many people on both sides of the debate are guilty of exactly the same error, which consists of assuming that *either* God created the universe and evolutionists are totally wrong *or* the universe evolved independently of divine activity and creationists are totally wrong.

The appropriate response to this, and to all other either/or thinking fallacies, is "Why can't each side be partly right and partly wrong?" In other words, in this case, is it not possible that God created the universe in a way which set the forces of evolution in motion? (Note that the fact that either-or thinking is a fallacy does not rule out the possibility that in some cases the truth may lie at one of the extremes.)

Stereotyping   Stereotypes are fixed, unbending generalizations about people, places, or things. A central feature of prejudice, stereotypes cripple observation. People who have a stereotyped view of Italians as violent, Jews as greedy, and blacks as lazy will find it difficult, if not impossible, to see any Italian as pacific, any Jew as generous, any black as industrious. No matter how many times they encounter challenges to their prefabricated images, they will either deny the reality before them or dismiss it as nontypical.

Nor are stereotypes limited to nationality, race, and religion. There are stereotypes of coaches, foreign film directors, feminists, fundamentalists, atheists, scientists, prostitutes, construction workers, homosexuals, marriage, government, and even of God and mother.

Attacking the Person   This fallacy consists of disposing of an argument by attacking the person who advances it. The validity of an argument does not depend on the character of the person who embraces it: a scoundrel may support a valid argument; a saint, an invalid one. The only legitimate basis for accepting or rejecting an argument is its own merit or lack of merit. This fact does not, of course, mean that a spokesperson's character should be totally ignored. If a man is a known liar, it makes good sense to examine what he says with care and, where possible, to seek corroboration. It merely means that it is incorrect to assume that past performance necessarily affects present statements or arguments.

Straw Man   This fallacy consists of changing other people's words or interpreting them in an extreme way in order to facilitate attacking the person's position. Consider this case: a mother says to her daughter "I think it would be a good idea if you stayed home this evening—you've been out every night this week," and the daughter responds, "Why are you opposed to my socializing—there's nothing immoral about enjoying myself." By misrepresenting her mother's position, making it seem much more extreme than it actually is, the daughter is guilty of the straw man fallacy. An actual example of straw man is the bumper sticker "Guns don't kill people, people do." Proponents of gun control do not argue that guns are the *agents* of killing, as the bumper sticker implies, but only the *instruments* of killing.

Shifting the Burden of Proof   The "burden of proof" is the responsibility for defending or supporting a position. In a general sense, everyone has such a responsibility: intellectual honesty demands that one have sufficient reason for any belief. Here, in the logical sense, however, "burden of proof" refers to the special responsibility of someone who makes an assertion in discussion or debate. If, for example, Sam says "Television viewing retards children's language development," it is reasonable for someone to ask him to support his assertion with evidence. If Sam responded to the request by saying, "I don't have to offer support—it's up to you to prove my assertion wrong," he is guilty of the fallacy of shifting to others the burden of proof that is properly his.

The burden of proof is increased when the assertion made challenges views widely accepted by informed people. Thus if Sam had said, "Television-viewing *enhances* children's language development," a view most informed people reject, his responsibility to support the assertion would be even greater and any attempt to shift the burden of proof would be a more serious error. Moreover, for his view to be persuasive, his evidence would have to be sufficient to outweigh the evidence supporting the more common view.

Double Standard   In his thoughtful study of mental maturity, Harry A. Overstreet observed that "a person remains immature, whatever his age, as long as he thinks of himself as an exception to the human race."[21] That, in essence, is the error of the double standard—thinking of one's self and those associated with one's self as exceptions. It is a common error. For example, Virgil and Edna both work and leave their children in a child-care center five days a week; they regard this situation as a necessary one and believe that their children benefit from it because they give them "quality time." Yet when their neighbors, a couple of similar age and with similar income, do the same thing, Virgil and Edna consider them materialists who neglect their children's needs.

The very language we use to describe friends and foes often suggests a double standard. For example, we call our friends outgoing, thrifty, persevering, and zealous; yet we call our foes loudmouthed, stingy, overly ambitious, and fanatical. When we attack others, we are "offering constructive criticism"; when others attack us, they are "nitpicking." At election time our candidates are "statesmen," the opposition's "politicians"; and when our party awards political jobs, it is "rewarding party loyalty", but when the other party does, it is engaging in "political patronage."

One of the most important characteristics of honest thinkers is that they use the same standard of evaluation for friends and foes alike. Moreover, in dealing with problems and issues they regard their own arguments and those of their supporters no less critically than the arguments of their opponents.

Contradiction   Contradiction occurs whenever a person makes two assertions that are inconsistent with each other. For example, a person says that corporations should never receive special tax advantages unavailable to the average individual taxpayer and then, at a later point in the discussion (or piece of writing) says that corporations should receive tax advantages only when foreign competitors are threatening their survival. The two assertions are contradictory.

You should explain to students that contradictions usually occur because we have not thought the subject through before speaking or writing about it and, as a result, change our position in the course of our presentation. If students apply the holistic approach described in Chapter 2 and carefully plan their spoken or written presentation, they will have little problem with contradiction.

Faulty Analogy   Analogy is a line of reasoning suggesting that things alike in one respect are also alike in other respects. If the similarities claimed are real, and there are no (unstated) dissimilarities that are important in the context in which the analogy is used, the analogy is reasonable. In a popular article on influenza research, for example, a science writer draws an analogy between the way the virus attaches itself to a living cell and the way a hijacker takes over an airplane and diverts it to his destination.[22] The analogy is reasonable because, though there are obvious dissimilarities between a virus and a human being, in this context those dissimilarities are not important. However, if someone were to use the analogy between a virus and hijackers (and other criminals) to argue that perpetrators of violent crimes should be denied all legal rights, the dissimilarities would be important enough to invalidate the analogy.

Because analogy is such a useful and frequently used device in both expository (explanatory) and persuasive expression, you should be sure students understand that analogy is by definition an *imperfect* comparison and exercise care in their use of it, especially as evidence for a line of argument.

Faulty Causation   The most common form of faulty causation is reasoning that if one event or condition occurs after another, it was caused by the other. This error undoubtedly underlies many superstitions; in other words, having bad luck after breaking a mirror or having a black cat cross one's path leads the person to see a cause/effect relationship where the most reasonable explanation is coincidence. Similarly, if a student was rude to her teacher yesterday and today receives a low grade on a composition assignment, she may conclude that the low grade was assigned because of the rudeness. (There may, of course, have been another reason.)

Faulty causation can occur in the formal reasoning of professionals as well as in everyday thinking. For example, malaria was long thought to be caused by damp night air because the onset of the disease occurred after the victim was out at night. The real cause, we now know, is mosquitoes, who are more active during evening hours.

Irrational Appeal   This error usually occurs in debating issues and consists of misusing a rational appeal. The most common kinds of irrational appeal are the following:

> An appeal to emotion that does not merely accompany thought, but substitutes for it.
>
> An appeal to tradition or faith that urges maintaining the practice or belief not because it is applicable to present circumstances, but merely because it has always been maintained.
>
> An appeal to moderation that is not offered because moderation represents the best approach to the problem or issue, but because it is a convenient way to avoid offending someone or to evade the responsibility of judging.
>
> An appeal to authority that fails to acknowledge the fallibility of people and their institutions and disallows reasonable questions and challenges. (Note that the appeal may be to eminent people, eminent books and documents, or eminent agencies, such as the Supreme Court.)

The best way to make students sensitive to the distinctions between rational and irrational appeals is to give them regular practice in identifying and evaluating the appeals in other people's arguments, as well as encouragement to recognize and evaluate their own appeals.

Hasty Conclusion   A conclusion is considered hasty if it is drawn before sufficient evidence is obtained to permit any conclusion or if it is drawn from two or more possible conclusions when the evidence provides no more support for one than for the other(s). Hasty conclusions are most commonly found in situations where prior opinions tempt a person to be uncritical.

Overgeneralization   Generalizations are a necessary and valuable product of thought. Here are some examples of acceptable generalizations: "Large bank loans are seldom obtainable without collateral"; "Democracies afford citizens greater personal freedom than other types of government"; "To create the illusion of depth, landscape painters make distant objects smaller than proximate objects"; and "The end of a sentence or paragraph carries greater emphasis than the beginning."

*Over*generalization is generalization that exceeds the scope of the evidence. It results from choosing a higher level of generalization than is warranted, sometimes because of carelessness, but often because force of statement is more highly valued than accuracy, as it is when strong feelings are involved. After several bad experiences with insensitive men, for example, a woman might say, "Men are coarse, insensitive, and unable to give affection freely." That, of course, would be an overgeneralization. Her experiences would justify her saying, "The last four men I dated were . . ." or "Some men are . . ." or, under certain conditions, "Many men who have been taught to equate machismo with masculinity are . . . ." But each of these statements is very different from saying that men in general have these characteristics.

Oversimplification   There is nothing wrong in simplifying: teachers and text-book authors do it all the time to make complex matters clear, particularly in introductory courses. Thus it is not simplification that should be avoided, but *over*simplification—that is, simplification that *mis*represents or distorts reality. Here are two examples of oversimplification: "If the students haven't learned, the teacher hasn't taught"; "We know ourselves better than others know us." There is an element of truth in each assertion. There are poor teachers and their incompetency often does prevent students from learning; similarly, no one else can know certain aspects of our selves (our dreams and hopes and experiences, for example) as well as we do. However, each assertion is guilty of a serious omission. Learning involves not only the teacher's effort, but also the students'. If that is lacking, students can fail despite the best efforts of the finest teachers. Similarly, there is an important side of ourselves that others know better than we do—the image we project, often unconsciously. By ignoring important aspects, the above assertions misrepresent the realities they purport to describe.

Each of the fallacies presented in preceding pages may occur either alone or in combination with other fallacies. Often one fallacy leads to another. For example, a person with an extreme mine-is-better attitude may make a remark *stereotyping* a race or ethnic group. When criticized by a friend for being preju-diced, he or she may attempt to save face by *attacking the person* (the friend) instead of dealing with the issue. Similarly, someone may draw a *hasty conclusion* or make an *oversimplification* and then later, after benefitting from thoughts expressed by others in the course of the discussion, *contradict* the original asser-tion.

Skill in Evaluating Arguments

This objective embraces a number of subskills, some of which we noted earlier: skill in summarizing extended arguments (précis writing): skill in recognizing assertions and differentiating between minor and major ones; skill in reading the structure of the argument—that is, the relationships among the assertions, partic-ularly "and-," "but-," and "therefore-relationships"; skill in the appraising the quantity and quality of evidence supporting the argument; skill in determining what other evidence, if any, is relevant to the argument; skill in raising worth-while questions about the accuracy of the author's assertions and his interpreta-tions of evidence; skill in testing arguments for fallacies.

The Ability to Make Sound Judgments

A sound judgment is one which is free of flaws in logic and fits the evidence better than any competing judgment. Such a judgment has three general characteristics.

First, its subject is appropriately specific. If the evidence is limited to students in the business management program of a particular two-year college in Virginia, the judgment would not begin "College students" or "U.S. college students" or even "Students at Virginia's Excelsior College." Each of those subjects would be too broad to fit the evidence. Secondly, in a sound judgment, the predicate makes an assertion about the subject that the evidence fully supports. Finally, a sound judgment contains all appropriate qualifications, including qualifications of time, place, and condition.

Two effective ways to help students develop the ability to make sound judgments are to give them exercises designed to teach flexibility in expressing ideas and to call attention to questionable or faulty judgments and demonstrate how to revise them. For example, you might ask students to explain the difference between the following original and revised sentences, and to discuss the kind(s) of evidence needed to support each of them:

Original	*Revised*
Children who are taught to be mannerly at home are mannerly elsewhere.	Children who are taught to be mannerly at home tend to be mannerly elsewhere.
Inner city residents stay off the streets after dark.	Inner city residents usually stay off the streets after dark.

You should also provide students helpful guidelines to use in making judgments. The following are recommended:

- *When the facts will not support any firm or final judgment, make the judgment appropriately tentative.* This is not an invitation to "ride the fence," refusing to take a stand that the facts permit us to take. It means recognizing when the facts do not permit us to take a conclusive stand.
- *When the facts will not support a generalized judgment, particularize the judgment.* One of the best ways to determine how broad a judgment the facts will support is to consider how large our sampling of the people or things is. If it is a relatively small sampling, and there is no good reason to believe the sampling is representative of the larger group, then we should particularize the judgment, saying, for example, "Several students in my dorm have voiced objections to the new dorm-fee policy," rather than "Students on this campus object to the new dorm-fee policy."
- *Even when the facts support a firm judgment, exercise restraint in judging.* The traditional way to show intellectual restraint is to use understatement; for example, where the evidence would support our characterizing a particular problem as "one of the most critical problems of this or any age," we might instead say it is "a problem of considerable importance."

The Ability to Recognize When Evidence Is Insufficient

No single formula can be given that is applicable in all situations. That is all the more reason why it is so important to avoid early closure, particularly on controversial issues. Yet that does not necessarily mean waiting for every iota of evidence. In many cases that would not only be impossible, but irresponsible: decisions must be made, action must be taken. Not to act often signifies, not neutrality, but endorsement of the existing situation. Avoiding early closure means, rather, accounting for all major interpretations and being sure no relevant and available body of evidence is overlooked. The best way to develop this kind of skill in students is to guide them to ask, over and over, in a variety of situations, "what other evidence should I obtain before passing judgment?"

Vigilance Concerning Students' Tendencies to Irrationality

Students should be kept mindful of two facts modern culture prompts them to forget. The first is that the irrationality likely to do them the greatest harm is not other people's, but their own. The second is that, whereas their ability to influence other people's thinking is at best minimal, nothing prevents them from bringing their own thought processes more fully under their control. In making the effort to control those processes, of course, it is necessary to be observant, for as Joseph Jastrow rightly notes, "Prejudice need not be crude and coarse and obvious and simple. It may be subtle, delicate, intricate, elusive. It intrudes at all levels in endless variety. We approach most matters with a somewhat predisposed set of mind, neither quite closed nor quite open."[23]

TWO ADDITIONAL GOALS

There are two additional goals that, while not formal objectives, are worth aiming for. One is to have students review their reading habits and make worthwhile adjustments. Surely many students need to do more reading, both of a general nature and of specific content areas of major concern to them, in order to become more informed, deepen their understanding, and stimulate their thinking. "New facts," Alex Osborn said rightly, "often trigger new ideas." Other students, however, may be reading *too much*. Such a view may seem heretical, given the place reading has traditionally occupied in European and American education. Yet not every scholar has been enthusiastic about reading's contribution to the life of the mind.

German philosopher Arthur Schopenhauer believed that "the safest way to have no thoughts of one's own is to take up a book every moment one has nothing else to do." Henry Hazlitt claimed that many learned men have read themselves into "dreamy stupidity." Ernest Dimnet believed that fiction was responsible for debasing both thought and the art of reading by making the reader a passive observer instead of an active evaluator of what is written. (Dimnet made this observation before the advent of television. How much harsher his judgment would likely be of television fiction, which so often substitutes glitter for substance!)

None of this is to suggest that you should offer general counsel against reading. Many, perhaps most, students need the opposite advice. It is rather to suggest that you urge students to read more alertly and actively, allowing time for reflection and the pursuit of whatever interesting questions and ideas may arise.

The other goal to aim for while pursuing thinking objectives in your courses is a spirit of entrepreneurship in students—that is, a readiness to move from thinking to doing. A notable example of this spirit occurred in 1985 when thousands of schoolchildren around the country conducted a fund-raising campaign to help relief efforts in Ethiopia, ultimately contributing millions of dollars. Though the situations in which the ideas generated in a course can be transformed into action may be relatively rare, you should always encourage students to look for opportunities to do so. Such encouragement helps overcome the dichotomy between the classroom and the "real world" and helps students regard solving problems and analyzing issues as more than academic exercises.

A NOTE OF CAUTION

This chapter is filled with the names of the dispositions and skills of effective thinking. Because of the overemphasis in our educational system on imparting information, teachers can easily make the mistake of approaching the dispositions and skills as terms for students to memorize. There is nothing wrong with learning terms, but compared to the primary goal of *acquiring* the dispositions and skills, knowing the terms is incidental. Students who have mastered only the terms will have failed to achieve the objectives.

APPLICATION

Review the specific instructional objectives detailed in this chapter. List those that are of special importance in your subject area or at your grade level. For each objective that you list, explain one or more specific situations that provide you an opportunity to pursue the objective.

chapter 5

INSTRUCTIONAL METHODS

If you want your students to learn to think more effectively, you must use methods proven effective in accomplishing that aim. This idea is a truism, to be sure, but one worth underlining. The failure to incorporate thinking instruction into curriculums for the past century has occurred amid continued affirmations of the importance of such instruction; indeed, amid numerous prescriptions for accomplishing that goal.[1] Thus the problem has not been teachers' refusal to teach students how to think; it has been misunderstanding about the methods that are effective in doing so.

Perhaps the single greatest impediment to thinking instruction has been misplaced faith in the efficacy of the lecture (or lecture/recitation) method. That faith rests on several unwarranted assumptions:

1. That learning a subject means being able to recall a large body of information. Recall is one kind of learning; another, arguably more important, kind is the ability to apply principles and concepts in solving problems and evaluating issues.
2. That being able to use the vocabulary of a discipline, say, sociology, with some precision means being able to think like a sociologist. This assumption ignores the distinction between parrotting words and speaking thoughtfully.
3. That having right answers is important, but having control over the process by which they are reached is unimportant. It is this unwarranted assumption which has produced the kind of graduate that business and the professions are most disturbed with—the kind who cannot take the initiative in solving problems and making decisions.

None of this is to deny the lecture method its place in education. It is, as Mortimer Adler and the Paideia group have noted, the appropriate vehicle for the acquisition of organized knowledge. The problem lies in what Adler describes as "the error of assuming that there is only one kind of learning and one kind of teaching, the kind that consists in the teacher lecturing or telling and the students committing to memory what they hear said or find in textbook assignments. There are two other kinds—coaching and discussing—both more important than the first kind because their results are long-lasting, as the results of the first kind are not."[2]

Lest it be thought that Adler's observation is only applicable to the liberal arts, consider the view of MIT's Andrea DiSessa, who argues that scientists and mathematicians should not be teaching "science" or "mathematics," but what scientists or mathematicians *do*. DiSessa explains:

> The point," "is to shift emphasis to activity and away from facts. After all, it is no doubt more correct to say mathematicians know how to generate proofs for x or y than that they know the proofs. Physicists generate solutions to problems; they don't *know* them. It is not that facts (or even calculational algorithms) are irrelevant, but that the higher level activity of deciding when to use a fact or invoke an algorithm is more characteristic of scientific knowledge than the retention of the facts involved. This of course is not surprising as *doing new things* is precisely the raison d'etre for scientific knowledge. In other fields even as far removed as the arts one sees clearly that the ability to *reshape* the old in the face of a new context better characterizes the successful practitioner than the ability to recall the old.[3]

Ideally, the three types of instruction work in harmony. Lecturing conveys what is commonly referred to as "subject matter" or "course content"; coaching develops intellectual skills; and discussing articles and books (other than textbooks) enlarges understanding of ideas and values.* Thus the three work in harmony: in Adler's words, "the knowledge to be acquired with the help of didactic instruction must be made secure by the skills to be developed by coaching and by the understanding to be achieved through seminar discussions on the one hand, and guided practice on the other."[4]

Since lecturing is not the appropriate teaching method for the acquisition of dispositions and skills, we will exclude it from consideration here. Further, since the kind of discussion that is used in skills teaching is somewhat different from the kind used in teaching for understanding, we will treat discussion as a companion method to coaching rather than as a separate method. Before turning to those considerations, however, let us address a question of understandable concern to many teachers: "Does content-learning suffer when the lecture method is curtailed to make room for thinking instruction?"

*Adler makes clear that the success of each kind of instruction depends upon having appropriate class size: for didactic teaching, from 35 or 40 students to a large lecture hall audience; for coaching, 5 or 6 students, certainly no more than 10; for discussion, from 15 to 25 students. For further discussion of this stipulation, see Chapter 9.

An unusually thorough study of the effects of such a change was completed by Ilma M. Brewer of the University of Sydney, Australia. Over the period 1968–1978, Dr. Brewer changed her teaching emphasis from recall of knowledge to comprehension and application of knowledge to problems. In 1968 her tests contained 0 percent comprehension/application problems; in 1978, 80 percent. During the same period student performance rose from 2 percent receiving grades of 80 and above to 31 percent receiving grades of 80 and above. The mean grade score increased 12.2 percent from 60.7 to 72.9.[5] These results suggest that an emphasis on thinking skills not only does not retard mastery of content; it significantly improves it.

COACHING STUDENTS

Because skills are acquired only through exercise, teaching students to think means, primarily, changing their role in the learning process from passive to active. This can be done only by changing your role as teacher from lecturer to coach. To appreciate the necessity of this change, consider how successful a basketball coach would be if he did nothing more than lecture his athletes on the requisite skills of the sport. On Monday, let us say, he lectured on dribbling; on Tuesday, on foul shooting; on Wednesday, on defense. However dramatic his anecdotes of exciting moments in the history of the game and however eloquent his urging to excel, his team's lack of opportunities for skill development would surely lead to their undoing in actual competition.

If, like most teachers, you have been trained exclusively in the art of dominating class time, giving up the podium will require an adjustment, but it need not be a traumatic one. As Adler points out, it is easier to learn to coach (or to lead discussions) than to learn to lecture.[6] Here are the essential activities of an academic coach:

> To break the habit many students have of leaning inordinately on their instructor and the textbook and to motivate them to become increasingly self-directing in their intellectual lives.
>
> To create an atmosphere conducive to creative and critical thinking; that is, an atmosphere in which process is valued above product and therefore mistakes are tolerated and students encouraged to face them honestly and learn from them, an atmosphere in which students are willing to be adventurous in their thinking because creativity is prized, an atmosphere in which criticism can be given and received without embarrassment or hurt feelings.
>
> To provide frequent challenges in the form of problems and issues appropriate to students' level of intellectual development, problems and issues that afford them practice in thinking skills.
>
> To allow them to struggle with problems and issues long enough to develop strategies for dealing with confusion and frustration, but not so long as to defeat them. To provide just enough assistance for them to overcome confusion and frustration and get started again.

To encourage students to extend their application of thinking skills beyond the particular exercises assigned to them; wherever possible, to reward that application.

As the above approaches suggest, the role of coach demands the exercise of restraint. No matter how far his team is behind and how inept their performance, an athletic coach cannot rush into the game, take the ball away from them and play the game himself. He may call a time-out and tell the team what to do, or he may make substitutions, but he cannot take over himself. Similarly, as an academic coach you must resist the temptation to deal with problems yourself and confine your assistance to calling "time-outs" and making suggestions, or "making substitutions" (in the sense of calling on other students). Like an athletic coach, too, you must demonstrate patience (or at least controlled impatience) and the ability to criticize constructively without discouraging students.

LEADING DISCUSSIONS

The principal classroom activity that characterizes thinking skills instruction is discussion. Therefore, in addition to becoming a good coach, you must become an effective discussion leader. That means meeting the following requirements:

Examine the subject of discussion carefully in advance.

It is difficult enough to lead a discussion effectively if you have command of the subject, but virtually impossible to do so if you have not given careful thought to the subject. Your preparation should include the same kind of thought that is expected of students—the application of the holistic process to a problem or issue, for example—in sufficient depth to learn what considerations are most important and what distinctions must be made, as well as which lines of inquiry are likely to be most fruitful. You must, however, avoid the temptation to let your examination of the subject close your mind to other ideas. Succumbing to that temptation will undermine your objectivity and ultimately stifle students' creativity.

Prepare a set of main questions to be addressed during the discussion.

Even though questions that can be answered by reciting factual information do little to promote cognitive growth, most teachers use these questions more than any other kind.[7] In preparing your main questions, avoid such questions. In their place use questions that require students to go beyond repeating what they have read or heard, questions that direct them to express and defend their own interpretations and judgments. These are the kinds of questions that have been shown to effect significant gains in cognitive performance.[8]

Main discussion questions provide a focus for discussion, serving both to get discussion started and to keep it organized; nevertheless, they account for a relatively small proportion of questions asked in a discussion. (Secondary or "follow-up" questions are more numerous.) It is therefore important both to limit the number of your main questions to four or five per discussion period and to speculate how students are most likely to respond to them. After you have gained some experience in this kind of speculation, you will be able to predict with some accuracy the kinds of follow-up questions you will need to ask.

After asking a question in class, listen carefully to the student's reply.

Only by grasping exactly what the student has said, fully and in all its implications, will you be able to determine what to say next. Since listening is one of the most neglected of basic skills (among teachers as well as students), you may need to devote special effort to improving your listening. You may, for example, find that you have to break the habit of using the time when a student is answering to plan what you will say next. Once the student has replied, consider what follow-up question you should ask. Though it would be impossible to present all the kinds of follow-up questions that you might ask, it is possible to identify some of the most useful ones, in one sequence in which they commonly occur.* They are as follows:

QUESTION: I'm not sure I understand what you are saying, Agnes. Would you mind expressing the idea again?
COMMENT: This question is appropriate whenever the student's response was vague or confused or when you sense that the rest of the class may not have grasped the meaning of what was said.
QUESTION: By what reasoning did you reach that conclusion? Please explain.
COMMENT: This question is appropriate regardless of the commonness or uncommonness, soundness or unsoundness, of the idea expressed. Often instructors inquire about the rationales underlying student views only when the views seem questionable; but good ideas are sometimes embraced for bad reasons and vice versa. Having students share with the class why they think as they do has several benefits: it reinforces the idea that they should have reasons for their views, gives them practice in formulating and expressing reasons, and expands opportunities for worthwhile class discussion.
QUESTION: Agnes, what evidence have you, other than your own reasoning, that your idea is sound?
COMMENT: Like the previous question, this one should be asked routinely, so that students derive the benefits previously mentioned and also develop the habit of testing their beliefs against some objective standard. This question also serves to reinforce whatever lessons have been presented about judgment criteria of special importance in your discipline.

---

*There is one occasion when follow-up questions should be avoided. That is when the purpose of discussion is to brainstorm as a group to produce various expressions of or solutions to a problem or issue; or to simulate the manner in which each student brainstormed individually. On this occasion the focus should be solely on the production of ideas, so the same question should be repeated with only slight variations again and again—"How many solutions can we produce?" "Agnes, what solutions can you add to the list?" "What are your solutions, Tom?" and so on. This approach is necessary to reinforce that efficacious yet difficult-to-practice rule of deferring judgment during idea-production.

QUESTION: [Turning to another student] Tom, do you agree with Agnes?
[Then, depending on Tom's answer] Why (Why not)?
COMMENT: Often Tom will respond as follows: "Yes, I agree with Agnes
for the reasons she gave." In that case, the appropriate question is "What
experiences have you had in your own life, what observations have you
made of others, that support Agnes' view? Describe one or more of them
in some detail for us and explain *how* they support Agnes' view." If he does
so, you may wish to probe his answer further or bring another student into
the discussion.
QUESTION: Can anyone think of any other interpretations of Tom's experiences than the ones he offered? Is it possible to see them as *refuting* rather
than supporting Agnes' view?
COMMENT: Suppose that Sally raises her hand and volunteers an interpretation that challenges Tom's. If her contribution was in any way vague or
ambiguous, you might ask her to explain further. Then you might call on
Tom to respond to her interpretation, or you might bring yet another
student into the discussion.
QUESTION: We have a conflict, Luke, between Tom's interpretation and
Sally's. Which do you find more reasonable and why?
COMMENT: Let's say that in answering, Luke cites a principle learned
earlier in the course, but he misstates it. Your first impulse may be to say,
"You've misstated that principle, Luke," but it would be preferable to keep
yourself out of the discussion and merely say, "Does everyone accept Luke's
answer?" Perhaps someone alert enough to have caught the error will speak
up and correct it. If no one does, it may be necessary to give a further clue:
"Rose, Luke mentioned the principle of _____ in his response. State that
principle in your own words." After the error has been corrected, you
would undoubtedly return to the conflict between Tom's and Sally's interpretations and discuss it further. And what then? You should be sensitive
to the fact that enough time had elapsed and enough terrain had been
covered since Agnes' initial statement that the issue ought to be clarified.
QUESTION: Let's return to Agnes' statement and re-examine it in light of
our discussion. Agnes, would you please repeat it for us?
COMMENT: After Agnes has responded, you might ask her whether she
wished to revise her original statement. (Of course, if you had taken the time
to write her statement on the board at the outset of the discussion, you could
dispense with her restatement and direct the class' attention to the board.)
Or you might instead put the same challenge to another student thus:
"Henry, in light of what has been said, how would you revise Agnes'
original statement?" If time permitted, you could have the class analyze
Agnes' or Henry's revision of the statement. Or you might sense that
discussion of the matter had reached the point of diminishing returns and
close it with a statement of the lesson it yielded.

Many instructors prefer breaking a class into several small discussion
groups to leading the entire class in discussion. They reason that in small groups

each student has more opportunity to contribute and therefore can practice his or her thinking skills more efficiently. Though this *can* be the case, there is reason to believe it is often not so. Dianne Common of Canada's Simon Fraser University presents evidence that small group instruction, as typically practiced in social studies classrooms, is more likely to corrupt than to enhance critical thought. This corruption occurs because the classroom climate and the nature of group discussion combine to "foster consensus and uniformity as a dominant group characteristic," a characteristic that is "antithetical to the spirit and practice of critical thought."[9] If you decide to use small group discussion in pursuit of thinking skills objectives, be sure to take suitable precautions against this effect.

EXTENDING WAIT-TIME

In using the kind of questioning illustrated above—indeed, in using *any* kind of questioning—be aware of the benefits of providing adequate wait-time for students to address the question and frame their response. One study revealed that the pace most teachers set for answering questions is much too fast: the teachers observed allowed students, on average, only one second to begin responding. If no response was forthcoming at that time, they either repeated the question or moved on to another student. If students did respond to the question, teachers waited an average of only 0.9 seconds before commenting on the response, asking another question, or moving to a new topic. Moreover, the teachers gave poorer students *less* time to answer and *less* helpful evaluative comments than they gave more proficient students.[10]

Students whose teachers extend waiting time in their questioning sessions master inquiry skills more effectively. That was one of the findings of the study just cited. And another study concluded that extending waiting time produces a number of specific gains: it increases the length of student responses, the number of unsolicited but appropriate student responses, the number of questions students ask, the number of experiments students propose, the number of times students make inferences and support them with evidence, and the number of contributions from slow learners.[11]

PLAYING DEVIL'S ADVOCATE

Many teachers employ the method known as "playing devil's advocate." This consists of the teacher entering the discussion and taking the neglected side of the argument in order to give students the opportunity of responding to an opposing view. The method can be effective in stimulating class discussion if certain cautions are observed. One caution is to limit the use of the method to those occasions when a student's position seems so obvious that no one in class can be found to oppose it. The reason for this caution is that when you as teacher enter a discussion, you both abandon the important role of moderator (and the objectivity that goes with it) and force most of the class to become passive spectators.

Another caution is to resist the temptation to maintain the devil's advocate role beyond its usefulness. It is easy to get so caught up in the game that you forget that its purpose is to challenge students, not to baffle and discourage them. Whenever you use this method, be sure to concede when the student has answered your mock objections and praise him or her for doing so; then make clear that you are returning to the role of moderator.

A similar admonition should be made clear to student participants in discussion. Many of the students who respond most readily to class discussion will have acquired a mistaken notion that the purpose of debate is to win at all costs. They will tend to argue for the sake of arguing, employ sophistry, and regard ideas that oppose theirs as an attack on their persons. Be prepared for such behavior and gently but firmly discourage it. Whenever possible, stress that the purpose of discussion and debate is to increase understanding and solve problems and issues, and that when that happens, everyone wins.

Now let us turn to the methods useful in teaching thinking skills, first identifying an effective overall approach and then considering a number of specific methods to be used within that approach.

AN OVERALL APPROACH

Any sensible approach to teaching thinking skills balances work on skill clusters (or individual skills) with work on holistic thinking. The former affords students a simpler, less confusing way of developing their skills, by working on one skill at a time and getting the extensive practice necessary to master it. The latter teaches students how to use skills in combination in ways that approximate real-life problem solving and decision making. The suggestions that follow will help you achieve this balance.

Suggestion 1   Early in your course introduce the five-stage holistic thinking process detailed in Chapter 2—Exploration, Expression, Investigation, Idea Production, and Evaluation/Refinement. Explain each stage and provide one or more examples of its application to problems and issues in your discipline. If possible, give students one or more exercises, preferably simple ones, in which they use the process. Keep your expectations for these exercises modest: it will be sufficient if students demonstrate that they understand how to use the process. Students will likely feel more comfortable and develop self-confidence more quickly if these early assignments are not graded.

Suggestion 2   As the course progresses, continue to have students use the holistic process for appropriate problems and issues, but give special attention to each of the five skills, in turn. Thus after the initial assignments, students will spend one or more weeks applying the holistic process to problems and issues, but paying special attention to articulation,* then one or more weeks applying the holistic process but paying special attention to investigation, and so on. As each stage of the holistic process becomes the focus of attention, provide the necessary classroom discussion and coaching to enable students to understand the stage and

*Since the first stage, exploration, involves finding problems and issues, students will not use it when dealing with problems and issues that *you* have assigned.

master the skills associated with it. Once each stage has been covered, you may reasonably require that students demonstrate their mastery of it in all future applications of the holistic process.

Suggestion 3 Your list of objectives will include certain dispositions and thinking skills that are important enough in your discipline that they deserve special emphasis. Moreover, your evaluations of class discussions and homework exercises will undoubtedly reveal thinking deficiencies that need special attention. The best response to both situations is to assign students skill-cluster exercises—that is, exercises which call for the use of a particular group of skills but not all the skills used in the holistic process. An example of a skill-cluster assignment is the common assignment in which students are asked to evaluate an argument on a controversial issue. The skills being exercised in this case would be those associated only with the evaluation/refinement (critical thinking) stage of holistic thinking.

This approach is useful not only in courses in which thinking objectives are the sole objectives, but also in courses in which they are secondary objectives. If your course is of the latter type and you cannot devote as much time to thinking as you would like, don't be concerned—just devote as much time as you can, paying proportionate attention to each of the three suggestions.

SPECIFIC TEACHING METHODS

The basic approach detailed above constitutes a broad methodology for teaching thinking, but it does not answer the questions that arise in day-to-day classroom teaching. In other words, it explains what to do, but not how to do it. That important question can only be answered by identifying particular classroom-tested teaching methods. Following is a collection of such methods. Not all methods will be suitable for every course at every level from elementary school to graduate school—at least not in the precise form suggested here—but the great majority can be made suitable for a wide variety of courses and levels with only minor adaptation. Where necessary for clarity, specific exercises that may be used with these methods will be noted here; for the most part, however, the discussion of exercises will be reserved for Chapters 7 and 8.

> *Inspire attitudes congenial to thinking and reinforce important lessons about thinking by posting interesting quotations and cartoons on the bulletin board.*

The kind of quotations and cartoons that work best for this purpose are those which are self-explanatory and therefore unlikely to provoke discussion.* (For quotations and cartoons intended to *provoke* discussion, see the method that follows this one.) Here are some examples:

---

*Of course, you should be willing, indeed pleased, to discuss any that students wish to discuss, even if their discussion takes the form of challenge. Challenge, after all, is a sign of intellectual vitality and interest.

The grand and indeed the only character of truth is its capability of enduring the test of universal experience, and coming unchanged out of every possible form of fair discussion. *(Sir William Herschel)*

I wish I could convey this sense I have of the infinity of the possibilities that confront humanity—the limitless variations of choice, the possibility of novel and untried combinations, the happy turns of experiment, the endless horizons opening out. *(Alfred North Whitehead)*

Compared to what we ought to be, we are only half awake, we are making use of only a small part of our physical and mental resources. Stating the thing broadly, the human individual thus lives far within his limits. He possesses power of various sorts which he habitually fails to use. *(William James)*

The man who does not read books has no advantage over the man who cannot read. *(Laurence J. Peter)*

2–4–82 ©1982 United Feature Syndicate, Inc.

12–8–80 ©1980 United Feature Syndicate, Inc.

Stimulate students' curiosity about ideas and promote discussion by posting discussion-provoking quotations and cartoons on bulletin boards and calling students' attention to them.

Because of their compactness of expression, quotations and cartoons are excellent devices to promote thinking and discussion. Here are some examples, each with an appropriate question to use to begin a discussion:

One of the saddest experiences which can come to a human being is to awaken, gray-haired and wrinkled, near the close of an unproductive career, to the fact that all through the years he has been using only a small part of himself. *(V. W. Burrows)*

DISCUSSION STARTER: How can we tell when we have realized our full potential?

It takes courage to be creative. Just as soon as you have a new idea, you are a minority of one. *(E. Paul Torrance)*

DISCUSSION STARTER: What has being in a minority got to do with having courage?

Most people are other people. Their thoughts are someone else's opinions, their lives a mimicry, their passions a quotation. *(Oscar Wilde)*

DISCUSSION STARTER: How well does this description fit the celebrities whose names fill the talk-show rosters and the pages of popular magazines?

Reason can answer questions, but imagination has to ask them. *(R. W. Gerard)*

DISCUSSION STARTER: What does it mean to say imagination must ask questions?

It's easy to be successful when things go right. The real challenge is to be successful when everything goes wrong. *(Anonymous)*

DISCUSSION STARTER: How is it possible to be successful when everything goes wrong?

I'm a great believer in luck, and I find the harder I work the more I have of it. *(Thomas Jefferson)*

DISCUSSION STARTER: Do you think Jefferson was joking when he wrote those words?

Reprinted by permission of King Features Syndicate.

DISCUSSION STARTER: Can you think of an occasion when you failed to persuade someone because you took the *wrong* approach? What might you have done instead?

DISCUSSION STARTER: How would a relativist react to the idea in the above cartoon? What makes you think so?

> *Encourage students to raise their own questions about your subject field and to do the necessary research to find answers to those questions. Whenever possible, give credit for such work.*

It is an educational truism that students do better work when they are interested in what they are doing than when they are not. This method ensures that they will be interested. You may wish to give them some assistance in finding a suitable question, for example by suggesting some possibilities: Why did dinosaurs die out? To what extent does English contain words borrowed from other languages? How are criminals treated in other cultures, "primitive" as well as advanced? (If your course is too tightly structured to allow regular credit for such work, you might consider using it for extra credit or makeup work.)

> **Get students thinking about problems and issues early in the course.**

It is not enough to encourage students to think or to be creative or critical: you must give them some idea of what you want them to think (or be creative or critical) about. And the more specific that idea is, the better. Throughout your course, therefore, from the very first week, you should present specific problems and issues for students to address and, whenever possible, a clear idea of what you want their thinking to yield. For example, if you are a history professor, you might make this announcement to your students:

> One of the problems all historians must grapple with is the fact that biases and assumptions, unconscious as well as conscious, can distort their interpretation of events. Over the next few weeks, I want you to decide what specific steps historians might take to reduce such distortions in their work. Prepare a written report of those recommendations by November 1. In addition to submitting that report, you may also be required to explain and defend your recommendations to the class.

Instead of a timeless problem like the one historians face, you may wish to use timely issues, such as the issue that is (once again) dividing sociologists: Is the discipline of sociology primarily a quantitative or a qualitative one? You might also wish to provide students with statements of opposing views to help them start their analysis. Or you might prefer to present them with the latest suggestions for reforming your discipline and direct them to investigate, as necessary, determine the pros and cons of each suggestion, and decide whether it should be accepted or rejected. Education professors might use such suggestions as the following, made by American Federation of Teachers president Albert Shanker: (1) that a national examination be developed and used to limit entrance into the field of teaching; (2) that a system be developed to allow students to choose the public schools they attend rather than attending in their districts; and (3) that impartial panels of veteran teachers evaluate the work of teachers accused of incompetence.[12]

The special value in this kind of assignment is that it conveys the message that your discipline is not a dead body of facts, but a living, growing field still being shaped by its practitioners—the kind of discipline that is open to new contributions, the kind worth getting excited about.

Model holistic thinking for your students.

Modeling the thinking process yourself will help persuade students of its importance, assist them in understanding how to use it themselves, and provide encouragement to them to use it. Here is how Lois Greenfield of the University of Wisconsin (Madison) suggests that modelling be done in an engineering class:

> Let the students watch and listen as the instructor, the expert, tackles a problem. Let students watch the way discrimination between the relevant and irrelevant information takes place in a problem-solving process, the way translation from the given problem description into a more workable form occurs, how the problem is redefined into terms for which equations can be developed, and how drawing diagrams, data tables or graphs helps in this process. Call the students' attention to the process by which a problem can be broken into more manageable parts. Permit the students to listen to the entire process of developing a plan, even when it leads to false starts, and to learn how it is recognized that the wrong problem-solving path has been chosen and how to check for consistency. *In other words, let the students see the scratch paper which was discarded, rather than just the elegant final solution!* [Emphasis added][13]

Instead of presenting conclusions or principles first and then examples, present examples and have students work out the conclusions or discover the principles.

This change from deductive to inductive format can transform a lecture into a discovery exercise which engages students' minds and allows them to exercise their thinking skills. Here is a nontechnical example of the inductive format:

QUESTION: Felix Carvajal, a Cuban postman, wanted to compete as a runner in the 1904 Olympics in St. Louis. Unable to afford a ticket, he begged money in the public square in Havana. When he arrived in New Orleans, he was fleeced by gamblers and thus was forced to travel on foot. He *ran* to St. Louis, begging food along the way, and arriving just as his event was about to begin in 100 degree heat. He finished fourth.[14] What does this unusual example demonstrate?

COMMENT: The answers will, of course, vary, from the foolishness of gambling to the heroic measures a person will take to achieve his goals if they are important enough to him, to the idea that the order of finish in a race is not the only indicator of success.

Lead in to the discussion of noteworthy experiments in your field or related fields by re-creating the challenges the researchers faced.

This method is related to the previous one; however, it deals specifically with experiments and it gives students less to work with at first. It can be presented in stages, if you wish, as shown in this example:

Stage 1   Tell students to design an experiment that will provide an answer to the question, "Do 'A' students spend more time, less time, or the same amount of time studying as 'D–F' students spend?"

Stage 2   After students present and discuss the experiments they designed, explain one educational researcher's actual experiment: he divided a group of students into four sub-groups according to their grade point averages: "A" students, "B" students, "C" students, and "D–F" students. Each student was asked to keep a careful, honest record of the amount of time he or she spent in study during a typical week. After explaining this, ask your students to speculate about the results of this study, stating which group studied most, which next most, and so on, and explaining the reasoning that underlies their choices.

Stage 3   After hearing students' speculations and reasoning, reveal the researcher's actual findings: the rank order was D–F, C, B, A, the D–F students having actually spent twice as much time studying as the A group did.[15] Next, ask what conclusion about grades the results of this study suggest. Discussion should lead to this conclusion, perhaps among others: that the amount of time spent in study is not of itself a guarantee of success, that the efficiency of the effort is at least as important.

Present common fallacies in your field and have students analyze them.

Every field has certain fallacies, including not only notions embraced by the ignorant, but also positions once held by scholars but since abandoned in light of later research. Here, for example, are several fallacies about the social sciences, as analyzed by Israel Sheffler.

IDEA: Objectivity is impossible in the social sciences because the subject matter is value-laden.

ANALYSIS: "To study values, we need neither to espouse them nor reject them any more than to study the law of falling bodies we need to jump from the tower of Pisa. In any event, scientific objectivity means not lack of values or interests, but rather their frank exposure and tentative espousal, and the institutionalizing of procedures for submitting valued hypotheses to test by investigators with counter-interests."

IDEA: Objectivity is impossible in the social sciences because social scientists, especially historians, select their material.

ANALYSIS: "But selection, on the level of choice of problem, is unavoidable even in the natural sciences; only selection in the sense of arbitrary avoidance of relevant evidence is pernicious. But why is *such* selection inevitable in the social sciences?"

IDEA: Because social phenomena are more complex than natural phenomena, they cannot be studied by logical method.

ANALYSIS: "But prior to Galileo, physical subject matter was thought complex, since its principles were unknown. Is the point of this argument perhaps that physics cannot explain social phenomena? But neither can social study explain physical phenomena. Is it rather that physical assumptions and controls enter into social investigations? But analogous assumptions about the observer must be made in physical investigations. Is the point that while physical things are completely explained by current physics, social objects are not? But not all aspects of physical things are explained by current physics, unless we trivially redefine 'physical things' to mean just those aspects so explained, or trivially reinterpret the claim so as to mean by 'physics' whatever does explain physical things completely."[16]

The best use of this teaching method is to present students with the fallacious notion without identifying it as a fallacy and without any interpretive comments, directing them to evaluate it in light of what they have learned so far in the course and prepare a defense of their position. Ideally, an assignment would present not just one, but several statements for evaluation, one or more of which are *sound*.

Use warm-up exercises occasionally to take the threat out of problem solving.

The shift from a relatively passive role to an active role will undoubtedly be upsetting to many students at first, including some high achievers. (Achievers often feel cheated when the process under which they have prospered for so long is suddenly changed and they must learn a new process and suffer for a time the uncertainty and fumbling with which slower students are all too familiar.) The use of ungraded warm-up exercises can have a calming effect on students by giving them an opportunity to develop thinking skills in a nonthreatening atmosphere and without the fear of receiving a low grade. The best kinds of warm-up exercises are those which invite playfulness, such as writing captions for cartoons and solving various kinds of puzzles. (For specific exercises, see Chapter 6.)

Have students form and test hypotheses of their own.

Gene D'Amour of the National Science Foundation recommends this approach, which he explains derives from Karl Popper's theory of the importance of the imagination in scientific theorizing. D'Amour explains the method as follows:

> The student, like the scientist, begins the learning experience by initiating a hypothesis. Next, he or she must attempt to refute this hypothesis by seeking empirical evidence of its untruth—its falsifiability. If the hypothesis stands the test, it may be accepted—but never as "knowledge," only as a hypothesis that has not yet been refuted. In this way, what the student comes to accept as 'scientific knowledge' rests upon his or her own efforts to disprove it—a method of instruction far more effective than the traditional memorization of pronouncements offered, *ex cathedra*, from the lectern. We posit, as indeed Piaget seems to have discovered, that the active participation of the student in a process of simultaneous criticism and discovery, produces better students—students with a sure and intuitive grasp of the fundamentals they will need to build upon later. That this accords with what can be shown to have been the actual history of the development of modern scientific theories should help explain its effectiveness as a teaching method.[17]

Present timely or timeless challenges in the form of dialogues for student analysis.

The dialogue is the most ancient and efficacious form of philosophical instruction, and is also one of the devices of literature, but its use needn't be limited to philosophy and English classes. Being more familiar to students than the essay, reflecting as it does the casualness, rapid exchanges, and spontaneity of everyday conversation, it is an excellent vehicle for teaching thinking skills.

By varying the issues you address, you can make your dialogues reflect everyday thinking situations or situations peculiar to your discipline. By varying the length of the dialogues, the complexity of the points included, and the amount of irrelevancy and ambiguity you build in, you can create suitable challenges for students at any level from kindergarten through graduate school. Here is an example of a relatively simple dialogue. Directions to students would typically call for careful evaluation of each person's views, appropriate investigation of the claims made, a decision as to what view—one of those mentioned or another view—is most reasonable, and the presentation of evidence to support that view.

BOBBI JO: You know, my Asian cultures course has changed my mind about marriage.

BILLY BOB: How so?

BOBBI JO: Traditionally, most Asian cultures have arranged young people's marriages. The parents would decide which boy would marry which girl. The kids themselves would have no choice in the matter. Many times they wouldn't even have met each other until the time of the wedding.

BILLY BOB: That's terrible. It leaves love and mutual attraction out of it altogether. How can they possibly know they're compatible unless they learn all about each other first and then decide whether they belong together?

BOBBI JO: I know it sounds odd when you first hear it. But it really makes good sense. Parents are older and tend to choose more sensibly. Anyway, history has proved the wisdom of the practice. Divorce is virtually unknown in those cultures.[18]

Present current local, national, or international problems or proposed solutions as thinking exercises for students.

The problems and solutions used in this method needn't come from feature articles in the newspaper. The news briefs found, for example, in the around-the-nation section of *USA Today* work very well. Here is one such item quoted in its entirety as it appeared in that section.[19] Directions for students are added in parentheses.

EUREKA SPRINGS, ARKANSAS. Passenger sitting behind driver in bus that fell into ravine killing 5 Ozark Bible Institute students Saturday, said he saw red light go on shortly before crash. Dashboard light indicates low pressure for air brakes. (Apply the holistic process, recording all your thoughts as you proceed.*)

You may feel uneasy about presenting problems that experts have not yet found answers to because, like most educators, you have undoubtedly been conditioned to value *product* (the "right" answer) more highly than *process*. If such is the case, remind yourself that there can be great value in struggling meaningfully with a problem, even if the struggle yields no definitive answer. Such activity rehearses students for life beyond the classroom.

Use a modified case-study approach.

The traditional case-study method demands little more than understanding the details of actual cases and being able to relate them to new situations. That approach gives inadequate training in higher-order thinking skills. Modification of the case-study approach, however, can produce an excellent method for teaching thinking skills. Nursing professor Bessie Marquis, of California State University at Chico, has developed such a modification for her nursing courses.

The approach reduces lecture time from 90 minutes (a full class period) to from 15 to 20 minutes. The remainder of each period is devoted to the examination of from three to five cases, the majority of them drawn from real-life experiences and involving the application of concepts currently being addressed in the course. These cases call for the resolution of various conflicts, some of them

---

*One approach is to define the problem as "How can bus manufacturers ensure that the driver is aware when the light goes on?" (A possible solution would be to build a shrieking alarm into the system so that he needn't rely on sight alone.)

ethical, none of which have a simple right or wrong answer. After addressing the problems before class (consulting materials in the bibliography given to them in advance), students attend class prepared to take an active part in the discussion. One student will present her analysis of the case and defend her proposed solution; then another student will be called upon, at random, to critique the first student's presentation. Later the instructor offers a critique, but otherwise acts only as coach and facilitator.[20]

Build a journal requirement into your course.

A journal is usually associated with a writing course, but it can be an aid to the development of thinking skills in virtually any course in the curriculum. A journal is the perfect place to have students do many valuable activities that otherwise could not be included in your course. (Examples of such activities will be noted as we identify other teaching methods.) Furthermore, it permits you to personalize instruction for students, allowing them to explore areas of special interest to them in greater depth. Nor are collecting and correcting journals necessarily formidable tasks. Instead of having students keep a book which you collect at term's end, you can have them keep looseleaf sheets, which you collect weekly or at longer intervals, perhaps storing them in folders in your office until the designated grading time(s). Grading, too, can be streamlined by using a mimeographed checklist containing not only criticisms, but also suggestions for improvement (to spare you writing similar comments again and again). If you decide to assign a journal in your course, be sure to provide students, at the beginning of the term, with a handout thoroughly explaining your expectations concerning its use.

Provide students with useful insights and have them build on them.

The insights presented may be about the process of thought as it is or should be applied, or about some important aspect of your discipline. In either case, the insights should be ones which you have reason to believe students can relate to their own experience. (If you would like to use this method, but have no room for it in your course, consider using it as part of the journal requirement.) Here is an example of how this method could be applied, in the form of an assignment to students:

Edwin Arthur Burtt, a scholar who specialized in the study of thinking once noted that we humans tend to justify our mistaken beliefs instead of correcting them. "Let a question be raised as to the soundness of [our notions on some subject], and at once we find ourselves filled with an illicit passion for them; we defend them just as we would a punched shoulder. The problem, how reasonable they are, does not trouble us. We refuse to learn truth from a foe. And indeed the hotter and more violent defense is provoked in favor of ideas with the least intelligent justification. . . . The reason for this supreme pitch of irrationality lies in the fact that beliefs reached through some thinking, however meager, we know can be doubted, while those absorbed as uncritically as the milk from our mother's breast are so firmly rooted in our entire make-up that to question them seems at first sight like scepticism carried to an insane degree."[21]

Think of one or more occasions when you responded in the way Burtt describes here. Provide sufficient details of the situation so that the reader will understand how inappropriate your reaction was. Then consider and record as many strategies as you can think of for avoiding such reactions in the future.

Add a thinking task to lecture sessions.

Purdue University's Sam Postlethwait, pioneer of the audio-tutorial method of instruction, used this approach successfully in his botany lectures. He cut his lecture time to 30 minutes (out of a 50 minute period), then remained silent as students devoted the rest of the period to dealing actively with the lecture. Their job was to identify the major question in the lecture and the source of the lecturer's information, state whether the presentation was believable and defend their view, summarize the presentation, and give a specific example of an everyday situation in their lives to which the lecture would be relevant.[22]

The pile of papers resulting from the regular use of this method would seem impossibly large, but Postlethwait devised an efficient system for his assistants to use in handling them: each paper was scanned and given one point for being submitted, one point if the student's identification of the question was consistent with the summary, and one point if an application to everyday life was made.

Another use of the latter part of the lecture period is to pose questions or outline problems to be thought about outside of class in preparation for small-group discussion periods, or to have students respond to such questions or problems in the journal.

Build thinking (and writing) exercises into reading assignments.

One of the most widespread assumptions of modern education is that reading is the most efficacious method of developing cognitive skills. This assumption underlies the emphasis on reading instruction in the schools, as well as the special concern over deficiencies in students' reading levels, a concern most clearly manifested in the amount of money spent on remedial and developmental reading programs. It is also responsible for the tendency of many educators to withhold instruction in higher-order cognitive skills until students have attained a fairly advanced reading level, *even if that attainment does not occur until age 20 or later.*

This assumption and the emphases it has produced have not gone unchallenged. Almost forty years ago, for example, Allison Davis argued after extensive observation that reading instruction is overrated as a means of developing thought processes. "Reading," she suggested, "offers too little skill in problem-solving (either of a rational, empirical, or inventive kind) to justify the first place it holds in the curriculum. Learning the skill of decoding written communication is important, but not so important for the development of mental ability as the pupil's analysis of his own experience, and his drawing of correct inferences from this analysis."[23]

To replace the emphasis on reading with an emphasis on problem solving and issue analysis would be to overreact, especially in view of the negative effects of television on many students' reading habits. The situation is best addressed by finding ways to broaden reading assignments to include thinking and writing exercises at every level of education. One effective way, recommended by Jack Lochhead, is to require students to write a summary and personal reaction to each reading assignment they complete.[24]

When students have unusual difficulty solving problems, have them think aloud while doing so.

Arthur Whimbey and other instructors in Louisiana's Xavier University use this method to teach analytical reasoning to educationally disadvantaged students. The students, sometimes working alone and sometimes in pairs (taking turns as vocalizer and listener), are asked to verbalize as much of their mental processing as possible, including counting, reading, arithmetic operations, and selection of equations. They learn each other's strategies for solving problems as they remain alert for errors. Moreover, they read transcribed protocols of effective problem solvers working on similar problems. The approach has proved effective.[25]

Pose problems for students to solve on their own, either in their journals for credit or for their own satisfaction.

Every day the media publicize another dozen or so interesting problems in various fields; unfortunately, they are usually presented more as laments than as challenges. By being aware of these and selecting ones appropriate for your course and your students, you can enliven your teaching and foster a problem-solving orientation in students. For example, the Highway Users Federation publicized the following statistics: only 15 percentage of Americans use seatbelts; if another 10 percentage buckled up, 1200 additional lives would be saved annually; if 80 percentage buckled up, over 10,000 lives would be saved on American highways annually.[26] This data could be turned into a variety of thinking problems.

In a psychology course, for example, students could design an experiment to determine what kind of appeal is most effective in getting people to wear seatbelts. In ethics, students could consider the morality of behavior that endangers one's self. In English, students could construct a persuasive argument for buckling up for those who oppose doing so. In advertising, students could create a single advertisement, or a larger advertising campaign, to get more people to wear seatbelts. Such assignments could be given as regular assignments or as journal assignments.

Assign directed wondering exercises.

It is a truism that most people lose their curiosity in early childhood and relatively few regain it, at least not without significant effort; it is also evident that educators are not likely to be successful in developing students' thinking skills unless they find ways to help them regain that curiosity. The directed wondering method is one way to do so. It prompts students to become curious about matters they were content to take for granted before; in time, with sufficient practice, they will acquire the habit of wondering.

One type of useful wondering concerns everyday phenomena: Why, for example, are our schools and colleges open only nine or ten months a year? When did that idea originate? Are the reasons that supported it then still valid now? Could society benefit from changing that pattern? And where did taxation originate? When did it start in our country? How has it changed since then? Why are people's incomes taxed? Why are people's properties taxed? Why do we have sales taxes? Are there preferable alternatives to the present systems of taxation? If you use this kind of directed wondering, be sure to direct students to go beyond merely obtaining information and accept the challenge of producing ideas for improving the phenomena they examine.

Another kind of directed wondering concerns new breakthroughs in concepts, products, and services. Everyone has experienced the "Why didn't I think of that?" reaction which comes immediately after learning of someone else's creative idea, particularly one significant enough to win the person fame and fortune. This reaction, unfortunately, is quickly forgotten (though traces may linger on in a vague feeling of envy). Directed wondering can be used to turn it in a positive direction by making it a spur to creativity. All you need do is direct students to watch for the "Why didn't I think of that?" reaction and immediately say to themselves, "What comes next?"—that is, how can the creative breakthrough itself be improved or extended?

For example, on reading that an educational researcher has suggested using retired people to assist kindergarten teachers, thereby reducing teaching loads without increasing school budgets, students would ask "Where else might retired people's services be put to use?" and produce, perhaps, the idea of having them give individual attention to older students with reading problems. Or, noticing a milk carton with pictures of missing children on the back, students would ask "What other kinds of public service ads might be placed on milk cartons?" and "Where else might the pictures of missing children be posted?" and think of putting anti-smoking ads on milk cartons and posting missing children's pictures in buses and subway cars.

Make students responsible for developing and posing questions about the lessons in your course.

As part of a reading or analysis homework assignment, have students raise as many relevant questions as they can about the material, with emphasis on higher-level questions. Then as part of class discussion, have them address these questions to one another. Judith Engel, a mathematics teacher at the Bronx High School of Science, uses such an approach, which she calls SQS (Students Questioning Students). She finds that it not only stimulates students to think more carefully about their lessons, but makes them more enthusiastic participants and more attentive listeners in class.[27]

Share with students your challenges as an instructor.

Instructors face dozens of challenges to their ingenuity every term they teach, challenges ranging from what to do about students who are consistently late for class and how to handle cases of plagiarism to how to help slower students understand principles and approaches they cannot seem to grasp. Such challenges make excellent problems and issues for student assignments, especially in advanced classes where "how would you explain" problems can focus on difficulties that occur in elementary courses. (This method should be used regularly in education courses to prepare students for the challenges they will face in their careers.) Naturally, prudence requires that some problems be disguised so that they do not embarrass students in the class, but that is relatively easy to do. Discipline and ethics cases can be given a fictional context—a different course, a different college, slightly altered circumstances; teaching dilemmas can be made hypothetical—for example, "How would you explain what a *concept* is to someone who didn't understand our textbook's definition?"

Encourage students to be alert for creative ideas—including established ideas whose creativity they have just come to recognize—and to record those ideas in their journals and consider ways their application might be extended to other fields.

Don't be concerned if many of the creative ideas students record are from other academic fields than your own. The enlarged awareness of creative achievements they gain from recording those ideas will ultimately make them more aware of creativity in your field as well. Besides, many creative breakthroughs occur by borrowing ideas from other fields. If students read of the Mattel toy company's nationwide contest to find a creative toy designer under 12 years of age, a contest with $300,000 in college scholarships as prizes,[28] it is but a short step to thinking of contest ideas to create new scholarships for young people with aptitudes for counseling or teaching or research.

Broaden the analysis-of-arguments method to include the use of creative imagination.

The analysis-of-arguments method is often used in *critical* thinking courses, but it is seldom used in a way that encourages students to exercise creative thinking as well. Here is how to achieve that broader aim: any time you assign students an argument (in essay or other form) to analyze, direct them not only to evaluate the argument and, if appropriate, advance a counter-argument, but also to *list the objections to their argument that the author of the original argument would likely express if he had the opportunity, and then discuss the merits of those objections as objectively as possible.* The effect of this approach will be not only an increase in students' imaginativeness, but also an improvement in their ability to examine their own arguments critically.

Involve students in the search for interesting problems and issues for class discussion and thinking exercises.

One of the criticisms of American education that has been expressed again and again in recent decades is that, even when students are given instruction in thinking, they are given ready-made problems and so never learn sensitivity to problems or the skill of defining problems. This method addresses that shortcoming directly and effectively. All you need do is to include finding problems and issues (or fashioning them from the material students find concerning creative breakthroughs in your discipline or other disciplines) as one of the approved forms of activity for their journals. Since students will likely find that activity among the most interesting on your list, they will likely choose it. In the process they will not only learn how to recognize and define problems, but also provide you with some excellent material for your future classes.

Encourage students to apply the holistic process to problems and issues in everyday life, including life at school or college.

This method for developing students' thinking skills may make you shudder. The prospect of students rushing in every day with ideas for changing *your* grading and attendance policies, *your* assignment schedule, *your* teaching methods, can be unpleasant. But that needn't be a problem as long as you announce at the very outset of the course that, whereas you will be happy to receive any creative ideas for improving your course in future terms, you will not alter the way you have decided to conduct the course this term. (Naturally, it would be a source of encouragement if you did receive whatever suggestions are offered to you with the same degree of openmindedness you urge students to demonstrate.)

Other protocols will undoubtedly be necessary, such as maintaining a focus on ideas instead of people and the studious avoidance of names of people or campus offices in discussions of practices in need of reform. But though such discussions will sometimes be delicate, they need not be avoided on that account. Properly handled, they teach students how to speak and behave maturely and responsibly.

"Stage" classroom events to dramatize the need for careful observation.

One of the first experimental demonstrations of the problems of eyewitness testimony took place in 1902 and was described six years later by Hugo Munsterberg. His account of that demonstration follows:[29]

A few years ago a painful scene occurred in Berlin, in the University Seminary of Professor von Liszt, the famous criminologist. The Professor had spoken about a book. One of the older students suddenly shouts, "I wanted to throw light on the matter from the standpoint of Christian morality!" Another student throws in, "I cannot stand that!" The first starts up, exclaiming, "You have insulted me!" The second clenches his fist and cries, "If you say another word _____." The first draws a revolver. The second rushes madly upon him. The Professor steps between them and, as he grasps the man's arm, the revolver goes off. General uproar. In that moment Professor Liszt secures order and asks a part of the students to write an exact account of all that has happened. The whole had been a comedy, carefully planned and rehearsed by the three actors for the purpose of studying the exactitude of observation and recollection. Those who did not write the report at once were, part of them, asked to write it the next day or a week later; and others had to depose their observations under cross-examination. The whole objective performance was cut up into fourteen little parts which referred partly to actions, partly to words. As mistakes there were counted the omissions, the wrong additions and alterations. The smallest number of mistakes gave twenty-six per cent of erroneous statements; the largest was eighty per cent. The reports with reference to the second half of the performance, which was more strongly emotional, gave an average of fifteen per cent more mistakes than those of the first half. Words were put into the mouths of men who had been silent spectators during the whole short episode; actions were attributed to the chief participants of which not the slightest trace existed; and essential parts of the tragi-comedy were completely eliminated from the memory of a number of witnesses.

This experiment has been adapted for use in numerous courses, including law and psychology. Though you may have to alter its form significantly to have it fit your course, the basic idea—staging an event and having students record it as accurately as they can, and then discuss the discrepancies—can provide a vivid lesson in the perils of careless observation. (If the use of live performers is too dramatic for your taste, you may wish to use videotapes, perhaps scenes from films.)

Have students debate important issues in the field.

In advanced courses or the latter part of elementary courses, one good way to have students exercise their thinking skills while enhancing their understanding of important course content is to have them debate current issues in the subject. To use this approach, first make a list of controversial issues, as many as you can accumulate (at least 25) in the form of statements; for example, "Abortion is murder," or "Legislation should be passed restricting ownership of handguns." Then distribute the list to students and give them a day or so to decide their position on each issue, responding *yes, no,* or *unsure.* Collect their responses, determine which students disagree over which issues, and make debate assignments accordingly. Debates should follow this format:

1. The "pro" debater makes a two-minute persuasive presentation. The "con" debater does likewise.
2. The "pro" debater is given two minutes to raise questions to which her opponent must respond. Then the questioning/answering roles are reversed.

3. For a period of five minutes the class is allowed to pose questions to which one or both debaters must respond.

4. Each debater gives a one-minute summary of his or her position.

If these times are adhered to, each debate will be completed in fifteen minutes. (Eliminating the class questioning period will reduce that to ten minutes.)

Have students design one or more assignments for next term.

Toward the end of any course, students are in an excellent position to share the challenge the instructor must face—how to improve the course for the following term or year. Naturally, they will lack the expertise to evaluate their own suggestions as a professional would; nevertheless, they can *make* suggestions. Moreover, inviting them to do so will not only give them another opportunity to exercise their thinking skills, but also boost their confidence by demonstrating that you respect them and value their contributions. You may wish to specify the kinds of suggestions you want: for example, suggestions for making the material more interesting, for helping slower students keep pace, and for permitting students to pursue matters of special interest to them without neglecting the main aspects of the course.

IMPORTANT CAUTIONS TO OBSERVE

To be successful in teaching students how to think more creatively and critically, it is not enough to use proven methods; you must use them in a context which enhances learning. By observing the following cautions you will ensure that such a context is present in your course.

Be sure that you reward what you claim is important.

It is all too easy when one becomes a teacher to forget what was abundantly clear as a student: the fact that teachers often punish the very behaviors they urge students to practice. For example, they say, "I want you to think for yourself," and then punish anyone who disagrees with them. Or they say, "Strive for originality of expression," and then they reserve the highest grades for those who regurgitate verbatim what was given in the textbook or in lectures. Or they say, "Feel free to question anything that you don't understand or that seems mistaken," and then they become offended when students raise thorny questions.

To be sure that your rewards and claims are consistent, examine every aspect of your teaching from time to time. Look at your objectives, the methods you use, and the manner in which you use them. Reflect on what you respond favorably and unfavorably to in students' homework and class discussions. Take a long and critical look at your grading policy and practice. And wherever you find inconsistencies, make changes. If, for example, you find yourself stressing that the process by which a problem is approached is more important than the product (answer) and then grading only on the basis of the product, change your grading policy so that students receive separate credit—and more of it—for the process.

A word about students' self-esteem is in order. The educational theory dominant since the 1960s holds that students' intellectual development (indeed, their happiness in life) depends upon their level of self-esteem and, therefore, that teachers should do everything possible to raise that level through constant praise and encouragement. In a closely reasoned article, psychologist-consultant Barbara Lerner challenges that view, arguing that children's self-esteem is normally "robust, not fragile and in imminent danger of collapse without constant reinforcement." Thus, she reasons, teachers can and should withhold rewards until students demonstrate real achievement. The result will be a more genuine, *earned* self-esteem rather than "feel-good-now" self-esteem.[30]

> *Be generous in communicating to students and make all your communications clear.*

If your course objectives are never stated clearly, students can hardly be expected to understand, let alone achieve them. If your explanations or assignment directions are vague or ambiguous, students will surely be confused and frustrated (as you will be when they fail to perform as you wish them to). It is therefore a good idea to play devil's advocate with all your communications to students before you deliver them, searching for errors of omission and commission and making necessary revisions.

So much for ensuring clarity of communication; but what of generosity? Being generous in communicating means going beyond necessary statements of objective, explanation, and direction and providing additional aids to learning. To illustrate the idea of generous communicating, here are two examples of actual teaching practices.

Example 1   John A. Ricketts, Simeon Smith Professor of Chemistry at DePauw University, faced with the difficulty of teaching material requiring formal operational thinking to classes in which 50 percent of the students are unable to operate above the concrete operational level, has decided that the solution lies in creating an atmosphere that encourages students' cognitive development. An important part of that atmosphere is providing explanations that help students understand what is expected of them and guide them in doing it. One of these explanations is a five-page prelude to the laboratory manual. Following are the first two pages of that prelude.

PRELUDE TO THE LABORATORY

The design of this laboratory differs from the normal. Not only is it structured to introduce the techniques used by the bench chemist, to illustrate certain chemical principles, but hopefully it will strengthen and sharpen the reasoning abilities of the student. The idea for this laboratory is based on the Piagetian model for cognitive development. Each experiment is organized as a Learning Cycle whenever possible. The approach is not the "cookbook" set of directions; a premium is placed on student initiative. To give meaning to what will happen in the laboratory, do the Frog Puzzle (shown below) and study the rest of the *Prelude*.

The following summarizes student answers to the Frog Puzzle. The numbers appearing at the end of the answer is the number of students giving this particular result. The sample consists of college freshmen from the University of Nebraska at Lincoln.

1. I have no idea. (3)

2. On the first trip 55 frogs were caught and banded; on the second trip 72 frogs were caught and 12 were banded. The ones that were banded were thrown back in after being banded. He probably had already banded the others on the second trip. The equation $55 + 12 = 67$ frogs. (1)

3. First trip 55. Second trip $72 - 12 = 60$ frogs unbanded. Total $60 + 55 = 115$ frogs. (6)

THE FROG PUZZLE

Professor Thistlebush, an ecologist, conducted an experiment to determine the number of frogs that live in a pond near the field station. Since he could not catch all of the frogs he caught as many as he could, put a white band around their left hind legs, and then put them back in the pond. A week later he returned to the pond and again caught as many frogs as he could. Here is the Professor's data.

First trip to the pond
    55 frogs caught and banded

Second trip to the pond
    72 frogs caught, of those 72 frogs
    12 were found to be banded

Total number of frogs in the pond

_____

The Professor assumed that the banded frogs had mixed thoroughly with the unbanded frogs, and from his data he was able to approximate the number of frogs that live in the pond. If you can compute this number, please do so. Write it in the blank above and in the space below explain in words how you calculated your result.

_____

_____

_____

_____

---

4. The first trip he caught 55 frogs. The second trip he caught 72 frogs 60 of which were banded. After banding he felt they had mixed thoroughly so there were about the same number of unbanded. Add the banded together and multiply by 2. 55 + 60 = 115 × 2 = 230 frogs. (2)

5. Out of 72 there were 12 banded which is 16 percent so you add 8 which is 16 percent of 55 to 55. Add 60 which is 72 − 12 and you get 8 + 55 + 60 = 123. (1)

6. The problem said the professor caught 72 frogs on the second trip, of the 72, 12 were banded, that's 17 percent of total frogs. Then I took 17 × 55 frogs caught the first time. (1)

7. I used the proportion, 12/72 = 55/x. x = 330. (11)

8. Fifty-five frogs were caught the first time. The second time out one-sixth of those frogs were recaptured; thus I believe the original 55 represents one-sixth of the total population, so 55 × 6 = 330 frogs equals the total population. (4)

Which of the above reasoning patterns did you use? Study the above solutions and analyze the reasoning patterns in each case. Which do you think is the most plausible? Why do you think that there is a marked difference in the approach to the same problem? Jean Piaget would assert that the difference in the reasoning patterns is due to the differing degrees of cognitive development within the individual. The following essence of Piaget's theory of intellectual development is adapted from the essay, *Piaget's Theory in a Nutshell*, which is contained in the materials that formed a workshop on the development of reasoning which was directed by Dr. Robert Fuller and Dr. Melvin Thornton of the University of Nebraska at Lincoln and was supported by the American Association for the Advancement of Science and the National Science Foundation. [Three pages follow these in the manual, explaining Piaget's theory.]

Example 2   James Bell, Professor of Psychology at Howard Community College in Maryland, teaches both creative and critical thinking in his psychology courses and uses various forms of communication to help students master course content and thinking skills. Following is a list of activities he uses in "General Psychology" to help students learn to think critically. Asterisks indicate unusually generous communication.

1. Show film in class entitled "Critical Thinking" as an overview of the importance of evaluating evidence.*
2. Students read and fill out the booklet "Getting the Facts" to learn what psychologists mean by evidence, to be able to identify psychological facts, and to be able to interpret psychological facts.*
3. In class group discussion guide sheets are used to help students learn the information in "Getting the Facts."*
4. Students turn in written work demonstrating they understand what a psychological fact is.
5. In class students practice identifying psychological facts in the textbook.

6. For homework students make observations of violence on television to better understand how psychologists collect their psychological facts.
7. Students read and fill out the booklet "Critical Evaluation" to learn the steps in critical evaluative thinking.*
8. In class, students discuss the difficult sections of the booklet "Critical Evaluation."
9. In class, students discuss the evaluation of an article.
10. Students turn in written work demonstrating they can critically evaluate.
11. In class, working alone, students critically evaluate an article not previously seen.
12. As a part of the final examination, students describe an example of how they have used their critical evaluative thinking outside of the course.

Fit your assignments to your students' level of understanding and skill.

Naturally, your goal should be to extend this level by providing challenging assignments, but the challenges should be carefully designed to be appropriate to their stage of development.† The best general approach is to begin by *asking less* of students and/or *giving more* in the way of assistance, and then as the term progresses and they learn more and grow in confidence and competence, *asking more* of them and/or *giving less* assistance. Here, to illustrate, is one example of how assignments might progress during a semester when students have had no prior training in thinking:

EARLY ASSIGNMENT: What do you think about _____ (a controversial issue)? Why do you think this? (This assignment calls only for stating and explaining their views.)

INTERMEDIATE ASSIGNMENT: What are the various views people have about _____ (a controversial issue)? What evidence do they offer for these views? Which views are most reasonable and what makes them so? (This assignment calls for observing, investigating, comparing, and judging.)

ADVANCED ASSIGNMENT: What is the best expression of this issue? What kind of evidence is necessary to make an informed judgment? What evidence is available and what is the most reasonable interpretation of it? What view is most defensible in light of the evidence? What objections might be raised to this view and how are they best answered? (This assignment calls for use of imagination, and for interpreting, evaluating, judging, speculating, and responding to objections.)

MORE ADVANCED ASSIGNMENT: Each of the following products was banned from television advertising in 1952: feminine hygiene products, hemorrhoid remedies, tampons and sanitary napkins, body lice cures,

---

†A related concern is the short attention span of many students. The best way to deal with this handicap, in addition to moving from easier to more difficult problems as the term progresses, is to avoid problems requiring lengthy analysis until students have had a chance to extend their attention span.

enemas, pregnancy test kits, jock-itch remedies, and incontinence products. Since that time the ban has been lifted on every one of these products.[31]

Whenever possible, let students discover their own mistakes.

It is easy to succumb to the temptation to point out students' mistakes directly, explaining that they have drawn wrong conclusions, explanations, or interpretations, or have been superficial in their analysis of a problem. Nevertheless, it is in students' interest to resist the temptation and merely provide guidance in finding the mistakes. Here are six ways of doing so, adapted from a list prepared by Howard Barrows and Robyn Tamblyn.[32] (Though these authors were writing specifically of medical education, the recommendations have general application.)

1. Ask the student how he or she arrived at that conclusion and whether there are alternative possibilities.
2. Ask another student whether he or she agrees with what was said.
3. Ask the speaker to explain something related to the issue, but which you know cannot be adequately explained by what he or she said.
4. Ask whether the student has ever thought about some related concern (one that holds the key to his or her error).
5. Ask whether the student is completed satisfied with his or her explanation (hypothesis, etc.) or whether there are aspects with which he or she is dissatisfied.
6. Ask the student to elaborate on his or her answer so that you (and the class) may understand more fully.

Practice what you preach.

Students are more likely to take principles and strategies seriously when they have evidence that others take them seriously, and they have a better chance of mastering them when they have frequent opportunities to observe them practiced. If, like most educators, you have had little formal training in thinking, you will undoubtedly have to devote some time to the same kinds of exercises you assign students in order to develop (or refine) your thinking dispositions and skills.

Until you have evidence that your own dispositions and skills have reached an advanced level, guard against negative modelling by (1) checking your urge to pretend certainty in matters about which your knowledge is limited; (2) giving a fair hearing to all ideas and viewpoints, especially imaginative ones, even if at first thought they seem improbable; and (3) excluding from your assignments any issue, no matter how tempting, which you believe has only one side to it. That belief is a sure sign that your bias will prevent you from being openminded.

Dare to be lively, dramatic, innovative in your teaching; let your enthusiasm and excitement about your subject show.

Among John I. Goodlad's findings in his 1984 study of more than a thousand schools are these:

There is a paucity of praise and correction of students' performance, as well as of teacher guidance in how to do better next time. Teachers tend not to respond in overtly positive or negative ways to the work students do. And our impression is that classes generally tend not to be strongly positive or strongly negative places to be. Enthusiasm and joy and anger are kept under control. . . . [In addition] students generally engage in a rather narrow range of classroom activities—listening to teachers, writing answers to questions, and taking tests and quizzes. Strikingly similar "schooling activities" transcend teachers, grade levels, and subjects.[33]

By lifting your teaching methods above this level you will increase your chances of success with your students.

APPLICATIONS

1. Review the suggestions for an overall approach to teaching methodology on pages 102–103. Then adapt those suggestions and develop an approach to teaching thinking skills in your course(s).

2. Review the specific teaching methods beginning on page 103, noting which ones are most applicable to your course(s). Then decide how each of those methods could best be adapted to your course(s).

chapter 6

BASIC
INSTRUCTIONAL
MATERIALS

A number of good thinking textbooks are now available and others will become available as publishers recognize and respond to the growing demand for these texts. Adopting such a book, either as the main text or as a supplement, offers two advantages: expert explanation of important principles and concepts (an important benefit if your training in thinking skills is minimal) and a considerable saving of preparation time. In selecting such a text, however, you should be aware that some thinking texts are narrowly focused—limited, for example, to critical thinking—and therefore will not provide effective instruction in holistic thinking. In addition, using any text, even an excellent one, can *reduce* teaching effectiveness if you are too dependent on it.

Unless you are unusually well prepared to teach cognitive skills, you will undoubtedly be most successful if you use a suitable textbook to introduce principles and concepts, but develop at least some of your own materials to ensure that all instructional objectives are served and that the course reflects your genius as well as the textbook author's. This approach will not only increase your self-confidence in developing students' thinking skills; it will also tend to produce exercises that appeal to students. After all, you have an undeniable advantage over even the most accomplished textbook author; you know what problems and issues your students are most interested in.

This chapter will suggest a number of useful approaches for developing general thinking exercises—that is, thinking exercises that require no special or technical subject-matter knowledge* and therefore may be used in virtually any course. (Chapter 7 will discuss approaches that have proven effective in specific courses or disciplines.)

FINDING MATERIALS

Perhaps the best source of exercise material for thinking instruction is media reports of current events. Exercises dealing with current events convey the unspoken message that thinking skills are relevant not only to academic matters, but also to everyday life. That is a message that can motivate students to apply their skills outside the classroom. (Many teachers will understandably dislike the idea of using relevancy as an appeal, yet the fact is that for many students this appeal will enhance learning.)

Finding exercise material in the media is easy. To illustrate this fact, here are some of the possibilities found in a single newspaper supplement, the October 13, 1985 edition of *Parade,* together with a brief indication of how they might be used in exercises:

ITEM: "The First Thing I Had to Conquer Was Fear," an article about a concert pianist who is afflicted with psoriatic arthritis and cannot make a fist, has only 40% mobility in his right wrist, one numb finger and fused joints in the remaining nine fingers and thumbs—and yet is acclaimed as a piano virtuoso.

EXERCISE 1: Think of someone you know who has overcome a serious handicap. If possible, talk to the person and determine the particular obstacles the handicap presented and the strategies the person used to overcome them. Decide in what other situations those strategies might also be used in the same or modified form. Explain your ideas fully.

EXERCISE 2: Why is it that some people manage to overcome severe mental or physical handicaps and accomplish a great deal while many people who are confronted with few, if any, obstacles never accomplish anything significant? Consider a number of possible answers; then take the one that seems most likely and test it by reading appropriate works and, if possible, interviewing informed people. Modify your original answer in light of your research.

ITEM: "The Police Officer of the Year," an article about the winner of the nation's highest law enforcement award, the Los Angeles officer who coordinated security operations for the 1984 Olympic games. A companion article detailed the heroism of the ten runners-up for the award.

EXERCISE 1: One of the greatest security challenges of the Los Angeles Olympic games was how to guard against terrorist attacks. List as many

---

*Some exercises, of course, will involve investigation of fact and opinion in one or more disciplines, but only the kind of investigation that can be completed by a novice using sources readily accessible to almost anyone.

specific dangers as you can that would have had to be considered to provide for the safety of the athletes.

EXERCISE 2: [First the details of one or more of the acts of heroism performed by the runners-up for the award would be presented, and then the following instructions.] Such heroism is rare. What personal qualities must people have to act heroically? In what ways could the various agencies of our society—home, school, church, government, and so on—develop those qualities in people? If you don't believe such qualities can be developed, explain why and support your answer with appropriate evidence.

ITEM: " 'Are You Going to Hurt Me Too?' " an article by an expert offering ten steps that can be taken to curb child abuse.

EXERCISE: Child abuse is a serious problem in our society today. Think of as many ways as you can to prevent or reduce it. Then select your best ideas and explain them, being sure to anticipate and answer the questions and objections others might raise. [After receiving and discussing the students' ideas, you might share the ten ideas offered by the expert.]

ITEM: The "Laugh Parade" section of this same edition included four cartoons. The first shows a king sitting on his throne and saying to a servant, "Bring me my pipe, my bowl and my rock videos." The second shows a bride and groom about to be married—she turns to him and says, "Now remember. Let *me* do the talking." The third shows two children standing outside a dog house, looking at a small cat lying in the entrance. One child says to the other, "I don't know how he did it, but he sublet his doghouse." The fourth shows a muscular health spa instructor looking down at a skinny man and saying, "Before we move to the heavy stuff, Mr. Gearhart, we start you off pumping aluminum."

EXERCISE: [After giving copies of the cartoons to students or posting one copy on the bulletin board, you would give these directions.] What, if anything, do these cartoons have in common? Are there any common elements to be found in all such humor? If so, what do they suggest about creativity in cartooning?

Current events are not found only in the news media. If you are alert, you will find many timely exercise possibilities in the problems and issues being discussed by students or by faculty. Whatever people are complaining or arguing about can usually be turned into a good assignment. For example, a visit to any teachers' lounge or other gathering place for educators is sure to reveal laments that many students never seem to participate in class discussions no matter how hard teachers try to motivate them. Here's how that lament might look as an assignment:

Professor Danielle Murphy teaches literature at a small liberal arts college. She begins every term hoping to do little lecturing and to devote the larger part of each period to class discussion. Yet she is invariably disappointed with student response. No matter what the assigned work of literature, only one or two students will volunteer their comments, and discussion quickly fizzles out. The rest of the class sit and stare at their desks, or cast nervous glances at the clock. Identify and solve Professor Murphy's problem, then refine your best solution.[1]

FITTING MATERIALS TO OBJECTIVES

All exercise material in a course should fit the objectives of the course; in the case of thinking objectives, that means exercises should be designed to develop one or more of the dispositions or skills discussed in Chapter 4. Given the large number of those dispositions and skills, it is not always possible to create exercises that cover every one of them. But that is no cause for concern; practicing individual skills and clusters of skills, particularly those with which one has experienced difficulty, can make a positive contribution to one's progress as a thinker. Pianists, after all, practice their scales, tennis players their serves, basketball players their shooting and dribbling.

Ideally, thinking instruction will give students regular opportunities to develop the various skills individually or in clusters, as well as regular practice in applying all their skills to whole problems and issues. Moreover, since thinking for one's self involves the risk of failure and that risk can generate fear and impede performance, you should do your best to create a nonthreatening atmosphere in which solving problems and resolving issues is not only challenging but pleasurable. One way to create such an atmosphere is to include a number of ungraded, "practice" assignments. Another is to include warm-up exercises designed to lower intellectual inhibitions and invite spontaneity and flexibility of response. Our consideration of exercise-constructing strategies will begin with warm-up exercises and then proceed to skill-cluster exercises and holistic exercises.

WARM-UP EXERCISES

An effective warm-up exercise is fun to grapple with and interesting to discuss, but unlikely to provoke confrontations. Students will thus be willing to take chances in responding to it, chances they might hesitate to take if the matter were more serious and "face" were involved. Here are some effective kinds of warm-up exercises:

Simple Science Questions

Example If hot air rises, why is it colder on mountaintops?

Example What effects would occur if the phenomenon known as friction no longer operated? (Consider subtle as well as obvious effects.)

Example Suppose you are looking at a star, say Sirius, on a dark night. Astronomers tell us that light waves started to travel from Sirius many years ago. After all that time they reach earth, strike your retinas, and cause you to say you are seeing Sirius. But the star about which they convey information to you, the star that existed at the time the rays began their journey, may no longer exist. To say that you see what may no longer exist is absurd. Therefore, whatever you see, it is not Sirius. Is this reasoning sound?[2] Explain your thinking thoroughly.

Logic Puzzles

Example A man is walking up on the down escalator, and it is moving down faster than he is moving up. Is he going upstairs or downstairs? Explain your reasoning.

Example A logician died and left this will: "I leave $1000 to be divided among my four daughters. Some of the money is to go to Annabel or Beatrice. I know that Beatrice and Clarissa are under Dierdre's thumb, so if any of the money goes to either of them, she is to have none. I want Beatrice and Clarissa treated alike—in fact, all four, or as many as possible, are to receive equal treatment." Who was the logician's favorite daughter, and what was the size of her legacy?[3] Explain your reasoning fully.

Explaining-Exercises

Example Your niece, a preschooler, asks you the following question: "Is it possible to remember the future?" Compose an answer simple and clear enough for her to understand.

Example Is it possible for you to think of a country that you have never visited? Why or why not?

Visual Problems

Example Take 8 toothpicks away in such a way that only two squares remain.

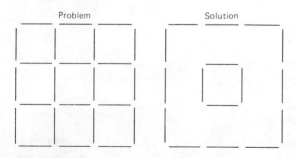

Example Four friends have a large garden in the shape shown on the following page. They want to divide it into four little gardens the same size and shape, but they don't know how. Show them.

Problem   Solution

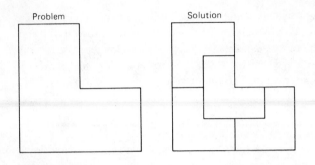

Cartoons Without Captions

Give students one or more cartoons without captions and have them write as many captions as they can think of for each and then choose their best ones. In using such an assignment, be sure to seize opportunities to encourage students and increase their self-confidence. Usually one or more student responses will permit you to say, sincerely, "Some of your responses were every bit as good as the original captions."

New Uses for Old Things

Example List as many uses as you can think of for old socks, stockings, or pantyhose. [Some items for additional assignments are old toothbrushes, inner tubes, jeans, wire coathangers.]

Substituting Original Expressions for Stale Ones

Example Each of the following expressions is overworked. Think of as many original substitute expressions as you can for the underlined words in each:

White as *a sheet*

Sticks out like *a sore thumb*

Slow as a *turtle*

Dark as *night*

Dead as *a doornail*

Other possibilities include, "right as rain," "strong as an ox," "smart as a whip," "busy as a bee," "plain as day," "cool as a cucumber."

Creating "Vanity" License Plates

Example Richard Simmons' license plates read YRUFAT, and Lawrence Welk's A1AnA2. But such creativity is not the province of celebrities only. An allergist might choose AACHOO, an attorney SUEM, an immodest Mensa member IQ200. Think of as many appropriate or just plain amusing possibilities as you can.

Recording Amusing "Inventions"

Example   Mock inventions can be amusing. Throughout the term record in your journal all such inventions you encounter in your reading or TV viewing. Or, if you feel so inclined, create some yourself. An example of such an invention is the phoneless cord for those who want to relax undisturbed. Among the inventions students might find are the following ones from the 1984 Nonsense Inventor's Fair in Austria: an umbrella with a big hole in it so the user can look up and see if it's still raining; a kitchen knife with ruled measurements on the blade to cut meat or bread precisely; and a pair of shoes with the proper steps for various dances painted on the soles.

Composing Clever "Comebacks"

Example   You are delivering a lecture to a large audience when a heckler in the crowd begins crowing like a rooster, making the audience laugh. Think of as many clever comebacks as you can to embarrass the person into silence; then decide which of them is most effective. [Henry Ward Beecher was in this situation and responded by carefully removing his watch from his pocket, looking at it intently, then saying aloud, "Dear me. My watch must have stopped. It must be morning instead of afternoon. The instincts of the lower animals are always infallible." In a similar situation, confronted by a heckler who was hissing, Charles Lamb said calmly, "There are only three things that hiss—a goose, a snake, and a fool. . . . Come forth and be identified."[4]]

Naming People or Places

Example   Some people's names fit their occupations or personal styles. Others seem to clash with them. Tyrone Power, for example, was an actor known for his rugged masculine roles. Storm Field is a TV weather forecaster. Both those names are appropriate. Arnold Schwartzenegger, on the other hand, seems an unlikely name for a bodybuilder. Think of appropriate (or humorously inappropriate) names for people in the following professions—the more names, the better:

> An athlete (specify the sport)
> A gospel singer
> A rock group
> A talk-show host (hostess)
> A college professor
> A movie star (macho male variety)
> A movie star (sexy female variety)

Example   Think of as many new names as you can for yourself. Consider names that best fit your personality and names that fit your intended profession. Decide which one you like best and explain why.

Example Think of as many names as you can for each of the following businesses: a toy store, a restaurant (you specify the cuisine), a crafts shop, a finance company, a health club.

Redesigning Things

Example Few people have enough space in their closets. Redesign your closet to make better use of the space there. You may add shelves, move the clothes bar, and make whatever changes you wish as long as the outside dimensions of the closet remain the same. Draw before and after pictures to illustrate.

Example Redesign your house to make better use of the space there. Make any changes you wish as long as the total square feet remain the same. Draw before and after floor plans.

Improving Efficiency

Example Most people spend a considerable amount of time in front of the TV set each day. At least a little of that time could be put to use without missing any part of the shows. List as many activities as you can think of that could be done conveniently while watching TV.

Example Review your daily routine on a typical day. List everything you do, hour by hour. Account for all your time. Place an asterisk by any activity you believe includes wasted or inefficiently used time. Then list as many ways as you can to use that time more efficiently.

SKILL-CLUSTER EXERCISES

Skill-cluster exercises are useful in providing a step-by-step introduction to the holistic process. As each stage in the process is introduced, exercises in the skills associated with that stage are assigned, all other skills being ignored at that time. A useful modification of this approach is to make exercise skills cumulative. In other words, as each stage in the process is introduced, exercises in the skills associated with that stage *and all previous stages* are assigned. Thus when students have been introduced to all stages, the exercises involve application of all thinking skills (or nearly all, depending on the nature of the problem or issue in the exercise).

Skill-cluster exercises are also useful in providing practice in those skills with which individual students or the entire class have experienced difficulty. For example, if students had difficulty producing ideas, their lists containing only a few ideas of the most common variety, you would assign additional exercises in idea-production, exercises that directed students to practice extending their effort at producing ideas, pressing for imaginative ideas, and deferring judgment.

As noted in Chapter 5, most assignment material can be fashioned to provide exercise in any individual thinking skill or cluster of skills by varying the number of steps demanded of students and the amount of work already done for them when the problem is presented. The most common example of doing preliminary work for the student is the practice of expressing the problem in the assignment directions. Following are some effective kinds of skill-cluster assignments. (To appreciate more fully the almost unlimited possibilities for shaping material to fit particular student needs, pause occasionally while reading these exercises and consider how you might alter them to serve different purposes.)

Exploring Attitudes

Example   Many studies have shown that some people profit from the experience of failure whereas others do not. The difference often lies in their attitude toward failure and the way that attitude makes them respond. Think of one or more cases in which you experienced failure and did not profit from it as much as you might have. Decide what attitude/approach would have been better.

Examining Thought Patterns

Example   Is there a characteristic pattern to the way you approach a problem or issue? Does an image come to mind first? Or perhaps a word? What comes next? And what after that? If you can't answer these questions completely, do this exercise: Flip open your textbook, pick a sentence at random, read it, and note how your mind deals with it. (Such thinking about thinking may be a little awkward at first. If it is, try the exercise two or three times.)[5]

Example   Do you find it difficult to ponder important matters? That is, are you able to prevent the casual, semiconscious drift of images from interrupting your thoughts? Do you have less control in some situations than in others? Explain.[6]

Taking Intellectual Inventory

Example   An occasional examination of your habits of mind can help you determine where there is need for improvement. Answer each of the following questions about your mental habits as honestly as possible: About what matters do you tend to accept rumor and hearsay uncritically? About what matters do you tend to exhibit mine-is-better thinking? In what situations do you tend to conform to the thoughts and actions of others? In what situations do you tend to save face? Practice self-deception? Assume too much? Look for overly simple answers to complex questions? Jump to conclusions? Overgeneralize? Add to each of your answers of the above questions a plan for overcoming your bad mental habits.

Recalling False "Knowledge"

Example   Everyone learns from time to time that his mind has played a trick on him by making him think he knew something that later turned out to be false. For example, until he was fifteen years old, the famous Swiss psychologist Jean Piaget had a vivid recollection of an incident that supposedly occurred when he was two years old. As he recalled it, he was sitting in his carriage, which his nurse was pushing, when a man tried to kidnap him. The nurse fought bravely, receiving various scratches, until a crowd gathered, a policeman came over, and the would-be kidnapper fled. When Piaget was fifteen, his parents received a letter from the nurse, who had since undergone a spiritual conversion and felt obligated to confess her lie. She had made up the entire incident which Piaget so vividly remembered. As Piaget explains, he undoubtedly heard her story as a child and projected it back into his visual memory.[7] Recall a situation where, to your surprise, you discovered that something you were sure you knew—an experience like Piaget's or simply a "fact" you thought you had learned—proved later to be false. Explain the situation and how you learned the truth.

Tracing Sources of Beliefs

Example Choose one of the following ideas and record your immediate reaction to it (whether you agree or disagree). Then try to recall where you first heard that reaction expressed. Don't be disturbed if the reaction did not originate with you—in most cases, we hear ideas expressed by parents or friends or authors of books or magazine articles before we embrace them ourselves. Finally, list as many specific occasions in which you have heard the reaction expressed since that first occasion.

> Every American has the right to own a gun.
>
> Drinking and driving don't mix.
>
> Seatbelts save lives.
>
> Atheists are bad people.
>
> Rock musicians are creative people.
>
> Teachers are overpaid.

Tracing the Consequences of Ideas

This kind of exercise is more ambitious than the one tracing beliefs; it involves some investigation. The examples given below are of general interest and could be used in any course. The history of the various academic disciplines will reveal many other ideas whose impact (favorable or unfavorable) has been dramatic.

Example Is intelligence inherited or acquired? The issue has had an interesting history, particularly in the past century, and its impact on education—most notably in the development and use of the intelligence *test*—has been profound. Begin your investigation by reading a contemporary critical overview of the issue—Stephen Jay Gould's *The Mismeasure of Man,* Norton, 1981, would be an excellent choice. Extend your investigation as far beyond such an overview as time permits. Then reflect on what you have read, as well as on your own experience and the beliefs you have acquired about the intelligence of humans in general and of particular races and nationalities. Finally, state and defend your conclusions about the relative worth of opposing answers to the question "Is intelligence inherited or acquired?"

Example   What attitudes toward Jews have you grown up with? (The answer you give if you are Jewish may be rather different from a gentile's answer.) In any case, answer as completely and as honestly as possible. Next, read a historical overview of the Jews in history—Cecil Roth's *A Bird's-Eye View of Jewish History,* Schocken Books, 1954, would be an excellent choice. Extend your investigation as far beyond the historical overview as time permits. Then reflect on what you have read and on the attitudes you have grown up with and, as best you can, trace the origin of the attitudes you have grown up with. In addition, decide which of your beliefs, if any, should be revised in light of your new knowledge.

Observing Others' Behavior

Example   Ask one of your instructors for permission to visit another of his or her classes. Go to that class and observe carefully the reactions of individual students to the lesson—for example, the subtle indications they give of attention or inattention. Record your observations.

Examining Advertisements

Example   Companies pay billions of dollars a year to advertise their products and services in such a way that people are motivated to purchase them. The appeals are sometimes rational, but more often emotional, playing on people's needs and desires and capitalizing on their suggestibility. For the next few weeks pay special attention to magazine and newspaper ads and television commercials. Try to identify the various strategies used to reach people. Record your findings in your journal, attaching the ads themselves or facsimiles whenever possible.

Directed Wondering

This kind of exercise gives students practice in speculating about possibilities and probabilities. Though it may be used with matters for which no answers are available or matters still being disputed, one effective use is as a lead-in to discussions of facts, as the following example illustrates:

Example   Suppose the shape or color of a container were changed—for example, the shape of an instant coffee jar or the color of a soda can. What effect do you think such a change would have on consumer reaction to the product itself? Explain your thinking.

After students have completed the assignment and discussed their answers, you might share these facts with them. An experiment in the 1950s put catsup in a milk bottle and milk in a catsup bottle. People called them red milk and white catsup, respectively. When "Taster's Choice" coffee was marketed, a square shaped bottle was used because research had demonstrated that people regarded that shape as "macho" and reacted more favorably to it. In addition, the coffee grains were left in large chunks because people believed large chunks were richer in flavor. A test in packaging orange soda revealed that changing the shade of the orange depicted on the can resulted in people saying the soda tasted different.

Other studies have further demonstrated that people's reactions to products are significantly affected by packaging. When the Camel cigarette package depicted smaller pyramids and a smaller tree in the background in the 1950s, people wrote the company complaining that the taste of the cigarettes had changed. When sales to Corningware's new "Gourmet dish" were below expectations, the company changed the name to "French white" and the picture on the label from shrimp to a pot roast, and sales doubled.[8] Students will usually be interested in probing why people react so irrationally and considering the implications of these facts.

Finding Instances of Creativity

Example The media often carry reports of new products and services designed to meet previously unmet needs; for example, the announcement that a soft drink manufacturer has marketed white chocolate soda that tastes like a cross between "chocolate and champagne."[9] Begin keeping a record in your journal of all such reports. Attach a newspaper or magazine clipping if possible.

Identifying Problems and Issues

Example List as many specific problems and issues as you can think of that are related to the following subjects:

Cigarette smoking
Drugs (including alcohol)
Sex
Education

Finding Unmet Needs

Example Someone once said that the simple prescription for success is to find a need and create a way to meet it. Many people have found that the prescription works—for example, the person who founded the first dating service and the person who founded "Rent-a-Heap," the cheap car rental agency. Use your creativity to identify as many needs as you can that are not presently being met, or met adequately. Consider both the need for products and the need for services.

Noticing Improvements in Things

Example It has been estimated that as many as 80% of all patents are awarded for improvements in existing things rather than for new things. There have been many variations on the bed since the days when someone first thought to heap straw in a pile, and many variations on lighting since the first campfire. List as many of those variations as you can think of for each and try to include some of the latest ideas. If your imagination needs stimulating, consult the Sears catalog. [Similar assignments could be done with methods of transportation and writing or shaving instruments.]

Improving Products

Example Take a walk through a department store, K Mart, for example, or flip through the pages of a department store catalog. Look carefully at the various items you find there, from file cabinets to shoe trees, with this question in mind, "Which of these things could stand improving in design or manufacture?" When something catches your eye, pause over it and consider how you might improve it, perhaps by adding or taking away something or by changing it in some way. Record your ideas.

Example List as many improvements as you can think of for automobiles, television sets, refrigerators, and watches.

Improving Systems and Processes

Example Choose a process or procedure with which you have some, but not necessarily a great deal of, familiarity. Three possibilities for your consideration are obtaining a driver's license, registering for the draft, and paying income tax. Investigate each process thoroughly enough to understand the basic rules, regulations, and procedures. Think of as many ways as you can to improve the system or process. Select your best idea and explain its merits.

Writing Headlines

Example [Distribute to your students one or more brief newspaper articles *minus the headlines.* Then give them this direction.] Read each of the following articles carefully. Then think of as many headlines as you can for each article. Select the one that best reflects the story's contents and best fits the space available for a headline. [Later, you might want to share with students the creative, if somewhat less than elegant, headline written by a *New York Daily News* staffer when an Italian prosecutor criticized a performance by Gina Lollobrigida: "Charges Gina/ Was Obscena/ on La Screena.]

Inventing New Things

Example Most of the sports familiar to us were invented some time ago, but from time to time new sports are invented. An example of a recent one is the part-volleyball, part-racquetball game called "Wallyball," invented by Joe Garcia in the 1970s. Your assignment is to invent another new game. Be sure to let your thinking range over as many possibilities as you can before settling on any one. When you find one that is both brand new and interesting, work out the rules of play.

Deciding What Comes Next

Example Everyone has said, on encountering a new product or service, "I wish I had thought of that." But most people never use the occasion to stimulate their own creativity. That is what you will be doing in this assignment. For each of the ideas listed below, a recent creative idea, ask yourself, "What comes next?"— that is, in what way the idea might be creatively extended either in the same area or an entirely different area. Be sure to extend your effort to produce ideas and defer all judgment until you have produced a good number of ideas.

> Kodak has developed two new products: one will allow hard-copy photographs to be made of the images on TV screens and computers; the other will allow 35 mm photographs to be displayed on a TV screen.[10]

> A Missouri experiment known as "New Parents as Teachers Project" has shown that students whose parents receive training in parenting do significantly better in school than students whose parents receive no such training. The training in this experiment was provided by child-development specialists who visited homes for a period of three years starting when the mothers were pregnant with the children.[11]

Handling Challenges to Ingenuity

Appropriate challenges can be designed for students of any age level. Ideally, they should range from everyday situations, such as being terrorized by the school bully, being urged by peers to take drugs, and having difficulty finding a summer job, to more unusual ones, such as the following.

Example You have just entered a cooking contest for which the first prize is an expensive new stove. The main judging criterion, aside from the quality of food preparation, is the creativeness of the recipe. Think of as many possible combinations of food that are both unusual and appetizing as you can. Then choose your best one and write a recipe for it. (There will be no penalty for actually cooking it and bringing a sample of the finished product to class.)

Example You are employed by the new products division of a toy and novelty company. Your assignment is to produce as many ideas as you can for new products for next year's Christmas season. Record all your ideas and be prepared to present the best idea in class, together with the arguments you would use to persuade your company's management to accept it.

Example Knowing of your success in your job with the toy and novelty company, a friend asks for your assistance on an assignment he is having difficulty with. He works in the new products division of a food company and has been told to devise several new products in the snack and cereal categories. Think of as many possibilities as you can. (If you wish, take a trip to the neighborhood grocery store to stimulate your imagination.) Record your ideas, choose your best one, and explain your choice.

Thinking of Illustrations

Example For each of the following ideas list as many cases as you can from your experience or observation that either support or oppose them. (Include vicarious experiences such as those from reading and TV viewing.) Use sentence fragments to save time.

> An old error is always more popular than a new truth. *(German proverb)*
>
> Wise men learn by other people's mistakes; fools, by their own. *(Proverb)*
>
> Show me a man who cannot bother to do little things and I'll show you a man who cannot be trusted to do big things. *(J. Braude)*
>
> It ain't what a man doesn't know that makes him a fool, but what he does know that ain't so. *(Josh Billings)*

Interpreting Statements

Example Explain the meaning(s) of each of the following quotations. Discuss any associations or implications that come to mind as you examine each quotation.

> He that is truly wise and great
> Lives both too early and too late.
> *(English proverb)*

> What was a lie in the father becomes a conviction in the son. *(F. Nietzsche)*
>
> Great minds are interested in ideas, average minds in events, small minds in people. *(Anonymous)*
>
> A stitch in time saves nine. *(B. Franklin)*
>
> It is human nature to hate those you have injured. *(Tacitus)*
>
> Habit is a second nature. *(Proverb)*
>
> What we have done is the only mirror by which we can see what we are. *(T. Carlyle)*
>
> An error cannot be believed sincerely enough to make it a truth. *(R. Ingersoll)*

Interpreting Political Cartoons

Example Read the following political cartoon carefully and decide what point the cartoonist is making. Then state that point clearly, adding whatever explanation would be necessary for someone who had read the cartoon without understanding it. [This cartoon was a reaction to President Reagan's military response to Libyan President Khadafy's provocations.]

© 1986, Boston Globe. Reprinted with permission of Los Angeles Times Syndicate.

Interpreting Fables

Fables offer excellent opportunities for developing and exercising students' skills of interpretation (particularly young students'). All you need do is give students the fables without the accompanying morals and have them construct appropriate ones. You may also want to have students consider what contemporary situations, beyond the most obvious ones, the fables cover. The class discussion following the assignment should focus on students' sharing their responses and the reasoning that underlies them.

Determining Effects

Example   What would the effects be if all types of examinations were eliminated from the nations' schools tomorrow? Be sure to consider effects on people other than teachers and students and long-term as well as immediate effects.

Example   What would libraries be like if there were no cataloguing systems (like Dewey Decimal or Library of Congress)? Who would be affected in such a situation and in what way(s)?

Investigating Viewpoints

Example   The purpose of this assignment is to give you experience in improving the quality of your opinions. First read the question presented below, give it a few moments thought, and record your answer in one or more complete sentences. Next consult the best sources of informed opinion available to you. Be sure you not only read books and articles in the library, but also interview appropriate professionals (for example, professors in related disciplines). Be sure, too, that your sampling of such views is reasonably broad. Finally, evaluate your original views in light of your investigation and make whatever revision is necessary. Keep in mind that there is no shame in revising a view that on closer examination proves to be flawed. [Note that though five questions are given here, only one or two would normally be used in this assignment.]

How many hours of work is it reasonable for a college instructor to expect of students each week in a three-credit hour course?

Why are so many marriages failing in our society today? What factors contribute most to this failure?

Should children be treated as adults when they commit crimes?

Should slow learners be placed in the same elementary and secondary classes as unusually able students?

What are the effects of Saturday morning TV cartoon shows on children?

Anticipating Objections

Example According to the leader of a NASA research team, the increased length of space flights—some projected for as long as 90 days—will make it likely that "intimate behavior" will occur between male and female astronauts. What objections might the space agency hear voiced from the public if they approved such behavior? Should they approve such behavior? Why or why not?[12]

Recognizing Fallacies

Example In your daily activities for the next week or two, be alert for examples of the fallacies we have studied in class; specifically, for any of the following: illogical conclusion, either-or thinking, stereotyping, attacking the person, straw man, shifting the burden of proof, double standard, contradiction, faulty analogy, faulty causation, irrelevant or irrational appeal, hasty conclusion, overgeneralization, and oversimplification. Record any that you find in the conversations you hear or participate it, including any that you find yourself committing. Be sure to explain the circumstances and context in which the errors occurred.

Analyzing Dialogues

Example Read the following dialogue carefully, reflecting on what each of the participants says. Then decide what position on the issue is most reasonable—that position may be one of the ones expressed in the dialogue or a third view. Defend your position as thoroughly and effectively as you can.

SAM: There seems to be a lot written today about workaholism. But I'm puzzled about what's being said.

EVELYN: What's workaholism?

SAM: Working extraordinarily hard at your job, so hard that you can be considered a work addict.

EVELYN: So what are you puzzled about?

SAM: My father and grandfather have always taught me that laziness is the affliction for which work is the cure. Now everyone seems to be saying the reverse. Work, it seems, is the new villain.

EVELYN: I know you have great respect for your father and grandfather, but their ideas seem a little dated.[13]

Writing a Dialogue

Example   Select a current issue—for example, the debate over whether or not the record industry should be required to put warning labels on albums that feature explicit lyrics. Investigate views on both sides of the issue. Then construct an imaginary dialogue between two informed people who disagree on the issue. Do not "load" one side of the dialogue; rather, present the strongest case you can for both sides, as the people themselves would do.

Taking a Position on Issues

Example   An Iowa legislator proposed that students, with parental permission, should be allowed to get drunk under hospital supervision to teach them their drinking limitations.[14] Do you believe the proposal is a sound one? Be sure that you not only state your position clearly, including important qualifications, but also explain the reasoning that underlies it. Be prepared to defend your position in class discussion.

Additional examples of issues for which the above format could be used are the following: Should schools have the right to keep students off the honor roll because of poor conduct in class? Should women in the military be assigned to combat roles? Should federal and state penitentiaries allow inmates to leave prison during daytime hours to hold jobs or attend college classes? Should parents spank children? Should juveniles who commit capital crimes be subject to adult penalties, including the death penalty?

"People's Court"

A good source for material for this kind of assignment, other than the television show "The People's Court," is newspaper accounts of court cases. The following is an example.

Example   Study the following case carefully, weighing the circumstances and actions taken. Then state what you believe is the fairest disposition of the case and detail the reasoning that supports that belief. If you lack enough information to judge fairly, use the "If . . . then . . ." format.*

> In Belvedere, California a woman confessed to an Episcopal priest that she had embezzled $28,000 from his church. The priest angrily advised her to get an attorney and later testified against her in court. She subsequently sued him for $5 million, arguing that he had breached the confidentiality he, as a priest, owed her.[15]

HOLISTIC EXERCISES

To be completely faithful to real-life situations, holistic exercises would, in most cases, give students no specific directions. In real-life, after all, though problems and issues occasionally come with directions—for example, when a professional person receives a specific assignment from a superior—they are more often discovered by the thinker herself. However, since to withdraw all or nearly all directions would create for many students a formidable obstacle to learning, the most reasonable approach is to use two formats for holistic exercises, a preliminary one for earlier assignments and an advanced one for later assignments.

- *Preliminary Format.* This format provides students with material that poses a holistic thinking challenge. The material may take various forms, ranging from the details of a news story to a provocative quotation or a dialogue. In most cases, students should be required to express the problem or issue themselves (instead of having it expressed for them). In addition, the preliminary format provides directions that mention the various steps of the holistic process and specify the requirements of the assignment ("Record all your ideas on paper," for example).
- *Advanced Format.* This format provides students with material that poses a holistic thinking challenge, but omits directions. Thus it leaves students to decide for themselves where to begin and how to proceed. Note: Before this format is used for the first time, you should explain that in real-life we have to figure out for ourselves what problems and issues, if any, are confronting us; no one helps us interpret what we encounter or decide a course of action in response to it. Further, you should explain that, henceforth, dialogues will be presented without comment or directions (except for an assignment due date), and each student will be responsible for identifying problems and issues, deciding which are most worthy of attention, and applying the holistic process.

Following are several types of assignments recommended for providing holistic thinking exercise. All of them can be presented in either preliminary or

---

*An example of the "If . . . then" format is as follows: "The case does not specify whether her confession occurred in a formal, sacramental context. *If* it did, *then* the woman's claim should be upheld. *If,* on the other hand, her confession was an informal admission, *then* the priest was justified in proceeding as he did."

advanced format. The particular format used in the examples is indicated in parentheses.

Brief Dialogues

Example (Preliminary Format) Read the following dialogue carefully and decide whether it presents a problem or an issue. Then express the problem (issue); investigate it, as necessary; produce as many ideas as you can; and evaluate/refine your best one. Remember to express the problem (issue) in many ways before deciding which expression is best. In addition, be sure to defer judgment and extend your effort to produce possible solutions. Record all your work.

> ZEB: There's one thing I don't think belongs in our Constitution.
>
> JEB: What's that?
>
> ZEB: The freedom of religion clause.
>
> JEB: But freedom of religion is one of the basic freedoms we all enjoy.
>
> ZEB: As I see it, it's a dangerous business allowing people to practice any religion they want with no restrictions. What if people want to worship the devil. Do you think that's right?
>
> JEB: No, I don't personally, but I wouldn't deny others the right to do so.
>
> ZEB: You're just repeating empty formulas you were taught. What if a group made sexual orgies their main ritual. Would you approve that?
>
> JEB: Hey, man. Where do I sign up for that religion?
>
> ZEB: Be serious. There were lots of religions in the past that practiced some pretty weird and disgusting things. Like the sacrifice of young girls to ensure a good harvest and the murdering of servants so some king or queen could be properly attended in the afterlife. Do you approve of that kind of stuff?
>
> JEB: No, I guess not, but . . .
>
> ZEB: Right. The more you think about the matter, the more you've got to agree my fears make good sense. We should change the Constitution.[16]

Example (Advanced Format) [The following dialogue would be presented without directions or comment.]

> BATHSHEBA: Have you seen Sandra lately? She's altogether different from the Sandra we knew last spring. She doesn't party anymore, she takes her studies seriously, and she's much more subdued. I don't mean she's depressed or anything like that. It's just that she's quiet and reflective where she used to be so talkative and zany.
>
> BARTHOLOMEW: I haven't seen her, but frankly I don't believe she could have changed that much over a single summer. People don't change their personalities. We're all products of our conditioning. No stimulus is strong enough to evoke such a radically different response in so short a time.
>
> BATHSHEBA: Whatever doesn't fit your behavioristic view of people,

you reject out of hand. People can change if they want to badly enough. They can take stock of themselves, will to be different, and set about changing their habits. And many psychologists share my conviction.

BARTHOLOMEW: There is such a psychological school, but it's archaic. Behaviorists like Watson and Skinner have demonstrated definitely that the notion of free will is a myth.[17]

To heighten the quality of realism, you may wish to include several dialogues in each assignment, only one of which contains a problem or issue of any significance (the others containing merely innocuous conversation). When this variation is used, of course, you should not penalize students who find and address minor problems or issues in the innocuous conversation. The point of the assignment is not to find the hidden problem or issue, but to regard everyday conversation alertly and use it a springboard to productive thought.

Extended Dialogues Reflecting Everyday Conversation

Extended dialogues afford you an opportunity to include the tangents, irrelevancies, and flaws in thinking that often characterize everyday conversation and thus challenge students to make important distinctions and interpret what they read and hear. Like brief dialogues, extended dialogues should be presented without comment or directions (except a general explanation of purpose given at an appropriate point in the course). Here is an example of an extended dialogue of moderate length.[18]

Example (Advanced Format)

LEO: Do you know what's insane?

EDWINA: What?

LEO: The treatment of insane people in our legal system. If a person commits a crime and is found to be insane, or even suspected of being so, he's allowed to plead not guilty by reason of insanity. That's crazy.

EDWINA: I don't think it's crazy at all. No other handling of such cases would be fair.

LEO: Face the facts. Most of those people who plead insanity are as sane as you and I. They're taking advantage of the loophole provided by the insanity plea.

EDWINA: I grant you that some are, but not most. And besides, the psychologists and psychiatrists brought in by the courts can detect when insanity is faked.

LEO: That's what you think. I've read lots of articles about how people fooled them. As a matter of fact, I can recall a case several years ago when some people, either journalists or graduate students, did an experiment to see whether professionals could be deceived. They didn't commit a crime, naturally, but they arranged to get themselves recommended for psychiatric evaluation. Then they faked insanity and managed to fool the professional staff of the institution again and again. Ironically, only the inmates recognized that they weren't crazy.

EDWINA: All right, I'll grant that psychologists and psychiatrists make mistakes. But such cases are the exception and not the rule. The fact is that there are specific kinds of mental illness, each with its own characteristic symptoms that can be recognized. More important, when people have such an illness they are not responsible for their actions.

LEO: You mean the law has chosen, insanely, not to hold them responsible for their actions.

EDWINA: I mean exactly what I said—they are not responsible for their actions. They don't know what they're doing, their sense of right and wrong is disconnected, and they act either out of compulsion or without awareness of the nature of their actions.

LEO: How can you pick up a knife and stab someone and not know what you're doing?

EDWINA: Easy. If you become convinced that many of the people around you are not people at all, but giant salamanders bent on taking over the planet and you grab a knife and begin stabbing them to save the human race, you don't know what you are doing. More exactly, you know in your own mind that you are doing one thing, but you don't know what you are *really* doing.

LEO: But you're saying that what should count when a sane person commits a crime is what he *does,* the reality, yet what should count when an insane person commits a crime is what he thought he was doing. That's inconsistent.

EDWINA: It's not inconsistent at all. It's judging different cases differently.

LEO: And what do you say about cases of temporary insanity? Don't they strain belief just a bit? They're so convenient. "Oh, your honor, I was insane just when I did that horrible deed. Right afterward, I regained my senses."

EDWINA: I don't see how they strain belief. We all experience a variety of emotions every day. If people can lose control of their emotions, why is it so difficult to conceive of someone's losing a grasp on reality temporarily?

LEO: It's so frustrating talking to you, Edwina. I have the feeling I'm dragging an impossible load up a steep mountain.

EDWINA: Maybe the load would be lighter if you unburdened yourself of your misconceptions.

LEO: Touché. I'll make one last attempt to get you to be reasonable. Won't you agree that there's something wrong with letting people go free after they've lost their sanity and committed crimes? Wouldn't it be better for them if they were kept in an institution and made to pay in some way for the crime? And wouldn't it be better for the public to be protected against the possibility of their losing control again?

EDWINA: To keep them institutionalized as long as they are insane makes sense. But they should be released as soon as they are diagnosed as sane. To keep them in one day longer because society is afraid or wishes to punish them is unjust.

Simple Statements Providing Information

In designing an exercise of this type, you needn't include all relevant information. (In the case where you find the information in a news account, you will often not have all relevant information yourself.) It is enough to teach students how to deal with situations in which they lack information—by investigating the matter further or using "If . . . then . . ." statements. In addition, you should, where possible, include some multi-logical problems—that is, problems that touch more than one academic discipline.

The following examples illustrate the variety of information in the news that lends itself to this kind of assignment. To save space, the advanced format is used for all of them. (Note that several of the examples deal with education. If you are reluctant to use such examples, reflect on the fact that of all the subjects from which problems and issues might be chosen, education is one of the few in which students have had considerable personal experience and observation. It is therefore an uncommonly good subject for problems and issues.)

- *Example.* In recent years there have been a number of educational malpractice lawsuits—that is, lawsuits filed by individuals who claim that the schools they attended fail to educate them properly and should be made to pay damages. Usually these suits are filed by individuals whose situations are in no way unusual. Occasionally, however, there are exceptions. One example is Frank Torres, 27 and illiterate, who was abandoned at age 7 and became a ward of the state. Torres claims the shelter ignored his inability to understand English, incorrectly classified him as retarded, and placed him in programs in which he couldn't understand what was being taught. Another example is Donald Snow, 22, who claims state doctors misdiagnosed him as a "hopeless imbecile" with an IQ of 24 when he was really only deaf.[19]
- *Example.* Professor and author Neil Postman proposes that a new subject be added to school curriculums. The subject, which he suggests be called "Media Ecology," or "Media Education," would have students investigate how the media handle discourse and affect beliefs and actions.[20]
- *Example.* The original purpose of tenure for teachers—that is, permanent appointment (usually granted after a probationary period)—was to guarantee academic freedom and ensure that no one would be fired capriciously. Contemporary critics argue that the main effects of the

tenure system are shielding incompetent teachers, preventing curricular flexibility, and preventing outstanding younger teachers from being promoted.

- *Example.* The New York State Education Commissioner has ruled that it is improper for teachers to adjust grades to reflect students' attendance records. "Final grades," he wrote, "should reflect a student's achievements and performance in the course. They should not be distorted by arbitrary penalties for absences or by arbitrary awards for exemplary attendance."[21]
- *Example.* In an effort to overcome the problem of illegal drug use, schools have taken a number of measures some find questionable, such as searching individuals suspected of (or reported for) using drugs on school property and conducting random searches of school lockers and desks. One New Jersey school even took the extraordinary measure of requiring all students to take blood and urine tests.[22]
- *Example.* The problem of fan violence in sports stadiums seems to have increased dramatically in recent years. A particularly horrible example of such violence was the riot that occurred in Brussels, Belgium, during the 1985 European Cup Final, in which 38 people were killed and 400 injured.[23]
- *Example.* A city-hired child psychiatrist in San Antonio, Texas, conducted a study on the effects of rock music on young people and concluded that "the glamorization of suicide, drug abuse, incest, rape, dehumanizing sexuality and violence as a way of life are potentially harmful influences on young people growing up." As a result of this study, the City Council considered passing an ordinance banning children under 13 from attending rock shows that depict violence and illicit sex.[24]
- *Example.* The National Council of Boy Scouts of America has ruled that a Charlottesville, Virginia, youth who doesn't believe in God must be expelled from the organization.[25]
- *Example.* A Connecticut law decreed that "those who observe a Sabbath any day of the week as a matter of religious conviction must be relieved of the duty to work on that day, no matter what burden or inconvenience this imposes on the employer or fellow workers." The law was challenged in the courts and the United States Supreme Court, invoking the principle of separation of church and state, declared the law unconstitutional. Specifically, they ruled that states may not force any employer to give workers their choice of a religious day off each week.[26]

Quotations

The quotations used need not be profound. In fact, an assortment of profound, superficial, questionable, and downright fallacious quotations is most preferable because it will provide students an opportunity to exercise numerous thinking skills, particularly evaluation and judgment. The following examples of quotations are all presented in the advanced format.

- *Example.* A person consists of his faith. Whatever is his faith, even so is he. *(Hindu proverb)*

- *Example.* Men who have been famous for their looks have never been famous for anything else. *(Arthur Ponsonby)*
- *Example.* Even God cannot change the past. *(Agathon)*
- *Example.* To be wronged is nothing unless you continue to remember it. *(Confucius)*
- *Example.* Pacifism is simply undisguised cowardice. *(Adolf Hitler)*
- *Example.* Winning isn't everything—it's the *only* thing. *(Vince Lombardi)*
- *Example.* If it feels good, it is good. *(Anonymous)*

There is another holistic thinking exercise that goes even further than those described above in freeing students from dependency on others' directions. This exercise consists of having students apply holistic thinking to problems of their own choosing, problems that arise, for the most part, from their day-to-day experience. Many instructors encourage such application, but do not include it as a formal assignment. Here is how to make it so:

Soon after the middle of the term (earlier, if desired), announce to students that they will be required to submit one or more reports of problems and issues to which they have applied the holistic thinking process learned in the course, stressing that it will be their responsibility to be perceptive and remain alert for possible challenges. Explain the guidelines students will be expected to follow in preparing the reports and the criteria on which they will be graded. Set specific due dates, perhaps two or three weeks apart. Collect the reports at those times and either grade them individually or treat them as a journal, assigning one grade for all the reports. If you wish, specify that these problems and issues should be at least indirectly related to the course. (Some instructors use this type of assignment strictly for make-up or extra-credit work.)

CONCLUDING SUGGESTIONS

All the holistic exercises presented above are designed to present more realistic problem-solving situations than are commonly used in thinking instruction. The obvious advantage of such situations is that they help prepare students to cope with the problems and issues they will encounter outside the classroom in their careers and personal lives. However, there is also a disadvantage: an increase in the confusion and frustration which students must face. That disadvantage is unavoidable. Confusion and frustration are, after all, precisely the difficulties students must learn to deal with effectively if their thinking skills are to have any practical value.

Students' success in doing such holistic exercises as these will depend in great measure on your sensitivity to the difficulty of the situation. You should develop exercises judiciously, according to students' ages and levels of emotional and intellectual maturity. The holistic exercises shown above will not be appropriate for all students at all levels of education. Where they are not, you should fashion other exercises, using the ones shown above as models of form and noting the sources consulted in creating them.

In addition, you should explain thoroughly and often, starting at the very beginning of the course, (a) that the exercises and assignments are designed to increase in difficulty as the course progresses; and (b) that students who put forth reasonable effort need not worry because they will grow in ability and thus be equal to the challenges at every level of difficulty. Moreover, as students proceed, you should coach them to competency, providing guidance and encouragement in proportion to their individual needs.

Finally, when you introduce holistic exercises like the ones detailed above, you should prepare yourself for divergent responses from students. Training in creative thinking will have taught students to value divergent thinking, and the absence of directions will increase the opportunity to approach problems and issues from a variety of perspectives. Being prepared for divergence does not, of course, mean that you should refrain from constructively criticizing deficiencies in student performances. (If anything, such criticism will be more needed at this stage than at earlier stages.) It means that you should maintain an open mind about the problems and issues you assign and refuse to decide in advance which approaches and solutions will be approved or disapproved. If you allow yourself to prejudge holistic exercises, your response to student work is almost certain to be, "You didn't do what I didn't tell you to do" or "You didn't guess the solution I had in mind." The principal effect of that response will be to persuade students that all the talk about creative and critical thinking is sham and what you really want is memorization and "right" answers.

APPLICATIONS

1. Review the numerous exercise headings included in each of the broad categories discussed in the chapter: warm-up exercises, skill-cluster exercises, and holistic exercises. Determine which of those exercise headings are relevant to your course(s).
2. For each of the exercise headings you listed in application 1, create one or more exercises of your own. Begin by producing as many ideas as you can for each heading, using the techniques for idea production explained on pages 40–44. Then evaluate your ideas and refine the best ones.
3. Begin today to look in newspapers and magazines and on radio and television for material that will be useful in creating thinking exercises for your course(s). In addition, keep a record of the ideas that occur to you, including those that arrive unexpectedly.

chapter 7

INSTRUCTIONAL MATERIALS ACROSS THE CURRICULUM

Chapter 6 discussed where to find and and how to develop materials of general interest—that is, materials that are useful both in courses devoted exclusively to the teaching of thinking and in the wide variety of courses in which thinking skills are an important secondary objective. This chapter will discuss finding and developing materials of special importance or interest to particular academic disciplines.

At the outset, it is worthwhile to recall a point stressed in Chapter 2, that teaching students thinking skills across the curriculum need not involve compromising regular course content. Though some time will usually be required to introduce or reinforce the principles and approaches of effective thinking, such time is minimal. (A strategy for introducing or reinforcing principles without spending class time on them is detailed later in this chapter.) Essentially, teaching thinking skills means *changing teaching methods* rather than adding content. To demonstrate this, let's consider a course that not only occupies a long and honored place in college curriculums, but that has important applications in most other courses at every level of education—ethics.

Traditionally, the ethics course has been taught by having students read either the works of great ethicists or textbook explanations of their works. The aim of the course has been to familiarize students with the great moral issues, the best known and most widely accepted responses to those issues, and the principles that have derived from the continuing work of knowledgeable people. Though this aim is certainly a worthy one, it does not encompass ethical analysis, and so in traditional ethics courses no special effort is made to have students become skillful in analyzing moral issues and making moral judgments. The overriding —in some cases, the exclusive—concern is having students know the whos, whats, whens, wheres, and whys of the history of ethics. (An unintended effect of this focus is the assumption many students make that ethics is of theoretical value only, with no practical dimension.)

How exactly could instructors go about changing ethics courses to emphasize thinking skills? For one thing, they could reduce the amount of reading students do for each assignment and add challenges in the form of cases calling for evaluation and judgment. Two typical forms for such cases are "Here are the facts: you judge the morality of the action taken," and "Here is a situation to which a response must be made: you decide what response is most defensible morally." In addition, they could devote some class time to discussing these cases, having students report on the judgments they reached and the reasoning and evidence that support those judgments, and encouraging questioning and debate.*

If instructors choose both reading assignments and cases judiciously, they will be able to cover the same course content covered previously, increase the students' understanding of the ethical principles and approaches by adding *knowing how* to *knowing that,* and at the same time contribute to their cognitive development. In addition, they will help students develop a better appreciation of the contributions of the great ethicists. Nothing, after all, creates more respect for achievement in a field than first-hand experience with its problems and issues.

FINDING MATERIALS

Though at first consideration it might seem difficult to find good thinking instruction materials for particular disciplines, once you learn where to look, you will find an abundance of materials. Here are the six best sources:

Professional Journals in the Discipline Journal articles often contain references to, and sometimes fully developed reports of, problems in the discipline and the approaches that have succeeded in solving them. Undergraduate students in all but the most advanced courses are not likely to be familiar with the problems discussed in journals, particularly problems only recently solved. You can therefore fashion such problems into new and interesting challenges for students. The problems might be either expressed for students or presented in rough form, leaving the task of expression to students.

Historical Works and Biographies These works will usually discuss numerous issues that provoked debate among famous scholars in the discipline. Some of these issues may be so well known as to be familiar to students and thus inappro-

---

*The approaches suggested here do not, of course, exhaust the possibilities; nor must these approaches be rigidly followed. Cases may be assigned *before* the relevant principles are studied, thus enabling students to better understand the principles. Similarly, if class time is not available for discussing every homework problem, you could allow ten minutes per period for discussing a single case; or, instead, call on a student to read his or her analysis of a case and invite the class to raise questions about it, but then leave the student to ponder those questions rather than respond to them.

priate to use as exercises. However, those that are unfamiliar can be presented to students for their analysis in this manner:

> You are a biologist (or sociologist, etc.). A controversy is raging over
> _____. You will be expected to have a position on the issue. Explain exactly how you would go about examining the issue. Then conduct your evaluation and go as far as you can toward developing a position. If you cannot develop a position, explain why not; that is, explain what prevents you from doing so and what you would have to know in order to do so.

Textbooks in Your Own or a Related Field   In academic areas which make use of experiments, notably the sciences and social sciences, textbooks are excellent sources of information about well-known and not so well-known, creative and uncreative, successful and unsuccessful research efforts. By browsing through textbooks for advanced courses, you can often find experiments not covered in your elementary or intermediate course textbook, experiments you can fashion into effective exercises for your students. Exercises can even be based on experiments covered in your own course texts, as long as you assign them before covering the chapters discussing the experiments.

For example, if you teach psychology you might note that one classic investigation of the extent to which behavior reflects fixed personality traits rather than relatively free responses to particular situations was Hartshorne and May's 1928 study of honesty in children. They put children in a number of situations in which they had a chance to be dishonest without, the children believed, being found out.[1] That study might suggest this exercise for students:

> You are a researcher interested in finding an answer to the question, "Is people's behavior more a reflection of fixed personality traits or of free responses to particular situations?" Apply the holistic thinking approach and design a carefully controlled experiment to help you reach an answer." [Similar exercises could be based on the work of Asch on conformity, Milgram on obedience, Seligman on "learned helplessness," and Festinger on cognitive dissonance.]

Scholarly Books in your Discipline or Related Disciplines   Occasionally, scholarly books will describe, in passing, effective assignments others have used. In *The Process of Education,* for instance, Harvard professor Jerome Bruner writes as follows:

> A sixth-grade class, having been through a conventional unit on the social and economic geography of the Southeastern states, was introduced to the North Central region by being asked to locate the major cities of the area on a map containing physical features and natural resources, but no place names. The resulting class discussion very rapidly produced a variety of plausible theories concerning the requirements of a city—a water transportation theory that placed Chicago at the junction of the three lakes, a mineral resources theory that placed it near the Mesabi range, a food-supply theory that put a great city on the rich soil of Iowa, and so on. The level of interest as well as the level of

conceptual sophistication was far above that of control classes. Most striking, however, was the attitude of children to whom, for the first time, the location of a city appeared as a problem, and one to which an answer could be discovered by taking thought.[2]

Another instance of an exercise being suggested in scholarly reading, in this case an exercise for college students, is found in the following passage from Israel Scheffler's *Reason and Teaching:*

Each student was therefore requested to acquaint himself with the philosophical literature bearing on the foundations of his own teaching subject, and was further asked to write a paper relating such literature to selected aspects of teaching. To facilitate this assignment, students were give bibliographies listing recent philosophical works bearing on the several teaching areas, e.g., books treating of philosophy of mathematics, philosophy of history, philosophy of science, philosophy of language, philosophy of art, etc. It was suggested to students that they might use the assignment as an opportunity to deepen or broaden their grasps of their subjects, and they were encouraged to integrate philosophical with any other materials they deemed relevant, in the writing of their papers.

Scheffler goes on to explain the effectiveness of the assignment in, among other things, producing insights about the relationship of philosophy to the various disciplines.[3]

Newspapers and Magazines   Ideas for materials are not only to be found in academic writing. Newspapers and magazines can yield numerous possibilities. To cite but one example, an article entitled "Synthetic Blood" in the popular press explains that chronic angina is sometimes treated by inserting a deflated balloon via a catheter into the plaque-filled coronary artery and then inflating the balloon to compress the plaque and thereby improve the blood flow. The article continues by noting that the procedure originally was complicated by the fact that when the balloon was inflated, oxygen supply to the other side of the artery was temporarily cut off, causing a sharp drop in blood pressure and harming the heart. The problem was solved by injecting artificial blood into the catheter so that oxygen can be provided while the normal blood flow is cut off.

   Either the original problem, how to deal with the problem of a plaque-filled artery, or the secondary problem, how to prevent blood pressure from dropping and the heart from being damaged during the corrective procedure, could be used as an exercise in a number of undergraduate science or engineering courses or in medical school courses.

Your Existing Teaching Materials   Yet another source of thinking instruction materials is your existing teaching materials. Materials that in the past you presented to be understood and remembered you might now present, in different form, as thinking challenges. If, for example, you have been in the habit of assigning readings expressing different viewpoints on important issues in your discipline, you can now direct students not only to read and remember the authors' arguments, but also to decide which position is more persuasive and why, and perhaps to supplement that author's arguments or compose their own rebuttal of the opposing position.

ADAPTING BASIC EXERCISES

Many of the basic exercises presented in Chapter 6 can be adapted for specific subject areas. As noted in that chapter, not all the exercises students are assigned need be holistic exercises. Warm-up exercises and exercises both in individual skills and in clusters of skills are also useful. The following adaptions are applicable to a wide range of courses.

Noticing New Things, Unmet Needs, and Improvements

This adaptation combines several exercises from Chapter 6 and is an effective way to make students notice the creative contributions being made in the systems, processes, and concepts of a particular discipline and of the unmet needs to which creative people will respond now and in the future. Moreover, it lays the foundation for the habit of seeking out problems and issues.

Improving Things (Including Systems and Processes)

This adaptation helps students apply their thinking skills to particular needs within the discipline and permits them to experience the satisfaction that comes from working for constructive change.

Inventing New Things (Including Systems, Processes, and Concepts)

This adaptation provides similar benefits to those found in improving things. In addition, it helps students learn how to deal with frustration and failure in a coaching context and thereby gain the guidance and encouragement necessary to develop self-confidence and perseverance.

Deciding What Comes Next

This adaptation teaches students to use other people's achievements as springboards for their own achievements, an indispensable skill for innovators. It also helps students recognize that the opportunities for constructive change in any field are never-ending and thereby encourages them to overcome any tendency they may have to passivity or boredom.

Handling Challenges to Ingenuity

This adaptation simulates for students the kinds of experiences faced by practitioners in a particular discipline. Thus it gives students practice in coping with the unexpected developments and dilemmas that arise in everyday professional life. Incidentally, providing such practice is a direct way of addressing the shortcomings in high school and college graduates most often cited by business and professional organizations.

Interpreting Statements or Political Cartoons

Interpreting statements is not an important activity in all courses and interpreting political cartoons is directly relevant to only a few courses. Nevertheless, where such interpretations are important, this adaptation will be useful.

Determining Effects

Ideas and the actions they lead to have consequences. This adaptation helps students become aware of this fact and develop skill in assessing those consequences in particular disciplines. It also increases students' understanding of the importance of sound thinking.

Investigating Viewpoints, Recognizing Fallacies, and Taking a Position

This adaptation combines several Chapter 6 exercises. In addition to those enumerated in the heading, it may also include the analysis of dialogues. It is of special importance in every subject in which there are issues that divide informed people; in other words, in *virtually every subject in the school or college curriculum.* Among the benefits students gain from this adaptation is skill in dealing with controversy rationally and responsibly, a skill of no small importance in professional life.

Holistic Exercises

This adaptation covers both forms of holistic exercise explained in Chapter 6. Its value lies in the fact that it simulates, better than any other exercise, the conditions under which problems and issues must be addressed in real-life situations. Thus it teaches students how to deal with problems and issues in the discipline *without depending on the instructor or the textbook author to find and express them in advance.*

EXERCISE IDEAS ACROSS THE CURRICULUM

By adapting the basic exercises detailed in Chapter 6 to fit the specific objectives and needs of your courses, you can develop a variety of assignments that simultaneously enlarge students' understanding of the discipline and provide meaningful challenges to their thinking skills. The following assignments, an assortment of skill-cluster and holistic exercises, demonstrate some of the possibilities that educators with experience in teaching thinking skills have found effective. These assignments are arranged according to broad academic discipline; however, it is important that you not limit your attention to those in your discipline. An idea in a different field, though not applicable in your course, will often trigger an idea that *is* applicable. Note also that though few of the exercise ideas are appropriate to every level of education in their present form, most can be revised to fit a number of levels.

The Humanities

Composition

Among the exercise ideas proven effective for teaching thinking skills in composition are the following:

Assign special exercises in brainstorming for unusual composition topics. Such exercises may be used as homework assignments or in-class activities. If the exercises are done out of class, responses should be shared in class so that students benefit from one another's creative efforts. The aim should be to produce as many good ideas as possible, ideas students can draw from when looking for a topic. A variation on this assignment is to have exercises in *approaches* to finding topics; the difference in this assignment is that it yields no specific topics, but only the *sources* of topics. An example of a topic source is the almanac, in which students can find what important events or achievements will soon celebrate a 25th, 50th, or 100th anniversary.

Such exercises have important benefits: they make the creative choice of topics a matter of prestige; they give students practice in several stages of the holistic process, including the first stage, exploration; they increase students confidence and interest in writing compositions; and they produce compositions that are interesting for instructors to read.

Assign special exercises in investigating, in which students are given topics (perhaps from the list of topics they produced in the assignments just described) and required to generate as many possible approaches to investigation as they can. In addition to getting and reading library books, they might list such approaches as interviewing knowledgeable people on campus or in the local community and contacting area professional associations—the medical or legal board, for example. Note that this exercise does not call for actual investigating—that might be done in a subsequent exercise—but merely for deciding what approaches to investigating are appropriate in a particular situation. Note also that though investigation is normally associated only with research papers, it has an important place in composition writing in general.

Have students provide, with every informative paper, a headnote explaining what audience they are writing for and what that audience is likely to know (and not know) about the topic. Though such considerations of audience are sometimes stressed in persuasive writing, they are seldom required in informative writing. Making students responsible for them will result not only in students doing some worthwhile thinking they might not otherwise do; it will also tend to eliminate padding from their writing.

Have students look for and keep a journal record of creative expressions they encounter in their reading.   An example of such an expression is this sentence from John Updike's *The Centaur:* "They are ex-heroes of the type who, for many years, until a wife or ritual drunkenness or distant employment carries them off, continue to appear at high school athletic events, like dogs tormented by a site where they imagine they have buried something precious." Their search, of course, should not be confined to works of literature. They might, for instance, include a sentence like this (from a *Time* article entitled "The Selling of the Super Bowl"): "Upon arriving they were given a designer carryall, a briefcase and enough press handouts to reconstruct a tree."

Literature

Have students address the problems facing literary critics or editors of literature anthologies.   For example, Professor Ann Trivisonno of Ursuline College designed the following exercises for her literature classes:

[For English Renaissance Literature] You are a renowned 17th century literary critic. A publisher has contacted you asking for you to help him make a decision about which of two manuscripts of poems he should publish. A young poet, Ben Jonson by name, has sent him a collection of his poetry; a friend whose name he will not reveal has given him a manuscript containing some unusual poems by a young poet named John Donne. The publisher wants to publish the poems which make the *most promising reforms* in English poetry, but he has a limited budget and can't afford to publish both. He needs your help in making his decision. Select a poem by Donne and one by Jonson (which we did not explicate in class) and point out the specific features of each poem which are innovative and unique. Then advise the publisher which poet to publish, giving reasons why the publisher should follow your recommendation. Write this feedback sheet in the form of a letter.

[For English Romantic Poetry] Imagine that you have been hired by a publisher to edit an introductory anthology of English Romantic Poetry. Your instructions are to bring together in a small, inexpensive volume those poems or parts of poems by Blake, Wordsworth, Coleridge, Byron, Shelley and Keats which best exemplify the characteristics of Romanticism and at the same time will have great appeal to the first-time reader of Romantic poetry. Select the poems that you would include in this anthology, arrange them in whatever order you prefer (it need not be either chronological or according to author) and write a well-organized three-page (typed) introduction to your anthology in which you identify the characteristics of Romanticism that are embodied in the poems, and indicate the special appeal of the poems you have selected to the first-time reader of Romantic poetry.

History

Have students adopt the perspective of an important historical person (or where appropriate, a government) and present a rationale for his or her actions in a situation that occurred during the period of time under study.   In a contemporary history course, for example, you might ask students to take the view of one of the allies of the United States who declined to join the United States in its early 1986 restrictions on relations with Libya. If you prefer, let the perspective be that of ordinary people of the time. That is the approach Deborah Morel of Angwin, California, uses in her junior high history class. After giving students a brief review of the historical background of the period, she directs students to write a dramatic narrative of two American colonists disagreeing over whether to support the revolution or remain loyal to the English crown.

To be sure students' responses are more than an exercise in imagination, require that wherever possible they cite specific historical facts that support the rationale they advance. In addition, during class discussions encourage students to challenge presentations that are not in keeping with the facts.

Philosophy

Assign students timely real-life problems with a philosophic dimension. For example, when the U.S. Supreme Court took up the issue of the constitutionality of a Pennsylvania law requiring that libel defendants sued by private citizens prove that the allegedly libelous statements are true, a philosophy instructor might have had students explore the case, identify the relevant philosophic concepts and principles, and discuss what bearing they should have on the outcome of the case.[5] This assignment differs, naturally, from one which addresses *legal* precedents and interpretations of constitutional law.

Ethics

Pose ethical dilemmas for students to develop positions on. Professor Richard M. Wolters of Doane College begins his ethics course with such a dilemma:

> You live in a small town which has been terrorized for years by a bully. He has come into town alone today, and a crowd has gathered around him. You have a rifle with you, and the opportunity to kill him with impunity. (Since all the rest of the people in the town hate him, they will not turn you in if you do so.) Do you kill him?

Wolters gives students about 15 minutes to respond in writing to the question, taking a position and explaining their rationale for it. He then leads them in discussion, which includes discovering strengths and weaknesses and extending their reasons to other situations. The next class day he puts them back into the same situation, but raises a different question: "Someone else has killed the bully. You know who it is. Do you tell, when put under oath, who killed the bully?" The discussion proceeds as on the first day.

In addition, in each of the four tests Wolters uses during the course, he repeats the situation outlined on the first day and directs students to re-evaluate their thinking on the issue in light of the ethical theories they have learned and the class discussions they have engaged in. Even if students' essential positions on the issue do not change, they are expected to see further implications of their answers, additional problems, and so on. Wolters finds these answers to be an excellent device for assessing each student's growth as a thinker.

Foreign Languages

Toward the end of elementary courses, or in intermediate courses, present students with a provocative assertion or even a fully developed argument and have them take a position regarding it and then support their view with reasons. In intermediate and advanced classes, use open-ended dialogues in which two individuals are disagreeing over something (for example, a moral judgment) but not resolving the matter. Distribute each dialogue in class and have two students read it aloud and then continue the discussion, each defending a different side of the argument. Another approach for intermediate and advanced classes is to pose problems and issues in the foreign language and have students solve them for homework and then, in class, discuss their application of the holistic process.

Music

Have students analyze works of music that are based on literature and identify/evaluate the specific adaptations that were made. Professor Anne Siegrist of Clarke College uses such an assignment in her course in Theatre Music. She has students read G. B. Shaw's *Pygmalion* and watch *My Fair Lady.* Then she has them write a paper that cites instances where the two differ in substance, arrangement (of scenes), setting, and characters; offers explanations of why the most significant changes were made; and examines in depth how the most important musical selections highlight, heighten, and complement the play's action.

The Social Sciences

Economics

Select problems currently vexing economists and have groups of students research and report on them. Take, for example, the problem of balancing the federal budget without seriously injuring any sector of the economy, or the problem of achieving a more favorable balance of trade with foreign countries without cutting American workers' benefits or merely setting high tariffs. Assign the problem to a problem-solving group of from three to five individuals within the class. Have them address the problem and make two presentations. In the first one they should explain salient facts about the problem, together with their formal expression of the problem and the line(s) of investigation and possible solutions they are pursuing, and then receive comments and suggestions from the class.

In the second presentation, scheduled perhaps two or three weeks later, they should present and defend their final conclusions about the wisest course of action regarding the problem. (A class of thirty students would thus be divided into six or seven groups, each responsible for addressing its own problem, and all responsible for understanding and evaluating the positions presented by the other groups.)

Sociology

Give students some current sociological data and have them interpret it in light of the principles and approaches they are studying in the course. An interesting study that could provide such data is one on shoplifting completed by George P. Moschis of Georgia State University and Judith Powell of the University of Richmond. They found that one out of every three students they interviewed admitted having shoplifted. (For those age 15–19, 43 percent admitted having done so.) Among their specific findings are that teenage boys are likely to plan their shoplifting, whereas girls tend to shoplift on impulse; that boys are more likely to have stolen than girls; and that girls are more likely to steal in the presence of friends, whereas boys are likely to steal alone.[6]

In this case, your directions to students might be to determine what factors in modern American society would account for (a) the high percentage of teenagers who shoplift, and (b) the differences between boys' and girls' shoplifting; and to prepare to defend their reasoning in class discussion.

Political Science

After lecturing on important topics, require students to pursue the topics further and attempt to solve the problems implicit in them. For example, if the lecture were on the phenomenon of political action committees and their increasing influence in American politics, you might direct students to apply the holistic process and submit their responses in writing. Such an assignment would presume earlier introduction to the process and some guided practice in using it. It would be up to the students to decide if they were dealing with a problem or issue and then proceed to address it. After they submitted their responses, class discussion could be used to explore the various views of the matter and their relative quality. You might wish to play devil's advocate during this discussion, adopting the position of a political action committee organizer.

Psychology

Have students address the questions psychological researchers have asked or (in the case of unsolved matters) are currently asking. Much of what students read in psychology classes is descriptions of experiments and the conclusions they yielded. How much more meaningful those experiments would be to them if they knew, first-hand, the difficulties and the satisfaction of designing good experiments. This approach provides them with this valuable experience, and at the same time lets them practice a number of thinking skills. Here are two examples of such assignments, together with the directions that might be included to guide student effort:

1. How aware are people of the important influences that affect their decisions? Two researchers, Wilson and Nisbett, designed an interesting experiment to find out. They asked shoppers in a large department store to examine four pairs of pantyhose hung on a rack and choose the pair they preferred. Their preferences, from the hose on the left to those on the right, were as follows: 12 percent, 17 percent, 31 percent, 40 percent. The fact that the four pairs of pantyhose were identical, a fact unknown to the shoppers, suggests that the shoppers were strongly influenced by position on the rack. Yet none of the shoppers indicated that position was a factor in her judgment. The study thus demonstrated that decisions can be affected by influences people are unaware of.[7] Your assignment is to design a different experiment to test the same question Wilson and Nisbett tested. Be as creative as you can and produce a number of possible experiments before selecting your best one. Submit all your ideas, even preliminary ones.

2. In 1958 Robert Fantz, a psychologist from Case Western Reserve University, found a way to study infant learning—by observing their eye movements in reaction to different objects. Since Fantz' breakthrough, other psychologists, aided by such technological developments as the videotape machine and the computer, have devoted their attention to this fascinating subject. Of course, breakthroughs in understanding usually depend on the designing of imaginative experiments. Think of as many creative experiments as you can to probe each of the following questions. Produce many possibilities before selecting your best one. Record all your ideas.

Are people conditioned to prefer certain aromas or foods?

Can infants distinguish the sound of human language from other sounds?

Can infants imitate adults' expressions?

Can babies tell the gender of other babies?

The Sciences

Geology

Have students form and test geological hypotheses that differ from prevailing ones. For example, after students have been introduced to the prevailing theory about the origin of petroleum—that it is the product of ancient decayed organisms—ask students to develop other hypotheses, being as bold as they wish, but raising all questions that geologists would raise and attempting to answer them, then deciding whether their thinking leads them to accept or reject the prevailing theory. After they have presented their views in class, introduce the new theory advanced by Cornell astronomer Thomas Gold, which suggests that natural gas is an inorganic component of the earth's mantle that is thrust toward the surface by geological and mechanical forces. (The Swedish government, supported by the U. S. Gas Research Institute, plans to invest $14 million to test the theory.)[8] Then have students critically examine Gold's theory.

Biology and Chemistry

Make students in laboratory courses responsible for identifying patterns of information, predicting effects and proposing possible causative factors, and presenting internally consistent arguments in support or refutation of an interpretation or conclusion. This is one of the approaches recommended by the Critical Thinking Network in Science, a group of biology and chemistry professors from around the United States organized under the auspices of Alverno College.

Have students respond to multiple choice homework (and exam) problems not only by choosing an answer, but writing out a justification for accepting or rejecting each possible answer in the problem. This approach is recommended by Walter R. Statkiewicz and Robert D. Allen of West Virginia University. They use four criteria in grading such work: appropriateness of concepts and information used in answering; quality of the arguments presented; consistency of the reasoning displayed in the response; identification of critical assumptions and contradictions within the problem.[9]

Here to illustrate this approach is an exercise developed by Clemson University biologist David Stroup:

The diploid number of chromosomes from a certain animal is twelve. You observe a cell which contains two distinct and separate groups of six chromosomes. This cell is:
1. In metaphase of mitosis.
2. In anaphase of mitosis.
3. In metaphase of the first division of meiosis.
4. In anaphase of the second division of meiosis.
5. Between meiotic divisions.

And here is an example of the kind of analysis Stroup expects students to produce in response to the problem: "Since the cell contains two distinct and separate groups of chromosomes, it is probably in anaphase or telophase of a division process. In metaphase all the chromosomes will be in one group. Since it is from an animal, it must have begun the division process as a diploid cell. The only haploid cells in animals are gametes, which do not divide. If a diploid cell with twelve chromosomes undergoes mitosis, each chromosome will separate into two and there will be two distinct groups of twelve chromosomes at anaphase. In the second meiotic division, the cell will begin with six chromosomes, each will separate into two, and two separate groups of six will form at anaphase. Thus 4 is the best choice."

Have students probe the ethical issues related to scientific inquiry and the applications that derive from such inquiry. Over the past few decades many spokespeople for the scientific community have urged that science instructors find ways to make students sensitive to ethical questions. Here are two examples of assignments that help students develop that sensitivity at the same time that they gain practice in thinking skills. (Note: Students will need to have had at least a brief introduction to ethical principles, in this course or a prior one, to be able to respond meaningfully.)

1. Research in genetics over the centuries has brought western medicine to the point where gene therapy in humans is feasible. Laboratories have recently begun trials in which healthy copies of an affected gene will be injected into the bone-marrow cells of a victim of a genetic disorder to begin producing the missing enzyme in sufficient quantities to effect a cure for the patient.[10] Naturally, ethical (as well as scientific) guidelines are necessary in such testing. Your assignment is to develop a set of guidelines that covers all important moral considerations. Be prepared to defend your guidelines in class discussion. [After students have presented and discussed their guidelines, you may wish to present the guidelines developed by the National Institute of Health for such testing.]

2. In recent years animal welfare groups have increased their protests about the treatment of laboratory animals. As a result of their efforts, federal research funding amounting to several million dollars was cut off at two prestigious medical centers.[11] Investigate this issue and write a report including the following: a clear statement of the issue, a summary of the positions advanced by leading spokespeople on both sides, your assessment of the reasonableness of each position, and your proposal for resolving the controversy. Be prepared to defend your proposal in class. [If students are aligned on one side of the controversy during class discussion, you may wish to play devil's advocate and defend the neglected side.]

Business

Business Management

Have students evaluate one another's analyses of problems. Kathleen O'Brien of Alverno College uses this approach. The checklist she developed for students to use in evaluating contains a number of specific criteria, including "Identifies important elements in the present situation which indicate a problem may exist." "Notes critical constraints in solving problems," "Explicitly states necessary assumptions, inferences," and "Indicates related managerial concepts and/or theory." In addition to checking off criteria the analysis has met, students assign each analysis an overall grade and have an opportunity to make specific comments.

Business Law

Have students address current problems that challenge the best minds in the field—for example, the problem of the rising cost of malpractice insurance plaguing doctors and hospital associations. Students can be directed to apply the holistic process to the problem, focusing on legislative solutions. (This problem could also be used in an insurance course; there, students would be directed to focus on solutions in the insurance industry.)

Marketing

Have students develop a marketing campaign for a product or service. Begin by having students read marketing reports and identify products/services that have failed to live up to expectations, and then apply the marketing principles and approaches they have learned to determine which products/services failed because of poor marketing as opposed, for example, to poor product design. Next, direct students to develop a new marketing campaign for the product/service of their choice and make a presentation to the class. The presentation period should, of course, include an opportunity for the class to raise questions and challenges and for the presenter to respond. (To reduce students' effort on the initial part of the assignment, so that they have more time to spend on the development of their marketing campaign, limit the assignment to a particular type of product or service: one that is usually interesting to students is *toys.*)

The Professions

Education

Have students analyze and attempt to resolve/solve current issues/problems in the field. An interesting issue concerns whether graduates of accredited education schools should automatically be certified to teach or whether they should also be required to pass a qualifying exam like the National Teacher Examination. An interesting problem is how to overcome shortages of qualified teachers in certain fields, notably science and mathematics.

Engineering

Assign students actual or simulated design problems. (Depending on the program and course, the problems might concern, among other possibilities, products, processes, workplace layout, or workflow.) One approach to this exercise would be to give students specific challenges—"create an original design for a sled," for example; another approach would be to have them seek their own challenges by visiting stores, looking through catalogs, and so on.

Law

Give students plausible "what if" scenarios and have them discuss the implications or consequences involved. For example, ask them what the impact on the legal system would be if it were established conclusively that the tendency to criminal behavior is not attributable to people's choice but is inborn. (A modified form of that view has been advanced by Harvard Professors James Q. Wilson and

Richard Herrnstein in *Crime and Human Nature,* Simon and Schuster, 1985.) Have them decide what changes would have to made in laws themselves and in the criminal justice system, what problems those changes would cause, and how they would recommend that those problems be solved.

Have students develop positions on contemporary legal issues. They might, for instance, be directed to familiarize themselves with legal initiatives (Montana's, for example[12]) prohibiting discrimination by sex or marital status in insurance premiums or policy benefits, then study the arguments on both sides of the issue and decide whether the legal initiatives are sound. Similarly, students might be directed to consider whether gambling or prostitution should be legalized.

Have students work out solutions to current legal problems. For example, the following paragraph, taken from a *Time* magazine article on the prison system, could be given without directions as an advanced holistic thinking assignment:

> [It costs] about $40,000 to build a cell and $16,000 a year to keep it occupied. Despite ambitious construction programs under way in some states ($1.2 billion for 19,000 prison berths in California alone), the crush shows little sign of easing. The inmate nation swells by 73 new members a day. At this rate, a new Folsom [prison] is needed every three weeks.[13]

Interdisciplinary Courses

Many problems and issues touch not one, but several disciplines. One such problem is the impending water shortage. Many experts believe that the world's supply of water for drinking, agriculture, and industry is reaching its limit and will fall short in both affluent and developing countries within the next twenty years.[14] Because it has several aspects—scientific, ethical, technological, and business—this problem would make an excellent exercise for interdisciplinary courses. Naturally, it could be used in other courses as well.

An especially timely interdisciplinary exercise for students is one developed, with other materials, by a team of College of St. Catherine professors: Mary Alice Muellerleile, William Myers, Kenneth Rich, George Rochefort, and Mary Thompson. It directs students to examine the various hypotheses, some quite recent, about the sudden extinction of dinosaurs some 63 million years ago and to explore the possible implications of these theories, as well as the implications of theories about the probable effects of nuclear warfare. The emphasis in this exercise is on students' analysis and judgment, which is required to be shared in class discussions.

The following two exercises, both developed by Alverno College's Jane Halonen, illustrate how everyday problems and issues can, if creatively handled, form the basis of unusual challenges to students' thinking. Halonen uses both exercises in her interdisciplinary course, The Person in the Environment.

A. The year is 1994. Global energy problems have created dramatic changes in our quality of life. Energy supplies have dwindled drastically, and population control is strictly enforced. Only one woman, drawn by lot out of every five, is allowed to have a child. The planet simply cannot sustain more people. In addition, citizens are entitled to live a specific number of years after which time they are expected to submit to euthanasia voluntarily. The length of Allocated Citizen Life (ACL) is exactly your age plus six months.

Each citizen is required to contact the Unitary Governing Board six months prior to the completion of ACL. At this time, you may exercise your option to appeal to the Board for an exemption from ACL requirements of termination if you can provide evidence that your death would create a significant loss for society. Successful appeals allow you to become a Revered Elder with special status and rights in society. If you decide not to appeal, the Board requests a full explanation of your decision. Regardless of the decision you make, your communication to the Board involves evaluating the quality of your existence in a society struggling with declining energy resources and examining society's adaptation to technological changes in light of your own values.

B. The following items are the creations of humans, but they also reflect our attitudes toward ourselves and our relationship with other aspects of the environment. With the other members of your group, read the list and select two items to discuss more fully:

Electric toothbrush

Vaginal spray

Valium (anti-anxiety muscle relaxant)

Remote control television switches

Zoos

Zippers

Drive-up fast-food windows

Panty-hose

Neutron bombs

Discussion Questions:

1. What is the explicit purpose of the item?
2. What attitudes of society are reflected in the development of the item? How might these go beyond the explicit purpose of the item?
3. Does the item reflect a specific "point of view" in its relationship to the environment? How well does this perspective match your own?
4. What would happen if there were an immediately-enforced ban on the continued use of items of this kind and they couldn't be replaced by something similar?
5. Would the world be better off without the item?

Mark E. Blum and Stephen Spangehl have developed an unusual interdisciplinary course at the University of Louisville. Offered in the university's Developmental Education Center, the course aims to develop in students the basic competencies required in all the liberal arts and other curriculums, the competencies of acquiring, producing, and using knowledge. The basic teaching approach is simple; students are given guided practice in using six inquiry methods used in the social sciences. Those methods are behavioral observation, survey, cultural analysis, performance testing, physical-artifactual testing, and simple statistical analysis. Students ask their own questions, collect their own evidence, and reach their own conclusions.[15]

In the special workbook Blum and Spangehl have developed for the course, students proceed through nineteen units of guided practice in inquiry. One example will suggest the structure of the exercises. Unit 4, "Guiding Research with Questions," presents five project ideas the authors note have actually been pursued by social scientists in recent years. After a brief general explanation of the types of questions they ask, the authors provide a specific demonstration with one of the five project ideas—"To study the conditions that are conducive to the development of cooperative behavior in young school children." They identify a number of questions a researcher might ask about this project idea, such as "What kind of behavior is cooperative?" and "What is the best condition in a school to further cooperative behavior?"

After showing students how to develop a comprehensive list of questions with one of the project ideas, the authors direct the students to develop their own lists for each of the other four project ideas. (The project ideas include "To examine the non-verbal behavior of young children as it relates to their decision-making processes" and "To study play from the point of view of the child in terms of the world of meaning he experiences in play situations.")

One worthwhile thinking skills assignment that is applicable in advanced courses in any discipline is to have students focus holistic thinking on the program they are in the process of completing, identifying the areas in which that program can be improved and producing a variety of suggestions for improving it. This assignment not only affords practice for students' thinking skills; it also produces ideas that can benefit the program and the students who subsequently enroll in it. Moreover, it speaks eloquently of the faculty's faith in the efficacy of the thinking process, in the essential integrity of their program, and in the abilities of their students.

FITTING ASSIGNMENTS TO COURSE TEXTBOOKS

The tradition of courses emphasizing only factual information has resulted, not surprisingly, in a parallel textbook tradition. Though some contemporary textbook authors have recognized the value of building challenges to students' thinking into their books, many others have not. As a result, many textbooks are so constructed that nothing more is required of students than memorization of their contents. In some cases, instructors are able to reject such texts and choose competing texts that include numerous challenges to students' thinking skills (some including helpful instructors' manuals). However, when all of the texts in a particular field, or at least all those that are thorough and accurate in their treatment, lack these challenges, instructors are left to their own resources to create thinking exercises and integrate them with textbook lessons. Let us now consider how this can best and most easily be accomplished.

The first step in integrating exercises with textbook content is to evaluate the text from the standpoint of thinking skills instruction, looking within each chapter, at the end of each chapter, and at the end of each section or unit, and determining whether it includes exercises that challenge students' higher order thinking skills. It is not enough that the chapter contains "review questions" that lead students to restate important ideas expressed in the chapter. It should also contain questions and/or exercises that call for the use of the skills of creative thinking, critical thinking, or both. Here, for the sake of comparison, are some examples of both types of questions:

"List the six structural features that all cell membranes have in common."[16] (*Comment:* Calls for remembering only.)

"Laws restricting marriage between close relatives (consangineous marriage) are widespread, the rationale being that such marriages generally lead to an increase in the incidence of genetic defects among offspring. Suppose that you are a carrier (heterozygous) for PKU. If you pick a potential mate at random from the population, what is the probability that he or she would also be a PKU carrier? If you marry your first cousin, do you think he or she would have the same probability of being a PKU carrier as your randomly selected mate? Why?"[17] (*Comment:* Calls for *application* of the chapter material to a new situation, as well as for an explanation of the students' answers.)

" 'To sensitive spirits of all ages, life is filled with cruel contradictions and bitter ironies' (Sec. 2). List some of these contradictions and ironies which you have come across in your own experience."[18] (*Comment:* Calls for application to students' own experience.)

"When we ask whether life has meaning, what precisely are we asking? What is 'meaning'? Is our question essentially logical or psychological? (Or both?) What might be the source(s) of meaning? How would we *know* if life has meaning?"[19] (*Comment:* Calls for investigation and analysis.)

"Pure speculation, but . . . *if* there had been as many women philosophers as men, in what ways do you think Western thought (philosophical and theological) might have been different?"[20] (*Comment:* Calls for speculation or creative imagining.)

If after evaluating your text, you decide it is somewhat deficient in thinking skills challenges, take the time to draft a brief letter to the editor stating the deficiencies you found and explaining that if they were eliminated in the next edition, the book would find wider acceptance among those who stress thinking skills in their courses. (Many publishing houses include the name of the editor on the back of the title page. Where that is not the case, use the appropriate *subject* designation: for example, "Biology Editor.") Publishers and authors are generally responsive to the criticisms they receive, but they can hardly be expected to address those that are left unexpressed.

The next step is to determine where and with what kinds of exercises each chapter should be supplemented. Following are examples of some of the most common opportunities for creating good thinking skills exercises, together with suggestions for capitalizing on them.

SITUATION: The text explains a common error made by novices in the discipline and shows how to correct it, but provides no exercise in correcting it.

EXAMPLE: A philosophy textbook explains that truth is not a subjective phenomenon created by each person, but *what is so* about something, the reality of the matter, as distinguished from what people wish were so, believe to be so, or assert to be so. It also explains that people often use the word *opinion* carelessly, and thus interpret having a right to their opinion as meaning their opinion is necessarily right (correct); it goes on to clarify the distinction between preference, which people should not feel obligated to defend, and judgment, which they should.

EXERCISE SUGGESTION: Construct a dialogue in which one or more of the participants demonstrate a typical misunderstanding of the points explained in the chapter. Require students to identify the error(s) and answer the participant(s), basing their responses on what they learned in the chapter, in this manner.

Read the following dialogue carefully, looking for flaws in thinking. If you find a flaw, identify it and explain why in sufficient detail to persuade someone who has read the passage without seeing it. (If you find two or more flaws, identify and explain your thinking about each.)

CLEM: Can you believe that stuff Chapter 2 says about truth and opinion. I mean, it's a lot of garbage.

CLYDE: I don't know . . . it sort of made sense to me.

CLEM: Come on, man, you've got to be kidding. How can some egghead textbook writer tell *me* what truth is for me? He's himself, not me. How can he see through my eyes or make up my mind? Only I can do that.

CLYDE: But wait a minute. . . .

CLEM: Wait, nothing. You're taken in by all the words, man. Like that stuff about opinion. This is a democracy, isn't it? Maybe in Russia the Politburo can say which opinion is right, but not here. My opinion is as good as anyone else's. It says so right in the Constitution.[21]

SITUATION: The text briefly describes historical situations, but does not discuss their causes or effects.

EXAMPLE: The following passage:

Evangelicalism drove many women of the Victorian leisured class out of their homes to do acts of charity for the poor. Visiting the poor in their homes, to bring comfort, food, and offers of work or of medical care for their children became a normal practice for thousands of women, especially as the increasing distance between the homes of the poor and the wealthy ended the daily contacts between classes that had been common in the eighteenth century. These often-criticized Lady Bountifuls also gave financial support to a large number of societies established for the benefit of the poor, and especially of poor women, such as the Society for the Suppression of Vice or the Invalid Asylum for Respectable Families. Several women with great personal drive, and often also personal wealth, undertook what were little less than public crusades on behalf of chosen causes, and became forces in public life as experts and advocates. Mary Carpenter fought for the widespread extension of the "ragged," or slum schools, to help save juvenile delinquents from the almost inevitable drift into a life of crime; and she argued, in *Reformatory Schools for the Children of the Perishing and Dangerous Classes and for Juvenile Offenders,* the revolutionary view that child offenders should not receive the same penal treatment as adults. Angela Burdett-Coults, the heiress to a banking fortune, worked with Dickens in aiding the ragged schools, set up the Destitute Children's Society, and, most important of all, was one of the principal forces behind the founding, in 1884, of the Society for the Prevention of Cruelty to Children. Octavia Hill saw the solution to the poor's problems in improved housing, especially for the so-called undeserving poor like the alcoholics. Hill began purchasing houses in which she could accommodate and supervise the most derelict cases, and showed her true Victorian spirit by organizing regular visits to them by rich ladies, in the genuine belief that the poor would be morally improved by regular contact with women of "higher standards." However condescending these attitudes may appear, in the late nineteenth century the unpaid work of thousands of members of Hill's Charity Organization Society undoubtedly helped make the lives of even more thousands of poor women tolerable during the infancy of state assistance programs.[22]

EXERCISE SUGGESTION: Have students choose one of the situations identified with a Victorian crusader and investigate the specific conditions she encountered. Then have them determine (1) the historical cause(s) of those conditions, and (2) the immediate and long-term effects of her achievement. Direct students to support their assertions.

SITUATION: The textbook presents a thought-provoking quote, but does not build upon it with an exercise.
EXAMPLE: In a history textbook, nineteenth century French author Alexis de Tocqueville is quoted thus: "Democracy does not always perish from weakness and inability to act. It is not in the nature of a democratic power to lack material means, but rather moral force, stability, and skill."[23]
EXERCISE SUGGESTION: Have students consider to what extent, if any, the condition of the United States in the 1980s bears out De Tocqueville's observation, and be prepared to defend their views in class discussion.

SITUATION: The textbook presents an interesting contrast, yet does not direct students to ponder the reasons for it.

EXAMPLE: The following passage:

In May 1918, again with Wilson's approval, Congress passed the Sedition Act, which made it a crime even to speak against the purchase of war bonds or to "utter, print, write, or publish any disloyal, profane, scurrilous, or abusive language" about the government, the Constitution, or the uniform of the army or navy. Mere criticism became cause for arrest and imprisonment. Socialist periodicals like *The Masses* were suppressed, and Eugene V. Debs was sentenced to ten years in prison for making an antiwar speech. Ricardo Flores Magon, an anarchist, was sentenced to twenty years in jail for publishing a statement criticizing Wilson's Mexican policy, an issue that had nothing to do with the war.

While legislation to prevent sabotage and control subversives was justifiable, these laws went far beyond what was necessary to protect the national interest. Some local officials used them to muzzle liberal opinion. Citizens were jailed for suggesting that the draft law was unconstitutional and for criticizing private organizations like the Red Cross and the YMCA. One woman was sent to prison for writing: "I am for the people, and the government is for the profiteers." Conscientious objectors were frequently reviled; labor organizers were attacked by mobs.

The Supreme Court upheld the constitutionality of the Espionage Act in *Schenck* v. *United States* (1919), a case involving a man who had mailed circulars to draftees urging them to refuse to report for induction into the army. Free speech has its limits, Justice Oliver Wendell Holmes, Jr., explained. No one has the right to cry *Fire!* in a crowded theater. When there is a "clear and present danger" that a particular statement would threaten the national interest, it can be repressed by law. In peacetime Schenck's circulars would be permissible, but not in time of war. The "clear and present danger" doctrine did not prevent judges and juries from interpreting the Espionage and Sedition acts broadly, and while in many instances their decisions were overturned by higher courts, this usually did not occur until after the war. The wartime hysteria far exceeded anything that happened in Great Britain and France, where the threat to national survival was truly acute. In 1916 the French novelist Henri Barbusse published *Le Feu (Under Fire)*, a graphic account of the horrors and purposelessness of trench warfare. In one chapter Barbusse described a pilot flying over the trenches on a Sunday, observing French and German soldiers at Mass in the open fields, each worshiping the same God. His message, like that of the German Erich Maria Remarque's *Im Westen nichts Neues (All Quiet on the Western Front),* written *after* the conflict, was unmistakably antiwar. Yet *Le Feu* circulated freely in France, even winning the coveted Prix Goncourt.[24]

EXERCISE SUGGESTION: Have students explore the situation in both France and the United States at the time in question, consider various possible explanations for the difference in their reactions to the exercise of free speech, and decide which of those reasons is most plausible. In addition, have students state their view of which nation behaved more reasonably and why.

SITUATION: The textbook mentions an important incident only briefly, in passing, and does not challenge students to think further about it.
EXAMPLE: The following passage:

> While World War II affected the American people far more drastically than World War I had, it produced much less intolerance and fewer examples of the repression of individual freedom of opinion. . . . The only flagrant example of intolerance was the relocation of the West Coast Japanese in internment camps in the interior of the country. About 110,000 Americans of Japanese ancestry were rounded up, simply because of the unjustified fear that they might be disloyal. The Supreme Court upheld the relocation order in the case of *Korematsu* v. *United States* (1944), but in *Ex parte Endo* it forbade the internment of loyal Japanese-American citizens. Unfortunately the latter decision was not handed down until December, 1944.[25]

EXERCISE SUGGESTION: Have students investigate the internment incident, studying the arguments advanced at the time and deciding precisely where the errors lay in those that prevailed. In addition, have them examine the alternatives to internment available at the time and decide which would have been preferable and why.

SITUATION: The textbook discusses a significant difference between two things, but doesn't challenge students to apply their thinking skills and analyze the difference further.
EXAMPLE: A marriage and family textbook spends several pages discussing the feudalistic Japanese practice of families choosing mates for young people rather than letting them choose for themselves.[26]
EXERCISE SUGGESTION: Have students consider how a Japanese person brought up in the feudalistic system would likely react to contemporary American marriage practices such as dating and cohabitation. Further, have them explain to such a person the rationale for American practices, admitting (where appropriate) the disadvantages in those practices and suggesting what changes would make for happier marriages and more stable family life.

SITUATION: The textbook traces the origin and development of a concept, but does not have students apply creative or critical thinking skills to the information presented.
EXAMPLE: A marriage and family textbook details the development of the concepts of childhood and adolescence over the last four hundred years.[27]
EXERCISE SUGGESTION: Have students determine what differences would

be found in the various agencies of society—including the family, the church, the state, the education system, the entertainment industry, business and the professions, and the media—if society's perspective on young people had not changed since the middle ages. In addition, have students decide which of those differences would be beneficial to young people and which detrimental.

IMPORTANT CONSIDERATIONS IN DEVELOPING MATERIALS

In most institutions it would be a mistake for instructors who are changing their courses from a lecture focus to a thinking-activity focus to assume that students have all the requisite skills to perform competently. Nor will the skills that need reinforcement consist only of thinking skills. Many students lack basic communication and research skills as well, including composition skills, speaking and listening skills, and interviewing skills. Before such students can be expected to do homework and classwork assignments adequately, they must have an opportunity to learn or refine these basic skills.

If the only way of introducing basic skills were to devote classroom time to them, instructors outside English courses would be justified in rejecting responsibility for doing so because accepting responsibility would be tantamount to abandoning their primary course objective—the presentation of their own subject matter. Fortunately, there are other ways that permit instructors to emphasize basic skills without devoting any time to them in class or in regular homework assignments. We will consider three such means—referral to the campus learning center, use of the campus library's reserve service, and the development of handouts that explain and illustrate what is expected of students.

Referral to the School or College Learning Center   Many schools and most colleges have a learning center or its equivalent, such as a developmental learning laboratory or a tutorial service. You should consider conferring with the learning center staff, explaining the specific communication and research skills students need for your course and discussing how the learning center might help remedy students' deficiencies. The most common approaches, in addition to offering credit and noncredit developmental courses, are to offer several-session skills workshops and walk-in tutorial services. In addition, you may wish to provide learning center staff with an outline or a more detailed treatment of the *thinking* skills you will be introducing or reinforcing in your course, so that students are able to obtain assistance even at times when you are unavailable.

Use of the School or College Library's Reserve Service   For research skills such as conducting materials searches and interviewing, as well as for the skills of listening, questioning, and debating, students will seldom need special workshops or tutoring. Reading a book, a pamphlet, or an article that explains the skill in question and offers suggestions for mastering it will usually be sufficient. You should either make such explanatory material available to students or let them know where and how to obtain it. (If you are unfamiliar with the print and nonprint materials commercially available or on hand in your campus library, consult the faculty in the appropriate departments or librarians, respectively.)

The Development of Explanatory/Illustrative Handouts   This means of emphasizing basic skills should be used even if the other two means are not deemed necessary. Thinking skills instruction is new to many students, calling as it does for *applying* what is learned and not merely committing it to memory; therefore, they may be confused or intimidated by it. They will likely have many questions, and the more of those questions you anticipate and answer on paper—once, for all students—the more time you will save in class and in student conferences.

The specific content of explanatory/illustrative handouts will naturally differ from course to course, but all effective handouts have at least these qualities in common: they eliminate confusion for students and help them understand important principles, concepts, and approaches; and they assist students in applying what they have learned to problems and issues in the course.

James Bell, Professor of Psychology at Howard Community College in Maryland, has developed an impressive assortment of handouts for his courses, which include Logic & Critical Thinking, General Psychology, and Advanced General Psychology. Space limitations prevent including the handouts here, but the following brief descriptions will suggest the importance of their contribution to students' learning.

In Logic and Critical Thinking, Bell provides students with a study guide to each of two course texts. (In most cases the authors do not provide study guides, so Bell writes his own.) In addition, he provides a special study guide for each of the several films he shows in class; these guides help students prepare themselves to interpret the films skillfully. He also provides a fifteen-page "Idea Notebook," the purpose of which he explains to students as follows:

> Your idea notebook is an opportunity for you to record your ideas and thinking related to this course. Besides noting interesting ideas, evaluating ideas, and applying what you are learning, also record your reflections about your own thinking processes. To increase what you learn from the experiences of this course, include in your Idea Notebook description, analysis, evaluation, interpretation, and reflection.

Bell's "Idea Notebook" not only details his requirements for students' notebooks, but also provides page after page of examples from the notebooks of former students. Thus it goes beyond merely telling students what to do, but demonstrates too, in a way that encourages them to meet the challenge of the notebook creatively.

In General Psychology, Bell uses a fourteen-page handout entitled "Learning to Get Better Grades in High School and College"; a fourteen-page "Group Discussion Manual," which includes a discussion of the psychological findings on small group dynamics and details a simple procedure for students to use in small group discussions in the course; a forty-seven page booklet entitled "Getting the Facts," which provides a clear and rather detailed discussion of the difference between scientific and nonscientific evidence and an introduction to four common research strategies; and several shorter handouts, including one on the scholarly observation of television and one on brainstorming.

In Advanced General Psychology, Bell uses an eight-page handout explaining some advanced considerations in the critical evaluation of sources and an ingenious thirty-four-page project booklet on the subject of punishment in human society. The latter is a carefully sequenced series of guided assignments that lead the students through a rather rigorous examination of the subject by means of a critical study of source material. Bell skillfully alternates between showing students how to proceed (by performing some tasks himself) and directing students to proceed on their own.

Instructors who invest the time to prepare such teaching aids are certainly to be commended, particularly when they do so while carrying the typically heavy elementary or secondary school teaching load. Yet it should be noted that though preparing teaching aids takes considerable time, having teaching aids available saves a significant amount of conference time *year after year* and improves teaching effectiveness.

It would be a mistake to think that students at every grade level or level of proficiency require the degree of assistance educators like Bell provide. Yet if the half dozen or so comprehensive studies of education that have been completed in recent years are to be believed, a great many students do require it, some of them desperately. Thus the success of your students in developing thinking skills in your course may depend, in large part, on the amount and quality of the assistance you provide.

APPLICATIONS

1. Consult the sources discussed at the beginning of this chapter ("Finding Materials") and find as many materials as you can that are relevant to thinking instruction in your discipline.
2. Decide which of the materials you found in application 1 lend themselves to one or more of the basic exercises discussed in the chapter ("Adapting Basic Exercises"). Then create one or more exercises using those materials.
3. Review the section of the chapter entitled "Exercise Ideas Across the Curriculum" and identify those that apply to (or can be adapted for) your discipline. Determine how you would use (or adapt) them.
4. Review the section of the chapter entitled "Fitting Assignments to Course Textbooks." Next, select a textbook in your field that is so constructed as to require of students little more than memorization; then design one or more thinking skills assignments as demonstrated in the chapter.

chapter 8

ASSESSING
STUDENT PROGRESS

The term *assessment,* quite fashionable now in education, obviously implies evaluation of some kind. However, unless the writer or speaker explains exactly what is being evaluated, by whom, and for what purpose, the term can create considerable confusion. The major varieties of assessment are as follows:

1. Evaluation of students' levels of proficiency by faculty (or administration) to determine course placement.
2. Periodic evaluation of students' performance in a course by the teacher to determine the extent of their progress.
3. Statewide evaluation of students' performance to develop comparative statistics on educational progress and establish a benchmark against which individual institutions can measure their students' performance.
4. Evaluation of teaching effectiveness by administrators to determine which instructors are succeeding in developing students' knowledge and skills.

The focus of this chapter is on the first two forms of assessment. The third will be examined briefly. (As we will see, the state of the art of thinking skills testing is not far enough advanced to permit the fourth kind of assessment to be made fairly.)

Assessment within a course should reflect the objectives of the course. In the case of assessment of thinking skills, it should therefore reflect the dispositions associated with effective thinking, the habits and skills of creative thinking, and the habits and skills of critical thinking, as detailed in Chapter 4. Moreover, it should reflect students' proficiency in combining those dispositions and skills in problem solving and issue analysis. If the problems and issues contained in the instrument reflect the important concerns of the particular discipline, the assessment will measure, not some generalized competency far removed from the primary aims of the course, but rather the higher level competencies in the specific discipline.

We have noted that teaching thinking skills in a course in which they were previously neglected means, essentially, changing methods and materials. Assessment of thinking skills demands a similar change—a change in approach and, in the case of testing, in the design of tests. Tests that have been designed to measure the amount of factual information students have learned have little value in measuring dispositions and skills; it is possible for students to be able to recite principles and explain concepts with precision and yet be unable to *apply* those principles and concepts to particular cases. This is not to say that knowledge is unimportant—in order to apply a principle or approach, students must first understand it—but only to stress that *the principal focus of thinking skills assessment must be on application.*

EVALUATING HOMEWORK ASSIGNMENTS

The first kind of assessment we will discuss is homework evaluation; that is, evaluation of the kinds of assignments detailed in Chapters 6 and 7. One of your paramount concerns as a teacher, a concern second in importance only to effective learning, is efficiency. As every serious study of education in recent years has shown, the average teacher at every level of education has too many students to do an effective job of teaching, particularly in light of the fact that many students have serious problems in basic skills. Adding thinking skills to a course not only makes the educational process more meaningful to students and more rewarding to teachers; it also creates more work for teachers. Skills can be acquired only through regular, guided practice, which means more papers for teachers to correct. An efficient method of evaluating homework is therefore imperative.* Following are guidelines for developing such a method:

Prepare directions for students to follow in doing homework assignments.

Make the directions as thorough as possible, explaining exactly how you expect students to respond and detailing the kinds of difficulties they are likely to encounter and how they can best overcome them. Where appropriate, include one or more examples of effective student responses with annotations explaining what makes them effective. In addition, state exactly what criteria will be used in grading student homework. This approach may seem too time-consuming to be practical; in reality, it will save considerable time. To begin with, it is a one-time effort that yields a quality handout that can be used, with occasional

---

*An efficient method of evaluating will not by itself solve the problem of excessive teaching loads. For further discussion of this problem, see Chapter 9.

modification, for years. Then, too, it significantly reduces the chance that students will be confused (or feign confusion) in doing homework, a reduction that translates to a considerable saving in time spent explaining the same points over and over to individual students. Finally, it enables students to form the habit of overcoming difficulties themselves, instead of depending on you to do so for them.

> *Wherever possible, require a response–format that facilitates evaluation.*

Evaluating time can be reduced considerably if student responses lend themselves to scanning; in just seconds, a trained evaluator can get an impression of the overall quality of the response and decide which parts of it bear closer inspection because of their unusual brevity or other characteristics. If you have four classes, a saving of a minute or two per paper—and even greater time-savings are possible—can amount to a saving of *several hours per assignment.* Two effective response formats which can be easily adapted to fit a variety of circumstances are presented on the next three pages.

1. The format on page 182 was first recommended more than thirty years ago for use in social science courses[1]
2. The format shown on page 183 was developed by Sam Postlethwait of Purdue University, the originator of audio-tutorial instruction, for use in large lecture classes. As explained in Chapter 5, Postlethwait confined his lectures to 30 minutes, leaving the final 20 minutes of the period for students to reflect on the lecture and complete this form, which he and his teaching assistants would subsequently grade. (The explanation headed "Writing a Summary," shown on page 184, appears on the back of the form.)

> *Streamline grading practices for routine assignments.*

Streamlining may be accomplished in any (or all) of three ways. One way is by simplifying the grading system. The most common simplification is assigning "check" if the work is done acceptably, "check plus" if it is done exceptionally well, and "check minus" if it is deficient in some respect. Numerical equivalents of, say, 75, 90, and 60, respectively, might be used. For grading students' lecture analyses, Postlethwait developed a variation of this approach: a three-point system (one point if the assignment is submitted, one point if the answers to questions one and four correspond, and one point if the student has answered question five) that enables a professor and his assistants to evaluate hundreds of papers in a reasonable length of time.

A second way of streamlining grading practices is by grading batches of, say, three or four assignments rather than each assignment individually. The obvious disadvantage of this approach is that students receive less feedback about the quality of their work, but that will not be a serious problem if the explanations in handouts are clear and complete enough that students know exactly what is

A Short Answer Form for Evaluating
Critical Thinking in Social Science

Name _____

Date _____

You will be given an opportunity to read and study a passage of social science writing, and to give your interpretation of it. Read through all the questions to see what is expected of you before beginning.

In the various questions which follow, you will be asked to examine the selection from several points of view. You may answer the questions in any order. There will probably be more things to note under some questions than under others, but you should make your coverage as complete as possible.

1. List any stereotypes or clichés which you can find in the selection.

2. List any examples you can find of emotional or biased statements in the selection.

3. Does the selection present unverifiable data as though they were facts? If so, list them.

4. What is the main point in this selection?

5. Are the facts which are presented in the selection as supporting the author's position pertinent to his argument? Explain.

6. What additional information is needed before passing judgment upon the author's position? Or, do you think enough data have been provided?

7. Is the presentation consistent? If not, list examples of inconsistencies.

8. Judging the selection as a whole, what are some of the ideas and beliefs which the author takes for granted?

9. What thoughts and feelings on the general subject did you have before you read the passage which may have influenced your reaction to the selection?

10. What are *your own* conclusions with respect to the main point of the selection?

[In reproducing this form for student use, space should be left between questions for students to write their responses.]

YOUR NAME_____ CODE NUMBER ____ TAB DAY____ TAB TIME____

YOUR TAB INSTRUCTOR'S NAME _____

THE NAME OF THE ARTICLE, MOVIE, OR LECTURE IS:

_____

It was written or presented by _____

1. Write what *you* think is the major question being addressed by the lecturer or article. (Write your answer as a question, followed by a question mark.)

_____

_____

_____

2. Where did the author get the information for this presentation? Check one, or more, as applicable:

_____ Experience   _____ Literature Survey _____ Other

_____ Scientific experiments_____ Personal Opinion_____

3. Do you think the presentation is believable? Briefly state why.

4. Summarize the article, focusing on what you see as the major question. Use facts to develop the ideas needed to answer the question you have written.

5. Give one example where this information has some relevance to your life in immediate, day-to-day situations (preferably a single situation). Be specific—give a personal and practical example.

WRITING A SUMMARY

Ask yourself, "What is the purpose of this information in the lecture or article?" It is important that you develop skills in detecting the central questions and ideas of an article, movie, or presentation. Learning how to be critical is a necessary part of personal and scientific endeavor.

1. **Major Question**

   A quantity of information from a lecture or an article can include answers to many questions. Most presentations concentrate on one major issue. Try to discover the issue and write what you perceive as the most fundamental question being addressed. Which of the following is a major question:

   a. Can herbarium collections be used to detect plants which are potentially useful to humans?

   b. Herbarium collections can be used to find new medicines and possibly new food crops.

   Statement (b), of course, is a conclusion, not a question. Statement (b) follows from Statement (a) after (a) has been put to the test.

2. **Source of Information**

   Humans have a tendency to accept statements because they sound authoritative or because they are written in magazines and newspapers (would they lie?). Paying attention to where information comes from is important in developing critical skills. Develop the habit of evaluating the source of information. Not all sources are equal.

3. **Believability**

   The nature of the source of information has a bearing on whether the author's conclusions are believable or are to be trusted. A presentation based on personal opinion is not as trustworthy as one based on several well designed experiments, or a review of other people's work.

4. **Summary**

   1. Keep your focus on the major questions and the ideas that follow from it.
   2. Use facts to support the answer to the question; don't use them "because they are there."
   3. Build the rough outline of your summary before you have to write it, not as you write it. Relate the different parts to the whole intent of the presentation.
   4. Try to detect the "key" elements of the presentation; words or ideas around which illustrations and facts seem to center. Use them in building your summary.
   5. Remember why you are writing the summary in the first place. Keep your writing on the right track; the one you started on. *Focus on answering the major question.*

5. **Application**

   Which of the following are *specific, personal* applications?

   a. Plants are necessary for humankind; they give us energy and nutrients from the soil.

   *b. The toast I ate for breakfast was mostly wheat endosperm.

   c. I learned that you can go to a herbarium and find out a lot about the plants that can be eaten and used for medicine.

   USE: I . . . me . . . my . . .   AVOID: I learned . . . now I know . . . you . . . we . . . humankind . . . people.

   *The best answer.

expected of them. If weaker students need more frequent evaluation, their needs can be accommodated while maintaining the streamlined approach with the rest of the class. There is an additional advantage to this approach; it enables you to see recurring errors and problems in students' work more clearly. Performance patterns are more discernible when several samples of work are examined than when a single sample is.*

A third way of streamlining grading practices is by using an evaluation sheet with explanations of common deficiencies and suggestions for overcoming them. One or two check marks on such a sheet, which is then attached to the student's paper, can thus provide an evaluation that would ordinarily take ten or fifteen minutes to write out. If an occasional paper contains an unusual deficiency not covered in the printed comments, you can add special comments.

Some teachers resist using streamlining approaches because they find them too impersonal. This view is understandable but unrealistic. Unless students have regular practice—indeed, much more practice than most teachers can provide under normal circumstances—they can have little hope of mastering the art of thinking. Streamlining grading practices is the only feasible way of providing that practice. You may wish to explain these facts to students as the reasons you will not be lavishing time on every paper, perhaps adding the promise that occasionally you will grade a paper in a less impersonal way.

EVALUATING PERFORMANCE IN CLASS DISCUSSION

Evaluating performance in class discussion is, at best, a difficult task. The most reasonable measure of performance in class would seem to be how many relevant contributions students make, but in this case what seems reasonable is not always fair. Some students are naturally more extroverted than others and thus are more ready to volunteer their ideas and ask questions than are the class introverts. Others, though they sit mute most of the time, can, by the quality of their attention to the instructor and other students, make a positive contribution to the class. To reward the voluble students and punish the reserved, therefore, seems as much an evaluation of genetic constitution as of performance.

Though there are no *easy* answers to the question of how to evaluate class discussion, there are answers. For example, you can have students take turns making formal presentations on the problems and issues in the course (for that matter, even on routine homework) and grade those presentations instead of students' unsolicited comments. The presentations need not take up a lot of time—two or three minutes will be sufficient in most cases. In addition, you can assign individual students special roles on a rotating basis—roles like that of discussion moderator and devil's advocate, the latter responsible for challenging presenters' remarks—and grade them on their performance. These approaches

---

*Note: Not collecting homework can make students lax about completing it on time. Therefore, if this approach is used, homework should be collected when it is due, even though it will not be evaluated then. Some instructors find it helpful to make a checkmark in their grade books at the time the work is submitted (a process that takes approximately ten minutes for a class of twenty-five or thirty students), and then file the work in students' individual folders for eventual grading.

offer an additional benefit in that they shift the burden of class activity from you to the students and thus free you to coach and guide the class.

If the nature of the course does not permit such approaches to be used, consider making this simple adjustment in your grading practice—instead of grading on the *quantity* of students' contributions, grade on the *quality* of their contributions and the quality of their attention to other contributors.

CHOOSING A COMMERCIAL TEST

The fact that the teaching of thinking has been advocated for almost a century and accepted as an educational imperative by an increasing number of educators for almost a decade might lead one to expect thinking skills testing to be highly refined and numerous commercial tests to be available. Such is not the case. To begin with, creative thinking has attracted the attention of an entirely different group of testing experts (indeed, a different group of scholars in general) than critical thinking. As a result, no one has developed a test that measures both creative and critical thinking! Even worse, as Robert Ennis, a director of the Illinois Thinking Project, and a leading author of thinking tests, reports, there are as yet "no fully comprehensive *critical* thinking tests [emphasis added]."[2] Similar criticism has been made by others about creative thinking tests.[3]

This is not to say that the tests that are available have no merit. It is merely to underline a *caveat* that you can ignore only at your own and your students' risk, as well as to state the challenge that continues to confront the testing experts. Following is a partial list of thinking tests currently available.

Creative Thinking

Creativity Tests for Children (1971–1976). Ten tests by J. P. Guilford and others. Sheridan Psychological Services. Grades 4–6. Measures "divergent [idea] production abilities."

Consequences. By P. R. Christensen and others. Sheridan Psychological Services, Inc. Junior high through college and adult levels. Measures ideational fluency and originality.

Flanagan Aptitude Classification Test No. 18–Ingenuity. By J. C. Flanagan. Science Research Associates. High school. Measures creativity or inventiveness.

New Uses. By R. Hoepfner and J. P. Guilford. Sheridan Psychological Services, Inc. High school, college, and adult levels. A measure of the structure-of-intellect ability of convergent production of semantic transformations.

Pertinent Questions. By R. M. Berger and J. P. Guilford. Sheridan Psychological Services, Inc. High school, college, adult levels. Measures conceptual foresight—the ability to see implications and consequences and to make predictions.

Seeing Problems. By P. R. Merrifield and J. P. Guilford. Sheridan Psychological Services, Inc. Junior high school through college and adult levels. Measures awareness of semantic implications.

Torrance Tests of Creative Thinking (1966). Two tests by E. Paul Torrance. Personnel Press, Inc. Grades K through graduate school. Measures creativity verbally and visually.

Utility Test. By R. C. Wilson and others. Sheridan Psychological Services. High school, college, and adult levels. Measures both ideational fluency and spontaneous flexibility in conceiving of new and unusual uses for familiar objects.

Critical Thinking

Basic Skills for Critical Thinking (1979). Five forms by Gary E. McCuen. Greenhaven Press, Inc. Grade: High school. Includes source of information, primary and secondary sources, fact and opinion, prejudice and reasons, stereotypes, ethnocentrism, library card catalogue, and *Reader's Guide to Periodical Literature.*

Cornell Class-Reasoning Test, Form X (1964). By Robert H. Ennis and others. Illinois Critical Thinking Project. Grades: 4–14. Seventy-two items each containing a premise asserting a class relationship, such as "No A's are B's."

Cornell Critical Thinking Test, Level X (1985). By Robert H. Ennis and Jason Millman. Midwest Publications. Grades: 4–14. Measures induction, credibility, observation, deduction, and assumption-identification.

Cornell Critical Thinking Test, Level Z (1985). By Robert H. Ennis and Jason Millman. Midwest Publications. Advanced or gifted high school students, college students, and other adults. Measures induction, credibility, prediction and experimental planning, fallacies (especially equivocation), deduction, definition, and assumption-identification.

Ennis-Weir Critical Thinking Essay Test (1985). By Robert H. Ennis and Eric Weir. Midwest Publications. Grades: 7 through college. Measures getting the point, seeing reasons and assumptions, stating one's point, offering good reasons, seeing other possibilities, and responding to/avoiding numerous logical fallacies.

Logical Reasoning (1955). By Alfred F. Hertzka and J. P. Guilford. Sheridan Psychological Services. High school and college students, adults. Measures facility with class reasoning, such as "No A's are B's."

New Jersey Test of Reasoning Skills (1983). By Virginia Shipman. IAPC, Test Division, Montclair State College. Grades: 4 through college. Measures syllogistic reasoning, assumption-identification, induction, good reasons, and kind and degree.

Ross Test of Higher Cognitive Processes (1976). By John D. Ross and Catherine M. Ross. Academic Therapy Publications. Grades: 4 through college. Measures verbal analogies, deduction, assumption-identification, word relationships, sentence sequencing, interpreting answers to questions, information sufficiency and relevance in mathematics problems, and analysis of attributes of complex stick figures.

Test on Appraising Observations (1983). By Stephen P. Norris and Ruth King. Institute for Educational Research and Development, Memorial University of Newfoundland. Junior high school through college. Measures ability to compare statements for their believability.

Watson-Glaser Critical Thinking Appraisal (1980). By Goodwin Watson and Edward M. Glaser. The Psychological Corporation. Grades: 9 through adulthood. Measures deduction, assumption-identification, deduction, conclusion-logically-following-beyond-reasonable-doubt, and argument evaluation.

To those who are considering adopting a commercial test for use in their institutions, Edward Glaser offers these suggestions:[4]

Read a comprehensive review of the tests available. He cites in particular, Bruce L. Stewart's *Testing for Critical Thinking: A Review of the Resources,* Rational Thinking Report Number 2, available from ERIC in either hardcopy or microfiche, Ed 183 588. (Note that this source covers neither creative thinking nor holistic thinking. As we noted earlier, there are no tests of holistic thinking yet available.)

Obtain a specimen set of each test and accompanying manual that seems appropriate for the particular grade level in question.

Evaluate the specimen sets/manuals to determine each test's relevance to the particular teaching situation. There are four specific areas of relevance to be evaluated: (a) relevance to the knowledge, skills, and attitudes in the objectives of the particular course or program; (b) norms and their pertinence for comparison with the categories of students to be tested*; (c) time required for completion on a power (not speed) basis; and (d) reading level and ease of scoring.

After deciding tentatively which test is most appropriate, take the test yourself and score it. This step provides additional evaluation of the test's suitability.

Before making a final decision concerning which commercial thinking test, if any, to adopt, reflect on the disadvantage Stephen Norris, of Newfoundland's Memorial University, has found in such tests. He writes:

Although most of these tests provide somewhat realistic situations, they are to a large degree sterile. In order to construct situations in which particular aspects

---

*Glaser adds that though such norms are desirable, they may not be essential. It may be sufficient that the test items are relevant to the course/program objectives and a baseline performance can be reliably established for each student, permitting a measure of the student's progress following instruction.

of critical thinking ability could be examined one at a time, a good deal of abstracting from the real world and idealizing of situations had to be done. So, if the interest of the evaluation is for an indication of critical thinking ability in use, that is, of students' ability to use critical thinking in real world situations, then something other than critical thinking tests ought to be used.[5]

Though this comment explicitly mentions only critical thinking tests, it may be applied to creative thinking tests as well.

DESIGNING YOUR OWN TESTS

Even if a commercial test proves suitable for diagnostic purposes, you will still have to design your own unit, mid-term, and final tests. It is therefore important for you to understand the kinds of tests commonly used and their suitability as measures of thinking skills.

The Objective Test

The objective test, whose main questions are multiple-choice, true/false, and fill-in, is the most widely used type of test in American education and the dominant type in commercial testing. Its popularity, however, should not be interpreted as proof of its superiority to other kinds of tests. In fact, for decades many respected educators have presented compelling arguments that the objective test has serious defects that not only fail to enhance students' intellectual development, but in many cases actually retard it. Those defects, which are likely to be especially pernicious in thinking skills instruction, are as follows:[6]

1. The objective test denies creative students the opportunity to demonstrate their creativity. The choices of answers open to them are so severely restricted, especially in true/false questions, that even where creativity is possible, it is punished. Sidney Parnes cites the example of a third-grader confronted by this question: "Passing the corner was a (steam) (team) (stream) of horses." The single right answer was, of course, "team"; thus a child who was attracted by the more poetic "stream" would be penalized for choosing it.[7]
2. It penalizes those who perceive subtleties unnoticed by most people. Perceptive students may, for example, see the need for a qualification which none of the multiple-choice possibilities express, so in answering, they are forced to deny their perception.
3. It is apt to be superficial and even dishonest, in that its questions are often constructed to be artificially difficult, with contrived ambiguity.
4. It often invites intellectual dishonesty in students by degenerating into a game in which students try to guess which answer the instructor wants rather than determine which answer is best.
5. It denies students practice in disciplined expression. Making check marks and circling choices offers no opportunity to develop the skills demanded of educated people in business and the professions—the skills of sorting out, organizing, and communicating ideas.
6. It penalizes students who do not share (or correctly guess) the test-

maker's frame of reference. As Robert Ennis explains, "Much depends on the background assumptions that a test-taker brings to a test. Current multiple-choice tests penalize a student who thinks well, but brings different background assumptions to a test."

7. It is not able to measure the thinking *dispositions* that influence the way students respond to problems and issues because, in Robert Ennis' words, "the person knows that he or she is being tested and might deliberately exhibit the appropriate behavior without having the underlying disposition."

8. It yields no information about one of the most important considerations of thinking instruction—how students arrive at their conclusions. "For most objective critical thinking tests," Stephen Norris notes, "such knowledge of subjects' thinking processes is not available. All that is available is the conclusions of their thinking."

If these defects of the objective test are well known, how is it that the test has remained so popular? Why haven't educators scrapped it in favor of types that enhance, rather than retard, students' intellectual development? There are a number of reasons. To begin with, the objective test is related in form to the test of which our society has long been enamoured, the intelligence test.* Moreover, like the intelligence test, the objective test is easy and economical to score, as Robert Ennis explains in comparing the grading efficiency of his own critical thinking essay test with that of standard multiple-choice tests. (The grading time he claims for his essay test is undoubtedly *less* than the grading time for many instructor-made essay tests.) Ennis writes:

> The economy achievable by multiple-choice testing is considerable. Grading the only standardized essay critical thinking test of which I am aware, *The Ennis-Weir Critical Thinking Essay Test,* takes a skilled and trained grader about six minutes on the average. Consequently 500 tests take about 3,000 minutes (fifty hours) of the time of a specialist in critical thinking with training in grading this test. On the other hand a modern test scoring machine can grade answer sheets at the rate of 10,000 per hour, and can be operated by a person who is not skilled in critical thinking (but does know how to run the machine). So the same number of tests (500) can be graded by the machine in three minutes. Hence the rate of grading one of the multiple-choice critical thinking tests is about 1,000 times that of the rate of grading the essay test. The cost of the personnel doing the machine grading is considerably less, although the machine itself is expensive. For purposes of rough approximation let us assume that the cost per hour of the operator plus machine is about the same as the cost per hour of the skilled and trained critical thinking essay grader. Under this assumption the multiple-choice method is economically superior by a factor of 1,000.[9]

Another reason for the popularity of the objective test lies in its name. The objective test is assumed to be more objective, more scientific, and therefore more

---

*According to creativity researcher E. Paul Torrance, Alfred Binet acknowledged the importance of such qualities as inventiveness and imaginativeness, but that understanding did not find expression in his intelligence test because (Torrance speculates) "it is quite likely that he was blinded to the inclusion of measures of this type because he was committed to a mental-age concept of mental development and such measures have never fit [that concept] very well."[8]

reliable than the essay test, which is scored by means of someone's "subjective" judgment. Is this assumption warranted? Ennis suggests it is not:

> There are often-unnoticed subjective features of multiple-choice critical thinking tests that are comparable to the subjective features of the open-ended approaches. For example the decision to include an item with its accompanying keyed answer is subjective. In making this decision one is judging that the student will understand the item as intended, that the keyed answer is correct for the level of sophistication desired, that the item tests for significant matters, etc.
>
> The interpretation of the resulting score is subjective as well. It means nothing by itself to say that someone got a score of 40 out of 52 on the Cornell Level 2 test, for example. One must "subjectively" judge how important it is that this score relates as it does to others' performance. Usually one must judge this not by looking at the items, but perhaps by looking at the credentials of the authors and publisher, people who recommend the test, and people who do not recommend it. Furthermore in mastery or competency testing one must "subjectively" judge what shall be the criterion for mastery or competency.
>
> So the "objective" label given to multiple-choice tests is somewhat misleading.[10]

Yet another reason for the popularity of the objective test, and perhaps the most significant reason, is that many educators have themselves taken more objective tests than essay tests and are therefore more familiar with them. In addition, those who have grown up with television have had that familiarity reinforced by the many game shows that use a form of questioning patterned after the objective test.

Whatever the reasons for the popularity of objective tests among educators, such tests are inadequate to measure the effects of thinking instruction. This is so not only because of the defects detailed above, but also because objective tests strongly suggest that effective thinking is a matter of having the right answer, a view sharply opposed to that taken by the great majority of authorities on thinking instruction and one that prevents students from acquiring the disposition to seek out problems and issues and apply the holistic process to them.

The emphasis on the right answer is the wrong emphasis. As Stephen Norris explains, "The criterion of having thought critically . . . cannot be that the truth was found, but rather that approaches which reliably lead to truth were followed. We now believe that many of Isaac Newton's theories are false, but surely his work must be one of the prime examples of critical thought in all of human history."[11] (Though Norris was referring specifically to critical thinking, both his assertion and his example of Isaac Newton apply equally well to creative thinking.)

The Essay Test

The essay test is free from most of the defects characteristic of the objective test. More specifically, the essay test allows students to express their creativity more or less freely and to express whatever subtleties they perceive; it affords practice in disciplined expression; and it permits the test scorer to evaluate students' intellectual dispositions and the process by which they arrive at their conclusions. The extent to which these ends are realized will naturally depend upon the quality of the test's design; that is, the relative significance of its questions, as well as their clarity and relevance to course objectives. Nevertheless, the test form itself poses no inherent obstacle to thinking skills assessment.

However, the essay test is not without its drawbacks. One is that, though essay responses allow students to express their thoughts fully, with careful regard for qualification and nuance, they also allow students to cover the absence of thought by multiplying words. Five paragraphs of empty verbiage appears, to the casual observer, indistinguishable from five paragraphs of profundity. Whenever you give an essay test, remember to make this distinction and let students know that content counts more than style. (In addition, be sure to set rigorous standards for style.)

The greatest drawback of the essay test is the time it takes to grade it. If you have a heavy teaching load, you will understandably be tempted to choose objective tests instead, particularly if, as often happens, administrators tempt you to do so by providing test-scoring services for your objective tests. (Ironically, the same administrators are usually unresponsive to pleas for assistance in the more time-consuming task of grading essay tests.)

The Combination Test

Fortunately, there is a third alternative—the combination test, which blends the best features of the objective test with the best features of the essay test. It would be impossible to list all possible kinds of combinations, but the following are some of the worthiest.

The modified true/false question.

Rather than the usual choice between two answers, "True" or "False," this modification offers three choices: "Completely true," "Partly true or true but needing qualification," and "Completely false." In addition, it requires students to add, in a space provided immediately beneath each question, an explanation of every "Partly true" answer. The explanation should outline the reasoning behind the choice, together with appropriate evidence, such as references to real or plausible hypothetical situations demonstrating exceptions to the assertion in the question. Here is an example of such a question and answer:

DIRECTIONS: Answer T if the statement is completely true; P if the statement is only true in part, or if it needs qualification; and F if it is completely false.
_P_ It is wrong to criticize another person's opinion because everyone is entitled to his opinion.

People are free to think as they wish, but this doesn't mean their thoughts are necessarily correct. Nor does such freedom deny others the right to disagree.

The modified true false question makes guessing difficult. Moreover, it motivates students to go beyond merely choosing answers to reflecting on *the reasons for their choices.* Thus it promotes deeper understanding of subject matter.

The modified multiple-choice question.

Similar to the modified true/false question, the modified multiple-choice question presents the usual a–d or a–e choices but also requires students to explain the thinking that underlies their choices. (A space is provided for such explanation after each test item.)

The brief essay-question.

This answer gives students practice in composing responses in their own words, with the qualifications and even brief examples or analogies they believe are most relevant; yet it does not create a lengthy reading assignment for the instructor. The directions that accompany this question should specify the word–limit, and state that responses that exceed the limit will be penalized. A twenty-five word limit is recommended for relatively simple matters, a fifty-word limit for complex ones. Holding students to word-limits does not only make grading easier; it also teaches students the value of brevity and precision and prepares those who go on to the professions for the exacting requirements of professional publication. Here are some lead-in phrases commonly used for brief essay-questions:

"What were the causes of . . . ."
"What were the effects of . . . ."
"Explain . . . (an important concept or principle in the course)"
"Suppose that . . . (a situation that challenges students to deal with a problem or issue)"

The guided-response question.

This type of question is answered by using a specific format, preferably a mimeographed sheet that permits the instructor to scan answers quickly and thus grade more efficiently. Since formats can be designed for responding to highly complex, as well as simple, challenges, the guided-response can be used in virtually any testing situation. An example of a guided-response format is the "Short Answer Form for Evaluating Critical Thinking in Social Science" on page 182 of this chapter.

The combination test offers a number of advantages not offered by the objective test. It gives students valuable practice in thinking and communicates the message that you expect thoughtful responses rather than guessing, that the process of arriving at the answer is as important as the answer itself. It also enables you to analyze students' responses to determine which questions (if any) ought to be rephrased to eliminate unnecessary confusion. In addition, it assists students in evaluating their own responses. When a test is handed back, they needn't wonder "Why did I choose that answer?" They can read their reasoning and see why it does or doesn't make sense. Further, by assisting students to evaluate their responses, the combination test helps prevent class discussion from degenerating into a series of attacks on the test questions.

Most important, the combination test enables you to perceive, not only which questions each student missed, but whether she missed it because of lack of preparation, carelessness, or honest confusion. The importance of that perception is difficult to overstate; it is the indispensable element in any successful effort to improve student performance.

GUIDELINES FOR TEST DEVELOPMENT

Following are guidelines for use in developing effective tests of thinking skills in courses across the curriculum. Some of the guidelines cover objective tests; others, essay tests.[12] Unless otherwise indicated, they may be used in preparing combination tests as well.

1. Test construction is itself an exercise in both creative and critical thinking. Therefore, it is important to take the necessary time to apply both kinds of thinking while you are constructing the test and (in order to refine it) after you have administered it to students.
2. Be generous in estimating the time necessary for students to complete the test. Consider exactly what they must do to answer a question and allow ample time for the reflection and pondering (yes, and the false starts and pauses) that are a natural part of thinking. Thirty seconds per question may be a reasonable allowance for a simple true/false question, but it is inadequate for a modified true/false question.
3. Make directions clear and explicit. To enable students to deal meaningfully with cases for which some information may be missing, direct them to make "if . . . then" statements, as needed. Here is an example of such a statement: "The case presented in this question omits reference to the person's state of mind at the time the act was committed. If it was . . . , then my judgment is . . . On the other hand, if it was . . . , then I say . . . ."
4. Recognize that the direction "evaluate the thinking in this passage" is ambiguous. Whenever using this or similar phrasing in a test question,

be sure to make clear whether you wish students to decide whether the argument that leads to the conclusion is sound, whether they agree or disagree with the conclusion, or both. It is unfair to penalize students for not including in their answers material that you did not direct them to include. (Remember, the fact that an argument is unsound does not necessarily mean that the conclusion should be rejected. If the conclusion is not supported by the argument presented, it might still be supported by some other argument.)

5. Consider basing one or more questions on errors in understanding made by former students in the course. Simply present the erroneous idea in one or more sentences and ask students to state their agreement or disagreement and support their position in a clear and persuasive manner. For best results, give several such problems, some of them expressing correct statements.

6. Whenever possible, include some test items that reflect the approach used with homework and classwork assignments—that is, skill-cluster exercises and holistic thinking exercises. If time limitations preclude using holistic exercises, be sure that skill-cluster exercises test the skills associated with all stages of the holistic process. (The investigation stage can be tested by giving students a problem or issue and having them explain how they would go about investigating it, without actually doing so.) To facilitate your evaluation of modified holistic items, direct students to do all their thinking on paper and then, when they have finished, to use the margins to label or briefly describe the stages of the process. Be sure to allow sufficient time for this labeling activity when planning the test.

7. To facilitate the evaluation of moderate-to-long essay responses, require students to include, at the beginning of each such response, a twenty-five to fifty word abstract of their main points or arguments.

8. After the test has been drafted, check the wording for clarity. Also, check the test items to be sure they cover what was taught and give emphasis to important matters.

9. Whenever possible, have several other discriminating people—such as other instructors or individuals with expertise in thinking instruction— take the test and critique it and (if appropriate) the scoring key. Then try it out on a group of students for whom it was designed, invite their criticism, and make whatever revisions seem desirable.

10. Use the test not only as a measuring device, but also as a teaching device. Whenever possible, return tests to students and guide them in analyzing their responses so that they can improve their application of thinking skills (and course concepts) in the future.

STATEWIDE TESTING

California, the first state to establish a thinking skills requirement in its state colleges and, later, in its public school system, is also the leader in statewide testing of thinking skills. Though the California Assessment Program (CAP) itself, today headed by Dale C. Carlson, was established in 1962, its expansion into thinking assessment is relatively recent. The first such test was developed for history–social science by Peter Kneedler and his staff and administered to California eighth graders in 1984–1985. It consists of 720 questions that emphasize higher-level thinking skills rather than rote memorization.

A number of other states are following California's lead and developing thinking skills programs and assessments of their own. The undertaking, of course, is large and progress will necessarily be slow. Nevertheless, by the end of this century such testing may be the rule, rather than the exception, in American education.

ASSESSMENT: THE LARGER DIMENSION

In the late 1960s the faculty of Alverno College, a liberal arts college in Milwaukee, began discussing the meaning of the generalizations often found in college catalogs about the importance of the arts and sciences, generalizations like "The liberal arts teach students to think clearly, develop a sense of values, and see themselves and the world around them from a broader perspective." Their discussions led them to wonder what a liberally educated person *does* that warrants the making of such generalizations and how that doing is best guided and measured.[13]

The result of those Alverno discussions has been the development of a unique approach to higher education that focuses on the development of eight specific competencies in students. No less unique than the approach itself is the fact that it has been used across every curriculum at Alverno since the early 1970s, more than a decade before the thinking skills movement gained widespread acceptance. The eight competencies are as follows:

Effective Communications Ability

Analytical Capability

Problem-Solving Ability

Valuing in a Decision-Making Context

Effective Social Interaction

Effectiveness in Individual/Environment Relationships

Responsible Involvement in the Contemporary World

Aesthetic Responsiveness

The faculty further examined the existing curriculum in each of the academic disciplines to determine the place of the various competencies in the curriculum. Here is how the faculty describe this effort:

> Traditionally, each department had described its curriculum as a structure of *knowledge,* beginning with basic general concepts and progressing toward more complex and specialized studies. This time, we worked from the assumption that there is also a progression of *abilities* implicit in the movement from introductory survey to advanced seminar. Our focus, then, was to discern the developmental patterns already embedded in the normal curriculum of our

disciplines, rather than to redefine our fields or to create a whole new curricular structure.

The examination of curriculums led to the identification of six performance levels for each of the competencies. These levels have become important reference points for curriculum development at the college and for one of the most important features of the Alverno approach—assessment.

Assessment, as the Alverno faculty defines it, is "a multidimensional attempt to discover and judge the individual learner in action." It differs from traditional testing in that it measures the dynamic—"how students seek out, integrate and use knowledge"—rather than the static—how many inert facts students have acquired. In every course students know at the outset which of the eight competencies they will be developing and how they will develop them, week by week, throughout the semester. Moreover, they know what criteria will be used to assess their progress (the criteria are developed outside the particular course and adapted to it) and by the time the assessment is made they have had practice in situations similar to those used in the assessment.

Assessment is an ongoing process at Alverno. In their four years at Alverno, students undergo well over 100 assessments, many of them tailored to the individual needs of students. About 75% of the assessments take place in the classroom, and the remainder in the Assessment Center. Assessors are often drawn from outside the classroom and even from off campus. Each assessor is responsible for "observing the student in action, carefully recording and evaluating her performance according to established criteria, and then working with her in feedback so that she learns to critique her own work objectively." The idea is to have assessment go beyond measuring the student's progress and develop in her the ability to assess herself, an ability crucial to continued development after graduation but one that is unfortunately ignored in the programs of most colleges.

It would be very difficult for you as an individual instructor to adopt the entire Alverno approach in your classroom because it is, in its very essence, a college-wide approach. (You may, of course, introduce the Alverno approach for consideration by your faculty or an appropriate academic committee.) However, you can take two steps to give assessment a larger dimension in your courses. First, approach all your evaluations of student learning from the perspective that the use of knowledge is more important than its mere possession. Secondly, encourage students to develop the habit of self-evaluation and provide opportunities for guided practice in such evaluation in your courses.

APPLICATIONS

1. Look back at a test you recently took in a course in your major field or, if you are now teaching, at a test you recently gave to your students. Analyze it in light of what you learned in this chapter; then redesign it to measure thinking skills more effectively.

2. List the changes you could make in your approach to evaluating student progress in your course without significantly increasing your workload. Don't limit your list of changes to adaptations of the ideas in this chapter. Apply your creativity and think of additional ideas.

chapter 9

DEVELOPING THE
THINKING PROGRAM

The worst mistake those in charge of a school's thinking program can make, next to assuming that all conscientious teachers automatically teach cognitive skills, is to assume that once a principal or chancellor has issued a directive calling for thinking skills instruction or a faculty committee has published a report recommending it, students' cognitive development is assured. The past hundred years of educational history provide repeated documentation that such is not the case. In order for a thinking skills program to succeed, a plan for program development must be carefully formulated and conscientiously implemented.

The first consideration in the development of a thinking program is the competency of faculty to provide thinking skills instruction. To date, no one has devised a standardized test to measure teachers' knowledge of creative and critical thinking, but the performance of teachers on the various basic skills or general knowledge tests that have become fashionable in recent years does not offer encouragement. (On one such general knowledge test, 300 out of 1514 applicants for teaching jobs failed the exam.[1]) Moreover, numerous studies, such as John I. Goodlad's unusually comprehensive *A Place Called School,* provide clear evidence that relatively few teachers from K through university are teaching thinking.

Why is thinking not being taught? A recent study by Gerald Unks, of the University of North Carolina at Chapel Hill, suggests the reason is a lack of competency. Unks noted that (1) the ability to think critically has been stressed in the social studies far longer (and more repeatedly) than in most disciplines; (2) studies show that despite this emphasis, little critical thinking actually occurs in the classroom; and (3) some studies suggest that poor teacher preparation is at least part of the problem.

Curious about these matters, Unks devised a study that centered on a single skill generally acknowledged as crucial to critical thinking, the ability to distinguish statements of fact from statements of opinion. Hypothesizing that social studies teachers cannot distinguish statements of fact from statements of opinion, he tested 293 social studies teachers from 43 randomly chosen school districts from around the United States and found that only 51.87 percent of the respondents could clearly differentiate statements of fact from statements of opinion.

Unks finds a number of troubling implications in the study, not least of which is the probability that many teachers are presenting opinionated material to students under the delusion that it is factual.[2] Nor is this situation likely to be limited to social studies instruction. Since few other disciplines have given as much emphasis to thinking skills instruction in their scholarly traditions, it is reasonable to conjecture that *even fewer* teachers in those disciplines are skilled at distinguishing fact from opinion. Moreover, since the ability to make this distinction is an elementary skill, those who lack it may be expected to have even less competency in teaching advanced cognitive skills.

To suggest that few teachers are at present competent to teach thinking skills is not an insult to the profession. Teachers understandably teach as they were taught (and as they were taught to teach), and in the vast majority of cases that has consisted of being provided with information and tested for its recall. The information, of course, has varied from course to course—historical data, scientific principles, philosophic concepts, literary themes and interpretations. Nevertheless, the skills involved have seldom extended very far beyond memorization and restatement.

RECOMMENDATIONS FOR STAFF DEVELOPMENT

Training large numbers of teachers to be effective in delivering thinking instruction is a challenging task, but not so difficult that a school or college need be daunted by it. All that is necessary is to provide appropriate opportunities for initial faculty training and ongoing development. The specific goals of the staff development program should be as follows:

To further develop in teachers the dispositions associated with effective thinking (see Chapter 4).

To further develop in teachers the habits and skills both of creative thinking and critical thinking (see Chapter 2).

To develop teachers' skill in coaching students and leading discussions (see Chapter 5).

To develop teachers' skill in creating challenging thinking exercises in their disciplines (see Chapters 6, 7).

To develop teachers' skill in constructing effective measures of students' progress in thinking (see Chapter 8).

The following recommendations represent the minimal initiatives a school or college should take in staff development.

Provide access to reading material on thinking and thinking instruction.

Though taking formal courses is certainly worthwhile, many teachers will either be unable to find such courses offered in nearby universities or unable to arrange their schedules to take available courses. By providing all teachers with access to appropriate reading material, a school or college can ensure that all teachers will be able to deepen their knowledge of the thinking process and the approaches proven successful in assisting students to master that process.

If the school or college library has a faculty reserve section, titles on thinking and thinking instruction should be added to that section (as well as to the general collection). Depending on budget constraints and whether the material is still in print, the library may either purchase books and pamphlets or order them through interlibrary loan. If the library has no such reserve section and lacks the space to establish one, another facility, a faculty lounge or meeting room, for example, may serve the purpose.

The bibliography at the end of this book is quite comprehensive and may be used as a guide for those charged with building the institution's collection of thinking skills and related materials. For institutions whose initial efforts must be modest, the following ten titles will provide a useful and reasonably balanced beginning. Those that are no longer in print can be borrowed through interlibrary loan.

Edward M. Glaser, *An Experiment in the Development of Critical Thinking,* Columbia University Press, 1941. An excellent historical summary of the thinking movement prior to 1941 by a pioneer in thinking skills testing.

Rowland W. Jepson, *Clear Thinking,* Longmans, Green & Co., fifth edition, 1967 (first published in 1936). A lively treatment of critical thinking, complete with many excellent thinking skills exercises.

Jacob W. Getzels and Philip W. Jackson, *Creative Thinking and Intelligence,* John Wiley & Sons, 1962. A detailed discussion of the early research on creativity.

E. Paul Torrance, *Guiding Creative Talent,* Prentice-Hall, 1962; also, *Rewarding Creative Behavior: Experiments in Classroom Creativity,* Prentice-Hall, 1965. A comprehensive treatment of classroom methods for developing creativity.

David Perkins, *The Mind's Best Work,* Harvard University Press, 1981. A contemporary examination of the research on creativity and an engaging discussion of its implications for education.

Richard J. Stiggins, Evelyn Rubel, and Edys Quellmalz, *Measuring Thinking Skills in the Classroom: A Teacher's Guide,* forthcoming from the National Education Association. A guide to the design and use of thinking skills assessments.

Stephen Jay Gould, *The Mismeasure of Man,* Norton, 1981. An analysis and refutation of various pessimistic views of human intelligence, including the misrepresentation of Binet's work on IQ.

Harry A. Overstreet, *The Mature Mind,* Norton, 1949, 1959. A thought-provoking consideration of the importance of psychological maturity in everyday life.

William Barrett, *Death of the Soul from Descartes to the Computer,* Doubleday, 1986. An admirably clear and concise exposition of the inadequacy of modern philosophy's view of human consciousness.

Peggy Rosenthal, *Words and Values: Some Leading Words and Where They Lead Us,* Oxford University Press, 1984. A searching examination of how certain popular words—for example, *self, development, opinion,* and *relationship*—subtly direct people's thinking and cause them to form harmful attitudes and illogical ideas.

In addition to obtaining these works for the faculty collection, the school or college should, if at all possible, provide each faculty member with a personal copy of two works. The first is the Paideia trilogy, all by Mortimer J. Adler et al.: *The Paideia Proposal,* 1982; *Paideia Problems and Possibilities,* 1983; and *The Paideia Program,* 1984. These books, all published by Macmillan, are of direct concern to elementary and secondary school teachers, but college instructors will also find them valuable. The program they detail is a balanced one, including not only didactic teaching (lecturing), but coaching and discussion, and applicable to a wide variety of disciplines and courses.

The second work is a booklet written by Debbie M. Walsh and Richard W. Paul and published by the American Federation of Teachers (1986), entitled *The Goal of Critical Thinking: From Educational Ideal to Educational Reality.*

Bring in workshop leaders to provide in-service training in the teaching of thinking.

Since teaching thinking skills involves not just understanding the objectives, methods, and materials appropriate to instruction, but also applying that understanding in specific courses, it is not enough for faculty to read books and listen to lectures. They should also have guidance in revising their courses. This is best done in workshops, with authorities on the teaching of thinking serving as leaders and offering suggestions and criticism as faculty participants design objectives and select materials and methods for their individual courses.

Obtain or develop audio-visual and computer program materials on the teaching of thinking.

Various commercial materials designed to aid in the improvement of teaching in general, and thinking instruction in particular, are now available. The quality of materials and their efficacy may, of course, vary a great deal and discretion should be used in their selection. One good source is Northwestern University's Center for the Teaching Professions in Evanston, Illinois. Though it does not specialize in thinking skills instruction, many of its materials are applicable. One is a series of eleven videotapes of college classes covering such aspects of teaching as "Using Questions to Stimulate Discussion," "Moderating

Disagreements Among Students," "Helping Students Clarify Ideas," and "Analyzing Questions Before Answering Them." (In addition, the Center's staff conducts research and prepares bibliographies on teaching, and offers a Visiting Scholars Program.)

In addition to buying or renting commercial audio-visual materials, schools and colleges should consider audio-taping or video-taping the classes of teachers. The ideal approach is to tape the classes of those experienced in thinking instruction and then to make the tapes available to teachers with little or no experience in such instruction. The implication that one is a master teacher can, of course, deter many who might otherwise volunteer. For this reason, in many institutions the taping/viewing is best approached differently—as an opportunity for those who wish to become effective thinking instructors, *but who profess no special expertise,* to receive constructive criticism from their peers.

Teachers who use computers in their courses should consider using some of the computer programs that focus on thinking skills. One notable example is Larry Hannah's simulation games, such as his "Quality of Life" spreadsheet activity, described in *The Computing Teacher,* December/January, 1985–1986, and his "Senate Committee Hearing" simulation, available from the publishers of *The Computing Teacher.* (A helpful preview guide to educational software is published by California TECC Software Library and Clearinghouse, San Mateo County Office of Education, 333 Main St., Redwood City, CA 94063.)

Send faculty to conferences on the teaching of thinking.

The number of regional, national, and international conferences on the teaching of thinking have multiplied in recent years. One of the most helpful of these conferences for classroom teachers is held annually at Sonoma State University in Rohnert Park, California, under the auspices of that institution's Center for Critical Thinking and Moral Critique, Richard Paul, Director. Others can be found advertised in the *Chronicle of Higher Education* or *Education Week.* By sending one or more faculty members to an occasional conference and having them share their experiences with their peers, a school or college will ensure that its thinking program continues to reflect advances in cognitive theory and teaching practice.

Establish a "clearinghouse" on campus to receive and disseminate information on thinking skills.

It takes considerable effort to remain abreast of developments in thinking instruction. In addition to dozens of books, hundreds of relevant articles are being published each year in the journals of virtually every academic subdiscipline. The most efficient way for faculty to become aware of these studies is to establish a "clearinghouse"—that is, one or more individuals who monitor the appropriate sources, such as RIE and ERIC in the library, and circulate worthwhile information to their peers. The individuals might be given reduced teaching loads to compensate them for their time; or they might be given the same "institutional service" credit given to members of standing committees.

Larger faculties will wish to go beyond this modest clearinghouse approach and persuade their administrations to establish formal offices of instructional and faculty development with one or more full-time staff members. A noteworthy example of such an office is the one at Oregon State University headed by Dean N. Osterman. Established in 1973, the office provides a variety of services designed to assist the university's 1200 faculty achieve excellence in teaching.

Establishing an office of instruction may seem suitable only for colleges and universities, but that is surely not the case. Elementary and secondary school faculties can profit greatly from the services such an office would provide. The fact that the idea is new should not be permitted to obstruct its endorsement. Nor should budgetary restrictions. Most budgets contain items of considerably less value to quality teaching than this, and those items can usually be trimmed to produce the funds necessary to create an office of instruction.

Provide opportunities for faculty to learn about one another's successful teaching methods and materials.

To be successful, the thinking skills program, like any new program, must earn the support of individual teachers. (For administrators to impose it on faculty is to doom it to failure, at least in the long run.) This support is not likely to materialize overnight, but its development can be expedited by providing opportunities for less committed and wary faculty members to see and appraise for themselves the initiatives being taken by those who are enthusiastic about the teaching of thinking. Perhaps the best way to provide such opportunities is to revise the agendas of department meetings and campus-wide faculty meetings to include presentations and demonstrations by faculty detailing their teaching strategies.

RECOMMENDATIONS FOR PROGRAM DEVELOPMENT

In teaching situations for which commercial programs will be adopted—that is, the situations that obtain in many elementary and some secondary schools—program development begins with the process of selecting the program. The fact that many programs have become available in recent years is a mixed blessing. On the one hand, the wider choice increases the likelihood that teachers will find a program that fits their students' needs. On the other, the varying quality of programs and the sometimes exaggerated claims in advertised materials require teachers to exercise great care in selecting.

Paul Chance has prepared a guide to assist teachers in finding the best commercial program for their students. Titled *Thinking in the Classroom: A Survey of Programs* (Columbia University Press, 1986), it examines eight of the best-known programs and answers the following questions about each:

What assumptions underlie the program?

What are the goals of the program?

How is thinking to be taught?

Who is to be taught?

Who is to teach thinking?

What benefits is the program said to produce?

What special problems will there be?

Moreover, Chance provides an evaluation of each program based upon careful examination of materials, manuals, and research reports, as well as upon conversations with program developers and thinking instruction experts. A close reading of this book is thus an excellent starting point in the selection of a program.

One program that deserves special mention is Matthew Lipman's Philosophy for Children. Lipman, director of the Institute for the Advancement of Philosophy for Children at New Jersey's Montclair State College, got the idea for the program in 1971. Since the publication of his first book for children, *Harry Stottlemeier's Discovery* (the name is a play on "Aristotle"), Lipman and his staff have developed and tested a number of books and teachers' manuals for students from grades 3 to 10. Many authorities consider Philosophy for Children the most effective commercial program available. For a concise introduction to this program, see Tony W. Johnson's *Philosophy for Children: An Approach to Critical Thinking,* a pamphlet published by the Phi Delta Kappa Educational Foundation. (The program is also reviewed in Paul Chance's book.)

After reading Chance's book and other relevant materials, such as Johnson's pamphlet, obtain sample materials for one or more programs that seem to fit your students' needs best. But don't rely only on such materials in reaching a judgment. Ask each company for a list of schools that have adopted its program and contact the teachers who have used, or are using, it. Question those teachers about the strengths and weaknesses of the program and whether they would recommend that you adopt it. Finally, if possible, arrange to use the program on a pilot basis before adopting it.

Keep in mind that few programs cover all aspects of thinking instruction thoroughly and well. For example, some may be very effective with critical thinking, but rather ineffective with creative thinking; others may cover both areas, but in a narrow way that neglects the dispositions required for successful application of thinking skills beyond the classroom. Accordingly, be sure to encourage all faculty who will use the program not to rely on it slavishly, but to develop their own specific thinking skills objectives and teaching methods, and to create some exercises themselves, especially in areas where the program's materials are limited or deficient.

THE ADMINISTRATOR'S ROLE IN THE THINKING SKILLS PROGRAM

Throughout this book the focus has been on the *teaching* of thinking—that is, on the concepts and principles teachers must understand, the objectives they should pursue in their classes, and the materials that have proven effective in courses across the curriculum. This focus is appropriate both because this book is written for teachers and because the success of a thinking skills program depends principally on the quality of instruction offered. However, there is another factor to be considered, a factor that is seldom recognized but nevertheless important—the amount and quality of support the thinking program receives from administrators.

Teachers should be aware of the ways in which administrators can assist them in developing the thinking program and should encourage administrators to provide such assistance. Here are the most important ways.

Administrators should acquaint themselves with the demands of thinking instruction.

The great majority of administrators, like the great majority of faculty, have received little or no formal training in thinking and thinking instruction. Therefore it is as mistaken for administrators as for faculty to assume that they already understand these subjects and need no further study of them. The only protection against the many misconceptions that have gained popular acceptance and can so easily undermine a thinking program is a special effort to learn the facts. Whether this effort is made through formal coursework, workshops and seminars, or private study is less important than than that it is conscientiously undertaken.

Foremost among the lessons administrators must learn is that an effective thinking skills program is not possible under the conditions found in many schools and colleges today. There is nothing novel about this idea, as Earl C. Kelley's words, written more than forty years ago, attest:

> The general notion that education can be done cheaply completely fails to take into account the extremely complex nature of a child's development. The teachers will have to have no more children in their classes than they can properly teach. This is a sound economic policy—no manufacturer would consider it good business to give a worker twice the amount of work that he could do. Yet we do this in schools. To illustrate, if we can say that a teacher can teach twenty-five pupils but cannot teach fifty, we often give her fifty and believe that we have saved the salary of a teacher. We have not in fact saved the salary of a teacher, but have *lost a teacher.* [Emphasis added][3]

Kelley's view is echoed in the most comprehensive plan of the 1980s for educational reform of elementary and secondary education—The Paideia Plan. Theodore Sizer, on behalf of the Paideia group, underlines the fact that intellectual skill training, the "backbone of basic schooling," is achieved by coaching, and he offers a number of maxims for successful coaching, among them the following:

1. Individual attention is crucial because teachers must know students' special strengths and weaknesses and meet their special needs, which can vary considerably from student to student.
2. Teachers must bring students to the point where they want to be coached and then encourage them to express their thoughts and develop the courage to accept coaching. This is a slow process.
3. Since skills are habits that are built only through repetition, frequent

drill is necessary, so teachers must constantly correct students' work. Moreover, because immediacy is important, correction must be thorough and prompt. Teachers' schedules must permit them time for such correcting.
4. The kind of criticism that coaching demands—not merely pointing out errors, but explaining why they are errors—is demanding and cannot be mass-produced.

Sizer argues that coaching students for "rigorous, resourceful use of the mind" cannot be done unless classes are small enough for teachers to "learn how each pupil's mind works."[4]

Despite the fact that Sizer's recommendations derive both from common sense and more than two millennia of teaching experience, many administrators will view them skeptically because studies by reputable scholars concluding that the effect of class size upon learning is minor continue to proliferate.[5] The crucial fact that must be stressed with such administrators is that those studies measure, not the mastery of higher order thinking skills and the disposition to use those skills, but the mere acquisition of factual information. That mind stuffing is as effective with large groups as with small should, after all, come as no surprise, and in no way challenges Sizer's claim. *The point is that the thinking program aims for a different, more valuable kind of learning and employs methods that demand smaller class size.*

Administrators should take the initiative in establishing the conditions necessary for the thinking skills program to be successful.

It is by now well established that one of the key components of excellence in an educational institution is the degree to which the administration becomes involved in the effort to develop and implement quality programs.[6] Administrators who view their role as merely devil's advocates to (or worse, active opponents of) reformers are hindering rather than helping the drive for excellence. The most helpful roles an administrator can fill are ENABLER and ADVOCATE. Being an enabler involves cutting red tape, removing roadblocks, guiding proposals through the bureaucracy; or, in more concrete terms, finding funds for bringing speakers and workshop leaders to the campus, purchasing books and other materials, and paying for faculty to travel to conferences. Being an advocate means championing the thinking program and arguing for the conditions necessary for its success with groups to whom faculty have little access—school boards, college governing councils, and legislatures.

Administrators should provide appropriate incentives for faculty to incorporate thinking instruction in their courses, and appropriate recognition for those who play leadership roles in the institution's thinking skills program.

Administrators should be sensitive to the fact that it takes time, effort, and courage for teachers to make significant changes in their teaching methods and materials. Accordingly, wherever possible, administrators should provide some incentives for doing so, even if the incentives are quite modest, such as a letter of commendation in each individual's personnel file or credit for professional development.

For the leaders of the thinking program the reward should be more substantial. Such individuals are those who not only revise their own courses, but also assist other teachers, help build the faculty reserve collection of thinking skills materials, or serve as a "clearinghouse" for information on thinking skills instruction. These people might be granted either a special monetary stipend or some reduction in teaching load.

The best incentive for college instructors to incorporate thinking instruction in their courses is for administrators to place as much emphasis on effective teaching as on publishing. Although the conventional academic view is that scholarship and publication enhances teaching effectiveness, research does not bear that view out.[7] Moreover, common sense suggests that the "publish or perish" standard undoubtedly detracts from good teaching by encouraging anyone who aspires to academic advancement to spend less time preparing for class. (Many would add that this standard does little more for scholarship than increase the amount of half-hearted and often trivial pursuits.)

Administrators should assist faculty in working out guidelines for the treatment of sensitive topics (where such guidelines are necessary) and make a commitment to support faculty should any controversy arise.

Controversies about classroom subjects and treatments are more likely to occur in response to elementary and secondary school programs than to college programs, but can occur in either. Although teachers should play a major role in writing the guidelines for treating sensitive matters in the classroom, administrators will usually be able to provide a perspective many teachers lack. Because they tend to have more contact with community groups, particularly in the context of complaints about classroom activities, administrators will usually be better able to recognize problem situations and anticipate the kinds of responses that may occur.

Together, teachers and administrators should be able to develop a set of guidelines that teachers can honor without compromising their academic freedom and that administrators can defend against criticism from any quarter.

Administrators should ensure that program evaluation results are used sensibly and fairly.

Administrators often wonder why faculty are so often suspicious of program evaluations. The answer in some cases, of course, is simple paranoia. But in many others it is a justifiable concern that faculty will be blamed for conditions over which they had no control, even over conditions for which administrators themselves should bear responsibility. A typical case concerns the teaching of writing. An English department will propose a program change that gives increased emphasis to composition, but note that in order for teachers to assign and grade the additional papers, some adjustment will have to be made in their teaching loads. The administration will respond that budgetary constraints will not permit any such adjustments to be made, but that the English department should proceed with the program change anyway. A year or two later, when memory has faded, the administration may evaluate the program and find that students' writing skills have not improved, and conclude either that the program was ill-conceived or that the English department was irresponsible or incompetent.

As Stephen Norris points out, when making any kind of evaluation of program, it is important to ask the right questions, including, "Were the teachers adequately trained?" "Did they have the time to teach properly?" and "Were the students ready for the program?"[8]

Administrators should show the priority they place on effective thinking by giving it special emphasis in the formal operation of their institutions, particularly in their dealings with faculty.

For at least a decade or two the prevailing view of the administration-faculty relationship has been the managerial view. Administrators have tended to view themselves as responsible for overseeing faculty activities *in much the same way as managers in a factory oversee the activities of assembly-line workers.* This view has been responsible not only for an increase in campus tension and antipathy, but also for a loss of effectiveness in addressing the problems and issues of education. Ironically, this managerial view has become more entrenched in recent years, at the very time when the business community has embraced the Japanese management perspective, which places great value on the contribution of every employee from the janitor to the company president. A further irony is the fact that the Japanese perspective originated with an American, W. Edward Deming, whose views were ignored by American business in the 1950s.

Administrators must realize that since the managerial view of educational administration fails to produce desirable effects from assembly-line workers, it is absurd to expect it to produce desirable effects from professionals. In Japan "quality circles," in which workers in the same production area meet several times a month to discuss company problems *on company time,* have contributed ideas that have improved product quality, raised worker outputs and lowered production costs, improved employee-employer relations, and stimulated invention. Nor have such groups been limited to product industries; they have been used successfully in service industries and even in education, with students addressing everyday problems and issues that arise in school. Moreover, quality circles are not limited in their effectiveness to Japanese culture. Experiments in American industries and in education have replicated their favorable results.[9]

Now if the involvement of production workers and of elementary school children has had a salutary effect on problem solving and decision making, what possible argument can be advanced for barring teachers from such involvement in their profession? Administrators will do well to go beyond singing the praises of creative and critical thinking and allow teachers to join the councils of "management" and contribute their intellectual skills to the consideration of significant problems and issues in their institutions.

Treating teachers as colleagues and partners does not, of course, necessitate replacing the committee format with the town meeting format; nor does it mean surrendering the final administrative authority to the faculty. It only means informing teachers of important challenges at the earliest possible time, inviting their ideas, and considering them fairmindedly before making a decision. To a secure, competent administrator, this approach constitutes no threat.

Administrators should articulate the program to the community.

The public's idea of the school's emphases is naturally drawn from their experiences in school. As we have seen, even the most highly educated people in our society have for generations been denied systematic training in thinking. What school means to the public at large is a number of discrete subjects learned by reading textbooks and listening to lectures and accepting what authorities say. Left to their own impressions, many people will understandably regard the idea of teaching students to challenge present realities and to question authority as irresponsible and dangerous remnants of 1960s permissivism.

Before the public can reasonably be expected to support a thinking skills program, there must be some assurance that they understand it and the thinking skills movement in general. The responsibility of building that understanding must be borne by every professional associated with education, but administrators have special opportunities and therefore special obligations. It is they who are in regular contact with school boards, advisory committees, legislators, and influential citizens. It is they who often have easy access to service organization leaders, the clergy, and the media.

Therefore, it is mainly administrators who must educate the public about the thinking skills movement, explaining the historic neglect of thinking in the schools, the abortive attempts throughout this century to place thinking instruction at the center of the curriculum at all levels of education, the frightening deficiencies in college graduates noted by business and professional people in the late 1970s, and the recommendations of numerous panels and commissions that schools and colleges revise their curriculums to give prominence to problem solving and issue analysis. Most important, it is administrators who must articulate the specific approaches their faculty have devised to carry out these recommendations, and administrators who must urge the public to pledge the moral and financial support essential for thinking skills instruction to succeed.

NOTES

Chapter 1

1. *How We Think* (D. C. Heath & Co. 1933), p. 4.
2. Presentation at Second International Conference on Critical Thinking, Sonoma State University, Rohnert Park, CA, July 9–13, 1984.
3. Ina V. S. Mullis, *What Do NAEP Results Tell Us About Students' Higher Order Thinking Abilities?* Unpublished evaluation of the National Assessment. (Mullis is employed by Educational Testing Service, the administering agency.)
4. Columbia University Press, 1941.
5. See, for example, Sidney Parnes, *Creative Thinking Guidebook* (Charles Scribner's Sons, 1967), pp. 53–60.
6. *Experiment in the Teaching of Critical Thinking,* pp. 69–70.
7. *A Place Called School* (McGraw-Hill Book Co., 1984), pp. 128, 215.
8. *Ten Philosophical Mistakes* (Macmillan Publishing Co., 1985); p. 50.
9. *Ten Philosophical Mistakes,* p. 81.
10. *The Art of Practical Thinking* (Simon & Schuster, 1940), p. 51.
11. Interview in *New York Teacher,* April 3, 1983, p. 4.
12. Albert Ellis, *A Guide to Rational Living* (Prentice-Hall, 1961), pp. 51, 13.
13. Simon & Schuster, 1982, pp. 160, 170, 253.
14. pp. 22–3.
15. St. Martin's Press, 1981. The following page/chapter references correspond to the five "that" clauses: pp. 15, 19, 55, Chapter 5, Chapter 6.
16. p. 40.
17. p. 57.
18. p. 56.
19. "McPeck's Mistakes," *Informal Logic,* 7, 1, Winter 1985, pp. 35–43.
20. The apt phrase "logically messy" was coined by Richard Paul.
21. "Intelligence as Thinking and Learning Skills," *Educational Leadership,* 39 (1), October 1981, p. 18.
22. *The Process of Education* (Harvard University Press, 1961), p. 33.

Chapter 2

1. *The Habit of Scientific Thinking* (Columbia University Press, 1935), p. 8.
2. "Research Synthesis on Right and Left Hemispheres," *Educational Leadership,* 40 (4), January, 1983, pp. 66–71.

3. Address at Second International Conference on Critical Thinking, Sonoma State University, July 9–13, 1984.

4. Cited in Paul Smith (ed.), *Creativity: An Examination of the Creative Process* (Hastings House, 1959), p. 17.

5. "Creativity in Self-Actualizing People," in Harold H. Anderson (ed.) *Creativity and Its Cultivation* (Harper & Brothers, 1959), p. 84.

6. *The Logic of Scientific Discovery*, rev. ed. (Hutchinson of London, 1968), p. 32.

7. Quoted in Clarence Tuska, *Inventors and Inventions* (McGraw-Hill, 1957), p. 88.

8. *Science and Human Values* (Harper & Row, 1956), pp. 30–1.

9. Eliot D. Hutchinson, *How to Think Creatively* (Abingdon-Cokesbury Press, 1949), p. 150.

10. *The Art and Science of Creativity* (Holt, Rinehart, and Winston, 1965), pp. 2–3.

11. See, for example, Sidney J. Parnes, *Creative Behavior Guidebook* (Charles Scribner's Sons, 1967), p. 32. Also E. Paul Torrance, *Rewarding Creative Behavior: Experiments in Classroom Creativity* (Prentice-Hall, 1965), p. 29; and Jacob W. Getzels and Philip W. Jackson, *Creative Behavior and Intelligence* (John Wiley and Sons, 1962), p. 25f.

12. *The Creative Process: A Symposium* (University of California Press, 1954), pp. 9, 15.

13. Cited in David Perkins, *The Mind's Best Work* (Harvard University Press, 1981), pp. 265–6.

14. Cited in E. Paul Torrance, *Guiding Creative Talent* (Prentice-Hall, 1962), p. 3.

15. *Creativity and Its Cultivation* (Harper & Brothers, 1959), p. 248.

16. Alex Osborn, *Applied Imagination*, rev. ed. (Charles Scribner's Sons, 1957), p. 172.

17. (Oneonta, New York) *Daily Star*, June 19, 1985, p. 1.

18. Interview in *Inc.*, December, 1985, p. 33f.

19. "Raising Kids," *Atlantic Monthly*, October, 1983.

20. *USA Weekend*, October 4–6, 1985, p. 29.

21. "Einstein's Creative Thinking and the General Theory of Relativity: A Documented Report," *American Psychiatrist*, 136:1, January, 1979, pp. 38–43. See also Rothenberg, *The Emerging Goddess* (University of Chicago Press, 1979).

22. Simon and Schuster, 1982, pp. 123–6.

23. Siegfried Giedion, *Mechanization Takes Command* (Oxford University Press, 1948), pp. 633–5.

24. Parnes, p. 57.

25. Quoted in Osborn, p. 149.

26. *The Creative Process: A Symposium*, pp. 20–1.

27. Cited in David H. Russell, *Children's Thinking*, (Ginn & Co. 1956), p. 265.

28. Robert Reinhold, "Texas Copes with the Cost of Criminals," *New York Times*, June 30, 1985, Section 4, p. 5.

29. Reported by John Stossel, *20/20*, ABC-TV, July 22, 1982.

30. *Eyewitness Testimony* (Harvard University Press, 1979), pp. 21, 22, 39, 55, 60, 235.

31. For a fuller discussion of these data, see Carol Tavris, *Anger: The Misunderstood Emotion* (Simon & Schuster, Inc. 1982), pp. 123–31.

32. (Oneonta, New York) *Daily Star*, August 28, 1984, p. 9.

33. Robert P. Crawford, *Think for Yourself* (Fraser Publishing Co., 1937), p. 175.

34. See, for example, Robert J. Sternberg, "Teaching Critical Thinking, Part 1: Are We Making Critical Mistakes," *Phi Delta Kappan*, November, 1985, p. 194f.

35. Quoted in Zbigniew Pietrasinski, *The Psychology of Efficient Thinking*, trans. by Boguslaw Jankowski (Pergamon Press, 1969), p. 129f.

36. William A. Henry III, "Libel Law: Good Intentions Gone Awry," *New York Times* March 4, 1985, p. 93.

37. Dan Kaercher, "School Closings: What Can Parents Do?" *Better Homes and Gardens,* August, 1982, p. 17.
38. Robert T. Kurlychek, "Toward Holding the Criminally Non-Responsible Defendant More Responsible: Some Therapeutic Concerns," *Corrective Psychiatry and Journal of Behavior Technology, Methods and Therapy,* 24 (4), 1978, pp. 144–45.
39. *Logic for the Millions* (Philosophical Library, 1947), p. 55.
40. "Coughlin: Prisons Should Incorporate," (Oneonta, New York) *Daily Star,* May 31, 1985, p. 9.
41. Sidney J. Parnes et al., *Guide to Creative Action* (Charles Scribner's Sons, 1977), p. 23.
42. Quoted in William J. Broad, "Tracing the Skeins of Matter," *New York Times Magazine,* May 6, 1984, p. 60.
43. See, for example, Hutchinson, pp. 35–40.
44. Hutchinson, pp. 182–3.
45. *Problem-Solving Processes of College Students* (University of Chicago Press, 1950).
46. See, for example, David Perkins, 1981.
47. "Verbal Reports as Data," *Psychological Review,* 1980, No. 87, pp. 215–251.
48. G. Fischer et al., *Aspects of a Theory of Simplification, Debugging, and Coaching.* Presented at the Second Annual Conference of the Canadian Society for Computational Studies of Intelligence, Toronto, July 1977.
49. "A Proposed Developmental Sequence for Problem-Solving Ability in Classical Genetics: The Trial-and-Error to Deductive Logic Continuum." Unpublished manuscript.

Chapter 3

1. Chester I. Barnard, *The Functions of the Executive* (Cambridge: Harvard University Press, 1938), p. 303.
2. Franz Boas, *The Mind of Primitive Man,* rev. ed. (New York: The Macmillan Co., 1938), p. 238.
3. Rowland W. Jepson, *Clear Thinking* (New York: Longmans, Green & Co., 1967), p. 81. (The first edition was published in 1936.)
4. Ernest Dimnet, *The Art of Thinking* (New York: Simon & Schuster, 1928), pp. 103–4.
5. Nancy Larrick, "Children of Television," *Teacher,* September, 1975, pp. 75–7.
6. Neil Postman, Keynote Address, Second International Conference on Critical Thinking, Sonoma State University, August, 1984.
7. Postman.
8. John Dewey, *How We Think* (New York: D.C. Heath & Co., 1933), p. 261.
9. Francis Bacon, quoted in Charles P. Curtis and Ferris Greenslet (eds.), *The Practical Cogitator* (Boston: Houghton-Mifflin Co., 1945), p. 18.
10. Parker J. Palmer, *To Know as We Are Known: A Spirituality of Education* (New York: Harper & Row, 1983), p. 83.
11. Peggy Rosenthal, *Words and Values: Some Leading Words and Where They Lead Us* (New York: Oxford University Press, 1984).
12. *Oneonta [NY] Star,* June 6, 1985, p. 1.
13. *Binghamton [NY] Press,* August 25, 1985, p. 1E.
14. *Oneonta [NY] Star* September 26, 1985, p. 1.
15. *Oneonta [NY] Star,* October 17, 1985, p. 20.
16. *Encyclopedia of Philosophy,* Vol. 3, p. 125.

17. See Peggy Rosenthal's discussion of these works in *Words and Values.*
18. Errol E. Harris, "Respect for Persons," *Daedalus,* Spring, 1969, p. 113.
19. "The Video Explosion," *Nova,* Public Broadcasting System, February 14, 1982.
20. Cited by Richard Paul, Opening Address, Third International Conference on Critical Thinking, Sonoma State University, July, 1985.

Chapter 4

1. *Problem-Solving Processes of College Students* (University of Chicago Press, 1950), pp. 30–1.
2. *The Art of Thought* (Harcourt, Brace, & Co., 1926), p. 139.
3. Carol I. Diener and Carol I. Dweck, "An Analysis of Learned Helplessness: II. The Processing of Success," *Journal of Personality and Social Psychology,* 1980, 39 (5), pp. 940–52.
4. *Synectics: The Development of Creative Capacity* (Harper & Brothers, 1961), p. 36.
5. *New York Times,* December 5, 1982, Section 4, p. 18.
6. William F. Buckley, Jr., "Crusader with a Purpose," *Reader's Digest,* May, 1980, p. 174.
7. Cited in John H. Douglas, "The Genius of Everyman (1): Discovering Creativity," *Science News,* 3 (17) April 23, 1977, pp. 257–72.
8. *Smithsonian World,* Public Television Series, WCNY (Syracuse, NY), December 12, 1984.
9. Harold Gilliam, "A Lesson from the 'Plain' People," *New York News,* July 21, 1985, p. 18.
10. *The Process of Education* (Harvard University Press, 1961), p. 13.
11. *Anger: The Misunderstood Emotion* (Simon and Schuster, 1982), pp. 229–30.
12. "Less Tilling Is Enough, College Study Indicates," (Oneonta, NY) *Daily Star,* November 8, 1985, p. 10.
13. See, for example, David Perkins, *The Mind's Best Work* (Harvard University Press, 1981).
14. *Anger: The Misunderstood Emotion,* pp. 213–14.
15. *Creative Behavior Guidebook* (Simon & Schuster, 1967), pp. 57–60.
16. *Problem-Solving Processes of College Students,* pp. 27–8.
17. *USA Today,* International Edition, September 18, 1985, p. 5.
18. W. Edgar Moore et al., *Creative and Critical Thinking,* 2nd ed. (Houghton-Mifflin, 1985), pp. 68–70.
19. Cited in Tavris, p. 138.
20. Dialogue with David Perkins, Third International Conference on Critical Thinking, Sonoma State University, July 20–23, 1985.
21. *The Mature Mind* (Norton, 1959), p. 51.
22. Harry Schwartz, "Medicine: Trying to Outsmart the Flu Virus," *New York Times,* December 29, 1968, Section 4, p. 9.
23. *Effective Thinking* (Simon & Schuster, 1931), p. 109.

Chapter 5

1. See, for example, S. C. Parker, *Methods of Teaching in High Schools* (Ginn & Co., 1915). Also, the same author's "Problem Solving or Practice in Thinking," *Elementary School Journal,* 21, 1920, pp. 257–73, in which he provides a detailed discussion of the rules for conducting problem-solving sessions.

2. *The Paideia Program: An Educational Syllabus* (Macmillan, 1984), p. 5.

3. "On Learnable Representations of Knowledge: A Meaning for the Computational Metaphor," in Jack Lochhead and John Clement (eds.), *Cognitive Process Instruction: Research on Teaching Thinking Skills* (The Franklin Institute Press, 1979), pp. 249–50.

4. *The Paideia Program,* p. 10.

5. *Learning More and Teaching Less* (Society for Research in Higher Education, 1985).

6. *Paideia Problems and Possibilities* (Macmillan, 1983), p. 57.

7. Cunningham and Weigand, cited in Robert Strom and Harold Bernard, *Educational Psychology* (Brooks-Cole Publishing Co., 1982), p. 311.

8. Nelson DuBois et al., *Educational Psychology and Instructional Decisions* (Dorsey Press, 1979), p. 299.

9. "Small Group Discussion in Social Studies Classrooms and the Corruption of Critical Thought," *Theory and Research in Social Education,* 10 (4), Winter, 1982, pp. 49–67.

10. O. Roger Anderson, "Wait-Time and Rewards as Instructional Variables, Their Influence on Language, Logic, and Fate Control: Part One—Wait-Time," *Journal of Research in Science Teaching,* 1974, 11 (2), pp. 81–94.

11. Robert Strom and Harold Bernard, *Educational Psychology* (Brooks-Cole Publishing Co., 1982), pp. 313, 315.

12. *New York Times,* April 28, 1985, p. 1f.

13. "Engineering Student Problem Solving," in Lochhead and Clement, p. 237.

14. David Wallechinsky and Irving Wallace, *The People's Almanac #2,* 1978, p. 1094.

15. James L. Mursell, *Using Your Mind Effectively* (McGraw-Hill, 1951), p. 3.

16. *Reason and Teaching* (Bobbs-Merril, 1973), pp. 102–3.

17. "Problem Solving Strategies and the Epistemology of Science," in Lochhead and Clement, p. 187.

18. Vincent Ryan Ruggiero, *Enter the Dialogue* (Wadsworth Publishing Co., 1985), pp. 15–16.

19. *USA Today,* International Edition, September 18, 1985, p. 5.

20. Paper presented at International Society for Individualized Instruction conference, Rutgers University, October 10–12, 1985.

21. *Right Thinking: A Study of Its Principles and Methods* (Harper and Brothers, 1946), p. 63.

22. Paper presented at International Society for Individualized Instruction conference, Rutgers University, October 10–12, 1985.

23. *Social Class Influences Upon Learning* (Harvard University Press, 1948), pp. 90–6. An interesting article which expresses a somewhat different, though complementary, argument about reading instruction is Martin Haberman's "The Reading Movement Has Gone Too Far," *Today's Education,* March–April, 1976, pp. 36–8.

24. Cited in "Thinking Through Writing," *On Campus,* April, 1986, p. 6.

25. *Teaching Analytical Reasoning in Mathematics,* in Lochhead and Clement, pp. 309–14.

26. *Reader's Digest,* December, 1985, p. 145.

27. Letter to author, December 27, 1985.

28. *On Campus* (A publication of the American Federation of Teachers), November, 1985, p. 2.

29. Elizabeth F. Loftus, *Eyewitness Testimony* (Harvard University Press, 1979), pp. 20–1.

30. "Self-Esteem and Excellence: The Choice and the Paradox," *American Educator,* Winter, 1985, pp. 10–16.

31. Exercise in Vincent Ryan Ruggiero, *The Art of Thinking* (Harper & Row, 1984), p. 195.

32. *Problem-Based Learning: An Approach to Medical Education* (Springer Publishing Company, 1980), p. 107.
33. *A Place Called School: Prospects for the Future* (McGraw-Hill, 1984), p. 124.

Chapter 6

1. Vincent Ryan Ruggiero, *The Art of Thinking* (Harper & Row, 1984), p. 151.
2. This problem appeared in Max Black's *Critical Thinking* (Prentice-Hall, 1952), pp. 156–7.
3. In Max Black, p. 157.
4. Quoted in Patrick Mahony, *Barbed Wit and Malicious Humor* (The Citadel Press, 1956), p. 155.
5. Vincent Ryan Ruggiero, *Beyond Feelings*, 2nd ed. (Mayfield, 1984), p. 17.
6. Ruggiero, *Beyond Feelings*, p. 17.
7. Quoted in Elizabeth F. Loftus, *Eyewitness Testimony* (Harvard University Press, 1979), pp. 62–3.
8. John Stossel, report on *Good Morning America,* November 9, 1982.
9. *USA Today,* July 17, 1985, 4D.
10. *USA Today,* International Edition, September 20, 1985, p. 1.
11. *New York Times,* October 6, 1985, Section 4, p. 6.
12. [Oneonta, New York] *Daily Star,* June 25, 1985, p. 1.
13. Vincent Ryan Ruggiero, *Enter the Dialogue: A Dynamic Approach to Critical Thinking and Writing* (Wadsworth Publishing Co., 1985), p. 91.
14. *USA Today,* International Edition, September 18, 1985, p. 5.
15. [Oneonta, New York] *Daily Star,* August 7, 1985, p. 5.
16. Adapted from an exercise in Vincent Ryan Ruggiero's *The Art of Thinking* (Harper & Row, 1984), p. 138.
17. Ruggiero, *Enter,* p. 114.
18. Ruggiero, *Enter,* pp. 141–3.
19. "Education Malpractice Suits Seldom Victorious," *Daily Star,* December 17, 1984, p. 29.
20. Address, Second International Conference in Critical Thinking, Sonoma State University, July 9–13, 1984.
21. "Teachers Can't Count Attendance in Grades," *Daily Star,* August 14, 1985, p. 10.
22. "Pro and Con: Testing for Drugs in the Schools," *New York Times,* November 10, 1985, Section 4, p. 8.
23. *Time,* June 10, 1985, p. 38f.
24. "San Antonio May Ban Kids from Rock Concerts," *Daily Star,* November 14, 1985, p. 1.
25. *Binghamton [New York] Press,* August 4, 1985, p. 7A.
26. "Supreme Court Overturns Connecticut Sabbath Law," *Daily Star,* June 27, 1985, p. 24.

Chapter 7

1. Discussed in John M. Darley, and others, *Psychology* (Prentice-Hall, 1981), pp. 418–19.
2. Harvard University Press, 1961, pp. 21–2.
3. Bobbs-Merrill, 1973, p. 34.

4. [Binghamton, NY] *Press and Sun-Bulletin,* November 18, 1985, p. 1D.
5. "Court Sets Stage for Key Libel Ruling," [Oneonta, NY] *Daily Star,* June 25, 1985, p. 2.
6. "Study Finds 1 Youth in 3 Shoplifts; Boys Are Worst," [Binghamton, NY] *Press and Sun-Bulletin,* December 22, 1985, p. 1.
7. Cited in Diane F. Halpern, *Thought and Knowledge: an Introduction to Critical Thinking* (Lawrence Erlbaum Associates, 1984), pp. 15–16.
8. Natalie Angier, "A Theory as Good as Gold," *Time,* September 9, 1985, pp. 70–1.
9. "Practice Exercises to Develop Critical Thinking Skills," *Journal of College Science Teaching,* 12 (4) February, 1983, pp. 262–6.
10. Natalie Angier, "Conquering Inherited Enemies," *Time,* October 21, 1985, p. 59.
11. Philip M. Boffey, "The Rights of Animals and the Requirements of Science," *New York Times,* August 11, 1985, Section 4, p. 8.
12. "In Montana, Unisex Insurance," *New York Times,* October 6, 1985, Section 4, p. 6.
13. Dan Goodgame, "Mayhem in the Cellblock," *Time,* August 12, 1985, p. 20.
14. Philip Shabecoff, "Experts See World Water Shortage," *International Herald-Tribune,* September 23, 1985, p. 3.
15. "A Developmental 'General Education' Course: Introducing Inquiry in the Social Sciences," *Journal of Developmental and Remedial Education,* 4, 23, Spring, 1981, pp. 24–6.
16. Cecie Starr and Ralph Taggart, *Biology: the Unity and Diversity of Life,* 3rd ed. (Wadsworth Publishing Company, 1984), p. 97.
17. Cecie Starr and Ralph Taggart, p. 246.
18. James L. Christian, *Philosophy: an Introduction to the Art of Wondering* (Holt, Rinehart, and Winston, 1977), p. 18.
19. Christian, p. 18.
20. Christian, p. 40.
21. Vincent Ryan Ruggiero, *The Art of Thinking* (Harper & Row, 1984), pp. 19, 25.
22. F. Roy Willis, *World Civilizations* (D. C. Heath and Co., 1986), Vol. II, pp. 338–9.
23. John A. Garraty, *The American Nation,* 4th ed. (Harper & Row, 1979), Vol. I, p. 324.
24. Garraty, Vol. II, p. 608.
25. Garraty, Vol. II, pp. 694–5.
26. Mark Hutter, *The Changing Family* (John Wiley and Sons, 1981), 208–10.
27. Hutter, pp. 336–45.

Chapter 8

1. Paul L. Dressel and Lewis B. Mayhew, *Critical Thinking in Social Science* (William C. Brown & Co., 1954), p. 12.
2. "Critical Thinking, Testing, and Evaluation: Status, Issues, Needs." Unpublished article.
3. See, for example, John French's review of *Creativity Tests for Children,* in Oscar K. Buros, *Eighth Mental Measurements Yearbook* (Gryphon Press, 1978), pp. 363–5. Also, the several reviews of the *Torrance Tests of Creative Thinking* in Buros, *Seventh Mental Measurements Yearbook* (1972), pp. 836–42.
4. Letter to author, November 29, 1985.
5. "Evaluating Critical Thinking Ability." Unpublished article.
6. This enumeration of defects is a composite. The first five are from B. Hoffman, "The Tyranny of Multiple-Choice Tests," quoted in E. Paul Torrance, *Guiding Creative*

Talent (Prentice-Hall, 1962), p. 21. Numbers 6 and 7 are from the Robert Ennis paper cited in note 2 above. Number 8 is from the Stephen Norris paper cited in note 5 above.

7. This example is cited in Sidney Parnes, *Creative Behavior Guidebook* (Charles Scribner's Sons, 1967), p. 32.
8. *Rewarding Creative Behavior* (Prentice-Hall, 1965), p. 29.
9. "Critical Thinking, Testing, and Evaluation." Unpublished article.
10. "Critical Thinking, Testing, and Evaluation." Unpublished article.
11. "Evaluating Critical Thinking Ability." Unpublished article.
12. Guidelines 8 and 9 were suggested by Edward Glaser in a letter to the author, November 29, 1985.
13. All the material on Alverno College's assessment program, including quotations, is from two informational pamphlets—*Assessment at Alverno College* and *The Volunteer Assessor at Alverno College*—both 1979 copyrighted publications of Alverno Productions.

Chapter 9

1. "300 Fail Teaching Exam," *Oneonta Star,* July 22, 1985, p. 10.
2. "Critical Thinking in the Social Studies Classroom. Do We Teach It?" 49 (3), March, 1985, pp. 240–6.
3. *Education for What Is Real* (Harper & Brothers, 1947), p. 75.
4. In Mortimer J. Adler, *The Paideia Program: An Educational Syllabus* (Macmillan, 1984), pp. 39–43.
5. See, for example, Harry E. Yuker, *Faculty Workload Research, Theory, and Interpretation,* Association for the Study of Higher Education, 1984, p. 37f.
6. See, for example, John Mangieri, and John Arnn, Jr., "Excellent Schools: The Leadership Functions of Principals," *American Education,* 21 (3), 1985, pp. 8–10. Also, John Roueche and George Baker, "The Success Connection," *AACJC Journal,* August, 1985, pp. 20–6.
7. David S. Webster, "Does Research Productivity Enhance Teaching?" *Educational Record* (Fall, 1985), pp. 60–2.
8. *Evaluation of Thinking Skills: Issues and Alternatives,* Address to Cincinnati Public Schools Thinking Conference, June, 1985.
9. E. Paul Torrance, "Education for 'Quality Circles' in Japanese Schools," *Journal of Research and Development in Education,* 15 (2), 1982, pp. 11–15.

BIBLIOGRAPHY

The following bibliography is divided into two lists: works published before 1950 and works published since 1950. This division is intended to encourage readers to resist the temptation to ignore older works. That temptation is rooted in the fallacy of fashionableness which argues that only the latest ideas are worthy of attention. As G. K. Chesterton rightly observed, we should not be concerned whether a work was written in our time, but whether it was written in answer to our question. The older works included here may include an occasional idea now known to be erroneous, but they will more often provide insights into the thought process and the teaching of thinking as valuable in their way as the latest research.

Works Published Before 1950

Adler, Mortimer. *How to Read a Book* (New York: Simon & Schuster, 1940).
Barnard, Chester I. *The Functions of the Executive* (Cambridge, MA: Harvard 1938).
Bartlett, Frederick C. *Remembering: A Study in Experimental and Social Psychology* (London: Cambridge, 1932).
Boas, Franz. *The Mind of Primitive Man,* rev. ed. (New York: Macmillan, 1938).
Bridgman, Percy W. *The Intelligent Individual and Society* (New York: Macmillan, 1938).
Burtt, Edwin A. *Right Thinking: A Study of Its Principles and Methods,* 3rd ed. (New York: Harper & Brothers, 1946).
Chrisof, Cleo. "The Formulation and Elaboration of Thought-Problems," *American Journal of Psychology,* 52 (1939), 161–85.
Clarke, Edwin L. *The Art of Straight Thinking* (New York: Appleton, 1929).
Columbia Associates in Philosophy. *An Introduction to Reflective Thinking* (Chicago: Houghton-Mifflin, 1923).
Crawford, Robert P. *Think for Yourself* (New York: Fraser Publishing Co., 1937).
Curtis, Charles P. and Greenslet, Ferris, editors. *The Practical Cogitator or The Thinker's Anthology* (Chicago: Houghton-Mifflin, 1945).
Davis, Allison. *Social Class Influence Upon Learning* (Cambridge, MA: Harvard, 1948).
Dewey, John. *How We Think* (New York: Heath, 1933).
Dimnet, Ernest. *The Art of Thinking* (New York: Simon & Schuster, 1928).
Duncker, Karl. *On Problem Solving,* trans. Lynne S. Lees. (Westport, CT: Greenwood Press, 1972). (Originally published in 1945.)

Hadamard, Jacques. *The Psychology of Invention in the Mathematical Field* (Princeton, NJ: Princeton, 1945).

Hazlitt, Henry. *Thinking as a Science* (New York: Dutton, 1916).

Humphrey, George. *Directed Thinking* (New York: Dodd, Mead, 1948).

Hutchinson, Eliot Dole. *How to Think Creatively* (Abingdon-Cokesbury, 1949).

Iles, George. *Inventors at Work* (Garden City, NY: Doubleday, Page, 1906).

Jastrow, Joseph. *Effective Thinking* (New York: Simon & Schuster, 1931).

Kelley, Earl C. *Education for What Is Real* (New York: Harper & Brothers, 1947).

Lippmann, Walter. *Public Opinion* (New York: Harcourt, Brace, 1922).

Mander, A. E. *Logic for the Millions* (New York: Philosophical Library, 1947).

Mearns, Hughes. *Creative Power* (Garden City, NY: Doubleday, Doran, 1935).

Noll, Victor H. *The Habit of Scientific Thinking: A Handbook for Teachers* (New York: Teachers College, Columbia University, 1935).

Osborn, Alex F. *Your Creative Power: How to Use Imagination* (New York: Scribner's, 1948).

Parker, Samuel Chester. "Problem-Solving or Practice in Thinking, IV," *Elementary School Journal,* 21 (1920) 257–72.

Phin, John. *The Seven Follies of Science,* 3rd ed. (Van Nostrand, 1912).

Platt, Washington, and Baker, Ross. "The Relation of the Scientific Hunch to Research," *Journal of Chemical Education,* 8 (1931), 1969–2002.

Robinson, James H. *The Mind in the Making* (New York: Harper & Brothers, 1921).

Rossman, Joseph. *The Psychology of the Inventor* (Washington, D.C.: The Inventors Publishing Co., 1931).

Sargent, Stephen S. *Thinking Processes at Various Stages of Difficulty,* Archives of Psychology, No. 249, 1940.

Science in General Education: Suggestions for Science Teachers in Secondary Schools and in the Lower Division of Colleges (New York: Appleton-Century, 1938).

Symonds, Percival M. *Education and the Psychology of Thinking* (New York: McGraw-Hill, 1936).

Thouless, Robert H. *How to Think Straight* (New York: Simon & Schuster, 1939).

Vigotsky, L. S. "Thought and Speech," *Psychiatry,* 2 (1939), 29–54.

Wallas, Graham. *The Art of Thought* (New York: Harcourt, Brace, 1926).

Weil, Richard, Jr. *The Art of Practical Thinking* (New York: Simon & Schuster, 1940).

Wertheimer, Max. *Productive Thinking* (New York: Harper & Brothers, 1945).

Works Published Since 1950*

Adler, Mortimer. The Paideia trilogy: *The Paideia Proposal,* 1982; *Paideia Problems and Possibilities,* 1983; and *The Paideia Program: An Educational Syllabus,* 1984. Macmillan.

_____. *Ten Philosophical Mistakes.* (New York: Macmillan, 1985).

Allport, Gordon W. *Becoming* (New Haven, CT: Yale, 1955).

Anderson, Harold H., ed. *Creativity and Its Cultivation* (New York: Harper & Brothers, 1959).

Barrett, William. *The Death of the Soul from Descartes to the Computer* (Garden City, NY: Doubleday, 1986).

Barrows, H. and Tamblyn, R. *Problem-Based Learning: An Approach to Medical Education.* (Westport, CT: Springer Publishing Co., 1980).

*This bibliography includes works published in 1950.

Bartlett, Frederick C. *Thinking: An Experimental and Social Study* (London: Allen & Unwin, 1958).

Bennett, J. and Peltason, J. *Contemporary Issues in Higher Education* (New York: Macmillan, 1985).

Beveridge, W. I. B. *The Art of Scientific Investigation* (New York: Norton, 1951).

Black, Max. *Critical Thinking* (Eaglewood Cliffs, NJ: Prentice-Hall, 1952).

Bloom, B. and Broder, L. *Problem-Solving Processes of College Students* (Chicago: Chicago University Press, 1950).

Bloom, Benjamin. *Taxonomy of Educational Objectives: Handbook I, Cognitive Domain* (New York: Longmans, 1956).

Blum, M. and Spangehl, S. "A Developmental 'General Education' Course: Introducing Inquiry in the Social Sciences," *Journal of Developmental and Remedial Education,* 4, 23, (Spring, 1981), 24–6.

Bronowski, Jacob. *Science and Human Values* (New York: Harper & Row, 1956).

Bruner, Jerome. *The Process of Education* (Cambridge, MA: Harvard University Press, 1961).

Common, Dianne L. "Small Group Instruction in Social Studies Classrooms and the Corruption of Critical Thought," *Theory and Research in Social Education* (Winter, 1982), 49–67.

Dimock, Marshall E. *A Philosophy of Administration* (New York: Harper & Brothers, 1958).

Dressel, P. and Mayhew, L. *Critical Thinking in Social Science* (Dubuque, IA: William C. Brown, 1954).

Ellis, Albert. *A Guide to Rational Living* (Englewood Cliffs, NJ: Prentice-Hall, 1961).

Feuerstein, Reuven. *The Dynamic Assessment of Retarded Performers* (Baltimore, MD.: University Park Press, 1979).

———. *Instrumental Enrichment* (Baltimore, MD.: University Park Press, 1980).

Flesch, Rudolf. *The Art of Clear Thinking* (New York: Harper & Brothers, 1951).

Gardner, Howard. *Frames of Mind* (New York: Basic Books, 1983).

———. *The Mind's New Science* (New York: Basic Books, 1985).

Gardner, Martin. *Fads and Fallacies in the Name of Science* (New York: Dover, 1952, 1957).

Getzels, Jacob W. "Problem-Finding and the Inventiveness of Solutions," *Journal of Creative Behavior,* 9 (1, 1975), 12–18.

Getzels, J. and Jackson, P. *Creativity and Intelligence* (New York: Wiley, 1962).

Getzels, J. and Csikszentmihalyi, M. *The Creative Vision* (New York: Wiley, 1976).

Ghiselin, Brewster, ed. *The Creative Process: A Symposium* (Berkeley, CA: University of California Press, 1954).

Gordon, William J. J. *Synectics: The Development of Creative Capacity* (New York: Harper & Brothers, 1961).

Goodlad, John I. *A Place Called School: Prospects for the Future* (New York: McGraw-Hill, 1984).

Gould, Stephen Jay. *The Mismeasure of Man* (New York: Norton, 1981).

Gruber, Howard E. et al., eds. *Contemporary Approaches to Creative Thinking: A Symposium* (Atherton Press, 1962).

Guilford, J. P. "Creativity," *American Psychologist,* 5 (1950), 444–54.

———. "Factors That Aid and Hinder Creativity," *Teachers College Record,* 63 (1962), 380–92.

———. "The Structure of Intellect," *Psychological Bulletin,* 53 (1956), 267–93.

Johnson-Laird, P. N. *Mental Models* (Cambridge, MA: Harvard University Press, 1983).

John-Steiner, Vera. *Notebooks of the Mind* (Albuquerque, NM.: University of New Mexico Press, 1985).

Kneller, George F. *The Art and Science of Creativity* (New York: Holt, 1965).

Koestler, Arthur. *The Act of Creation* (New York: Macmillan, 1964).

Kolb, David A. *Experiential Learning* (Englewood Cliffs, NJ: Prentice-Hall, 1984).

Krishnamurti, J. *Education and the Significance of Life* (New York: Harper & Brothers, 1953).

Krulik, Stephen. *Problem Solving in School Mathematics* (Reston, VA: National Council of Mathematics, 1980).

Krutch, Joseph Wood. *The Measure of Man.* (New York: Bobbs-Merrill, 1953, 1954).

LaBar, Carol et al. "Practical Reasoning in Corrections Education," *Canadian Journal of Education,* Summer (July 1983), 263–73.

Larrabee, Harold A. *Reliable Knowledge,* rev. ed. (Chicago: Houghton-Mifflin, 1964).

Lochhead, J. and Clement, J., eds. *Cognitive Process Instruction: Research on Teaching Thinking Skills.* (Philadelphia: The Franklin Press, 1979).

Loftus, Elizabeth. *Eyewitness Testimony* (Cambridge, MA: Harvard University Press, 1979).

MacKinnon, Donald W. "The Nature and Nurture of Creative Thought," *American Psychologist,* 17 (1962), 484–95.

Maltz, Maxwell. *Psychocybernetics* (New York: Simon & Schuster, 1970).

Maltzman, Irving, et al. "Experimental Studies in the Training of Originality," *Psychological Monographs,* 74 (1960), 1–23.

Maslow, Abraham. "The Creative Attitude," *The Structurist,* 3 (1963), 4–10.

Mason, J. et al. *Thinking Mathematically* (London: Addison Wesley Publishers, Ltd. 1982).

McPeck, John. *Critical Thinking and Education* (New York: St. Martin's Press, 1981).

Meichenbaum, D. *Cognitive-Behavior Modification* (New York: Plenum Press, 1977).

Moore, Brooke. "Critical Thinking in California," *Teaching Philosophy,* 6 (4, October 1983), 321–30.

Mursell, James *Using Your Mind Effectively* (New York: McGraw-Hill, 1951).

Nickerson, Raymond S. et al. *The Teaching of Thinking* (Hillsdale, NJ: Erlbaum, 1985).

Osborn, Alex. *Applied Imagination* (New York: Scribner's, 1957).

———. *Your Creative Power: How to Use Imagination* (New York: McGraw-Hill, 1947).

Overstreet, Harry. *The Mature Mind* (New York: Norton, 1949, 1959).

Parnes, S. and Noller, R. "Applied Creativity: The Creative Studies Project, Part II," *Journal of Creative Behavior,* 6, (3, 1972), 164–86.

Parnes, Sidney. "Effects of Extended Effort in Creative Problem-Solving," *Journal of Educational Psychology,* 52 (1961), 117–22.

———. *Creative Behavior Guidebook* (New York: Scribner's, 1967). (Also see the workbook that accompanies this book.)

Patrick, Catherine. *What Is Creative Thinking?* (New York: Philosophical Library, 1955).

Perkins, David. *The Mind's Best Work* (Cambridge, MA: Harvard University Press, 1981).

Perry, William G. *Forms of Intellectual Development in the College Years: A Scheme* (New York: Holt, 1970).

Pietrasinski, Z. *The Psychology of Efficient Thinking.* Trans. B. Jankowski. (New York: Pergamon Press, 1969).

Popper, Karl. *The Logic of Scientific Discovery,* rev. ed. (London: Hutchinson, 1968).

Postman, Neil. *Amusing Ourselves to Death* (New York: Viking, 1985).

Powell, Arthur G. et al. *The Shopping Mall High School* (Chicago: Houghton-Mifflin, 1985).

Ricketts, John A. "PSI and Piaget," *Proceedings of the Indiana Academy of Science,* 83 (1984) 379–84.

———. "The High School Chemistry Laboratory Can Strengthen Abstract Reasoning Skills," *Proceedings of the* Indiana Academy of Science, 83 (1984) 385–89.

Rosenthal, Peggy. *Words and Values.* Oxford, 1984.

Rothenberg, Albert. *The Emerging Goddess* (Chicago: University of Chicago Press, 1979).

Rubinstein, Moshe F. *Patterns of Problem Solving* (Englewood Cliffs, NJ: Prentice-Hall, 1975).

Russell, David H. *Children's Thinking* (New York: Ginn, 1956).

Samson, Richard W. *The Mind Builder* (New York: Dutton, 1965).

Sheffler, Israel. *Reason and Teaching* (New York: Bobbs-Merrill, 1973).

Shulman, L. and Keislar, E., eds. *Learning by Discovery: A Critical Appraisal* (Chicago: Rand, McNally, 1966).

Siegel, Harvey. "Critical Thinking as an Educational Ideal," *The Educational Forum* (November 1980), 7–23.

Sizer, Theodore R. *Horace's Compromise: The Dilemma of the American High School* (Chicago: Houghton-Mifflin, 1984).

Smith, Paul, ed. *Creativity: an Examination of the Creative Process* (Hastings House, 1959).

Stein, M. and Heinze, S. *Creativity and the Individual* (New York: Free Press, 1960).

Sternberg, Robert. "Teaching Critical Thinking, Part 1: Are We Making Critical Mistakes," *Phi Delta Kappan* (November 1985), 194f.

Taton, Rene. *Reason and Chance in "Scientific" Discovery.* Trans. A. Pomerans. (New York: Philosophical Library, 1957).

Taylor, C. and Barron, F., eds. *Scientific Creativity: Its Recognition and Development* (New York: Wiley, 1963).

Thinking: The Expanding Frontier. Proceedings of the International, Interdisciplinary Conference on Thinking. (Philadelphia: Franklin Institute Press, 1983).

Thorndike, Robert L. "How Children Learn the Principles and Techniques of Problem-Solving," *Learning and Instruction: 49th Yearbook,* N.S.S.E. (Part I, 1950) 192–316.

Thring, M. W. "The Encouragement and Development of Originality and Inventiveness in Engineering Students," *International Journal of Educational Sciences,* 2 (September 1968), 195–9.

Torrance, E. Paul. *Guiding Creative Talent* (Englewood Cliffs, NJ: Prentice-Hall, 1962).

———. *Rewarding Creative Behavior* (Englewood Cliffs, NJ: Prentice-Hall, 1965).

———, editor. *Talent and Education: Present Status and Future Directions* (Minneapolis: University of Minnesota Press, 1960).

Tuska, Clarence. *Inventors and Inventions* (New York: McGraw-Hill, 1957).

Vinacke, L. S. *The Psychology of Thinking* (New York: McGraw-Hall, 1952).

Whimbey, A. and Lochhead, J. *Problem Solving and Comprehension* (Philadelphia: The Franklin Institute Press, 1980).

Wolfard, Merl Ruskin. *Thinking About Thinking* (New York: Philosophical Library, 1955).

Yamamoto, Kaoru. "Threshhold of Intelligence in Academic Achievement of Highly Creative Students," *Journal of Experimental Education,* 32 (Summer, 1964), 401–5.

Zirbes, Laura. *Spurs to Creative Teaching* (New York: Putnam's, 1959).

About the Author

Vincent Ryan Ruggiero, Professor of Humanities at State University of New York at Delhi, is an internationally known writer and education consultant. Professor Ruggiero has been a pioneer in the movement to make thinking skills instruction an important emphasis at every level of education. He has published *The Art of Thinking: A Guide to Critical and Creative Thought,* available from Harper & Row. Other works by Professor Ruggiero include *The Elements of Rhetoric, The Moral Imperative, Beyond Feelings: A Guide to Critical Thinking, The Art of Writing, Enter the Dialogue,* and *Composition: The Creative Response.*

A founding member of the National Council for Excellence in Critical Thinking Instruction, Professor Ruggiero also holds memberships in the American Association for Higher Education, the Association for Business Communication, and the Intellectual Skills Development Association.